Housing in the European Cou

There are many facets of housing pressure in rural areas, not all of which are the consequences of economic or market forces. Changing demographics and migration, cultural and societal attitudes towards rural and urban living and property acquisition, land use planning regulatory controls, the difficulty of securing affordable housing provision, a desire for urban containment and countryside protection, the decline of traditional rural employment, the closure or absence of rural services, community uncertainty and social exclusion and the constant environmental and social pressure placed on rural areas by tourism and economic development, will each affect the prosperity of rural dwellers and affect rural space and residential property. Many of these issues will be evident in most countries; other countries may experience one set of pressure problems.

Housing in the European Countryside provides an overview of the housing pressures and policy challenges facing Europe, while highlighting critical differences. By drawing on contemporary research work of leading authors in the fields of housing studies, rural geography and planning, the book offers an introduction to housing issues across the European countryside for those who have hitherto been unexposed to such concerns, and who wish to gain some basic insight.

This in-depth review of housing pressure in the European countryside will reveal both the form, nature and variety of problems now being experienced in different parts of Europe, in addition to outlining policy solutions that are being provided by member states and other agencies in meeting the rural housing challenge now and in the years ahead.

Nick Gallent is a Senior Lecturer in Planning at the Bartlett School of Planning, University College London. **Mark Shucksmith** is Professor of Land Economy, University of Aberdeen and Co-Director, Arkleton Centre for Rural Development Research, University of Aberdeen. He is Programme Adviser, Joseph Rowntree Foundation 'Action in Rural Areas' programme, and Programme Chair, World Rural Sociology Congress 2004 and Executive Member of IRSA. **Mark Tewdwr-Jones** is Reader in Spatial Planning and Governance at the Bartlett School of Planning, University College London.

Housing, Planning and Design Series

Editors: Nick Gallent and Mark Tewdwr-Jones,
The Bartlett School of Planning, University College London

This series addresses critical issues affecting the delivery of the right type of housing, of sufficient quantity and quality, in the most sustainable locations, and the linkages that bind together issues relating to planning, housing and design. Titles examine a variety of institutional perspectives, examining the roles of different agencies and sectors in delivering better quality housing together with the process of delivery – from policy development, through general strategy to implementation. Other titles will focus on housing management and development, housing strategy and planning policy, housing needs and community participation.

Housing in the European Countryside
Edited by Nick Gallent, Mark Shucksmith and Mark Tewdwr-Jones

Forthcoming:
Decent Homes for All
Nick Gallent and Mark Tewdwr-Jones

Housing Development
Edited by Andrew Golland and Ron Blake

Housing in the European Countryside

Rural pressure and policy
in Western Europe

Edited by Nick Gallent, Mark Shucksmith
and Mark Tewdwr-Jones

LONDON AND NEW YORK

First published 2003
by Routledge
11 New Fetter Lane, London EC4P 4EE

Simultaneously published in the USA and Canada
by Routledge
29 West 35th Street, New York, NY 10001

Routledge is an imprint of the Taylor & Francis Group

Typeset in Galliard by
Florence Production Ltd, Stoodleigh, Devon

Printed and bound in Great Britain by
St Edmundsbury Press, Bury St Edmunds, Suffolk

British Library Cataloguing in Publication Data
A catalogue record for this book is available from the British Library

Library of Congress Cataloging in Publication Data
Housing in the European countryside: rural pressure and policy
in Western Europe/edited by Nick Gallent, Mark Shucksmith and
Mark Tewdwr-Jones.
    p. cm. – (Housing, planning and design series)
  Includes bibliographical references and index.
  1. Housing, Rural – Europe, Western. 2. Housing policy – Europe,
Western. 3. Urbanisation – Europe, Western. I. Gallent, Nick.
II. Shucksmith, Mark. III. Tewdwr-Jones, Mark. IV. Series.
HD7289.E85 H68 2002
363.5′094′091734–dc21   2002068192

ISBN 0–415–28842–8 (hbk)
ISBN 0–415–28843–6 (pbk)

Contents

List of contributors   vii

Preface   xi

Acknowledgements   xiii

1   Introduction   1
Nick Gallent, Mark Shucksmith and Mark Tewdwr-Jones

2   Theories and levels of comparative analysis   13
Chris Allen

Part One: Cohesive Cultures, Regulatory Regimes   **23**

3   Norway   29
Lars Gulbrandsen

4   Sweden   44
Gärd Folkesdotter

5   The Netherlands   60
Saskia Heins

6   France   71
Elizabeth Auclair and Didier Vanoni

Part Two: Atomistic Cultures, Laissez-Faire Regimes   **87**

7   Italy   91
Liliana Padovani and Luciano Vettoretto

8   Spain   116
Manuel Valenzuela

9   Ireland   129
    Joe Finnerty, Donal Guerin and Cathal O Connell

Part Three: Divisive Cultures, Unstable Regimes   **147**

10 England   153
    Keith Hoggart

11 Scotland   168
    Mark Shucksmith and Ed Conway

12 Wales   188
    W.J. Edwards

13 Housing pressure and policy in Europe: a power regime
    perspective   208
    Nick Gallent and Chris Allen

14 Conclusions   226
    Mark Tewdwr-Jones, Nick Gallent and Mark Shucksmith

References   237
Index   259

Contributors

Chris Allen lectures in the Department of Sociology at Bradford University. His main research interests are in the areas of housing and community care, housing needs, housing policy and housing and social exclusion. He has recently completed a project on 'managing risk' for the Housing Corporation and is currently undertaking an ethnographic research study of everyday life in three foyers in the north-west of England.

Elizabeth Auclair is Professor of Geography at Cergy-Pontoise University. For the last 15 years, she has conducted research in the fields of regional planning, local development and rural geography. Elizabeth is Director of a Master's degree course in cultural and tourism development and teaches a variety of courses in rural geography and regional planning. She was formerly a researcher at *FORS Recherché Sociale* and has been the scientific partner in several European research programmes.

Ed Conway graduated in Land Economy from the University of Aberdeen in 1992. He then worked as a research officer in that department for several years, working on a variety of projects including studies of rural sub-post offices; Wildlife Crime; evaluations of LEADER1 programmes in Lochaber, the Western Isles and Skye and Lochalsh; Disadvantage in Rural Scotland; the evaluation of Scottish Homes' rural demonstration areas; the evaluation of a local housing agency; the relationship between housing and economic development in remote areas; the evaluation of Scottish Homes' Rural Policy; a scoping study of rural partnerships; and the use of social indicators of rural development. He subsequently retrained as a primary school teacher, and now lives in Inverness.

W.J. Edwards is Lecturer in Geography at the Institute of Geography and Earth Sciences, University of Wales, Aberystwyth. His research interests are in social geography with particular emphasis on rural community development, rural social problems and rural housing.

Joe Finnerty is a Lecturer in Social Policy at the Department of Applied Social Studies, University College, Cork. His main research interests are in the areas of housing policy (with particular focus on the private rented sector), poverty and social exclusion and in the development of social indicators.

Gärd Folkesdotter holds an MA in Architecture from the Royal Institute of Technology in Stockholm and a PhD in Planning from the Nordic Institute for Studies in Urban and Regional Planning. She spent a number of years as an architect and planner, before embarking upon a research career, which has involved projects concerned with development and planning, urban renewal and local politics and gender and power. She is a member of the Swedish society for Town and Country Planning and the International Planning History Society and is also chairwoman of the Women's Building Forum – a Swedish association for women interested in building, housing and planning.

Nick Gallent is a Senior Lecturer in Planning at the Bartlett School of Planning, University College London. His principal research interests include: UK housing policy, housing and the planning system and planning and affordable housing. Other recent books published: *Rural Second Homes in Europe* (with Mark Tewdwr-Jones) and *Working Together: A Guide for Planners and Housing Providers* (with Matthew Carmona and Sarah Carmona). He is currently undertaking research on second homes and the planning system in Wales and England.

Donal Guerin is Social Inclusion Officer with Cork Corporation. He has written several books and reports on housing and social policy in Ireland.

Lars Gulbrandsen gained both a Master's degree in Political Science and a doctorate from the University of Oslo. His doctoral work focused on the changing housing market in Oslo throughout the twentieth century. Since 1997, he has been Research Director at NOVA – Norwegian Social Research. His research is centred on household finances, the impact of inheritance and inter-generational transfers.

Saskia Heins is an Urban Geographer and is currently completing doctoral research at the Urban Research Centres, Utrecht University. Her research interests are in housing and migration, particularly in rural areas. Her PhD Research deals with countryside images, preferences for rural living and moving to rural residential environments.

Keith Hoggart is Professor of Geography at King's College London. His research interests focus on housing, migration and social change in rural areas, as well as on local government policy and rural development. His current research projects include a British Academy-funded project on the provision of rural public housing in twentieth-century southern England, and an EU-funded project on the dynamics of residential, employment and service change in peri-urban areas. He has published six books and edited five volumes, including *Rural Europe: Identity and Change* (1995, with Henry Buller and Richard Black, Arnold) and *Researching Human Geography* (2001, with Loretta Lees and Anna Davies, Arnold). He has been a Fulbright Fellow to two US universities and held a Commonwealth Scholarship in Canada. He is past Chair of the Royal Geographical Society's rural geography research group.

Cathal O Connell is a Lecturer in Social Policy at the Department of Applied Social Studies, University College, Cork. His main research interests are in the areas of housing policy and urban and rural development issues.

Liliana Padovani is Associate Professor in Urban and Regional Policies at IUAV, Venice, Italy. She is active, as Vice-Chair of the Co-ordination Committee, in the European Network for Housing Research. She has been involved in research projects and has acted as consultant in Italy and abroad. Publications include: editing *Urban change and housing policies. Evidence from four European countries* (1995, Collana Daest n. 19, Venezia); 'Italy' in *Housing policies in Europe* (1996, ed. P. Balchin, Routledge); 'Le partenariat pour rénover l'action publique. L'expérience Italienne' (2000, *Pole sud*, n. 12). She is a member of the editorial board of *Housing Studies* and the *Netherlands Journal of the Built Environment*.

Mark Shucksmith is Professor of Land Economy, University of Aberdeen and Co-Director, Arkleton Centre for Rural Development Research, University of Aberdeen. He is Programme Adviser, Joseph Rowntree Foundation 'Action in Rural Areas' programme, and Programme Chair, World Rural Sociology Congress 2004 and Executive Member of IRSA. He was formerly Vice-Chairman and Council member, Rural Forum (Scotland), is a member of the EU LEADER group for North and West Grampian, and a member of several national and international learned societies. His main research interests are: poverty and social exclusion in rural areas, rural development, agricultural change and rural housing.

Mark Tewdwr-Jones is Reader in Spatial Planning and Governance at the Bartlett School of Planning, University College London. His main interests are in the fields of planning, government and politics, and he is currently undertaking work on: second homes; city regions and governance in the European Union; and devolution and decentralisation of policy-making within the UK. He is European Editor of *International Planning Studies*. Other recent books include *Rural Second Homes in Europe* (2000, with Nick Gallent, Ashgate), *The European Dimension of British Planning* (2001, with R.H. Williams, Spon Press), *Planning Futures* (2002, with Philip Allmendinger, Routledge) and *The Planning Polity* (2002 Routledge).

Manuel Valenzuela is Professor of Human Geography at the Madrid Autonomous University where he leads the Research Laboratory on Urban, Social and Tourism Geography. His major fields of research interest relate to urban geography and tourism and leisure geography. His recent studies have examined the quality of life in cities from the point of view of different social groups. Other work has focused on social housing needs, second homes and changing housing quality in Spain. He is a member of the Spanish Committee of the Habitat UNO Agency and has been an active member of the European Network for Housing Research (ENHR) since 1990.

Didier Vanoni is Director of *FORS Recherché Sociale*, a private research institute in the social sciences, situated in Paris. Past research has focused on housing and social policy and housing strategies for disadvantaged groups. The institute mainly engages in research on behalf of public bodies, state agencies and local communities. Didier is a specialist in housing and social exclusion and has worked extensively in the field of housing policy, acting as consultant for a range of NGOs. He also teaches sociology at Cergy-Pontoise University.

Luciano Vettoretto is Associate Professor of Urban Planning in the Department of Planning at the Istituto Universitario di Architettura, Venice, where he is co-director of the Master's programme in Urban and Regional Policy Evaluation. He is a member of the Editorial Board of *Archivio di Studi Urbani e Regionali* and author of numerous essays, on topics such as planning theory and methods and social geographies of recent spatial development.

Preface

This collection of national overviews of rural housing pressure and housing policy in Europe began life in 2000 as a study of European responses to the problems of living – or more specifically gaining access to suitable housing – within the European countryside. The study was commissioned by Scottish Homes and the research team comprised Mark Shucksmith, Mark Tewdwr-Jones and Nick Gallent. The intention, quite simply, was to see how other countries deal with housing pressure, how they define this pressure and how effective local and national strategies have been utilised in improving the lot of those residing in non-metropolitan areas.

The project was essentially a fact-finding mission with an extremely tight schedule: the original attempt to secure written contributions yielded just five chapters, with two of these drawn from the Republic of Ireland and the United Kingdom. But even from this small sample, it was clear that different countries in Europe have wildly differing takes on rural housing problems and the necessary responses. At the most basic level, there is very little general agreement on what constitutes housing pressure or a clear problem requiring some form of redress. To some, in-migration is a threat to the stability of rural communities; to others it is an opportunity or lifeline to be grasped. Conversely, out-migration is viewed in some areas and regions as part of the natural ebb and flow of people affecting all of Europe; elsewhere, it represents damaging change that must be stemmed at all costs.

This book expands the original research report to Scottish Homes by increasing the original five contributions to ten. The book has two aims. First, it attempts to provide an overview of the housing pressures and policy challenges facing Europe, while highlighting critical differences. Second, it offers an introduction to housing issues across the European countryside for those who have hitherto been unexposed to such concerns, but who wish to gain some basic insight.

There are many causes of housing pressure in rural areas. Changing demographics and migration, cultural and societal attitudes towards rural and urban living and property acquisition, land use planning regulatory controls, the difficulty of securing affordable housing provision, a desirability for urban containment and countryside protection, the decline of traditional rural employment, the closure or absence of rural services, community uncertainty and social exclusion and the constant environmental and social pressure placed on rural areas by tourism and economic development, will each affect the prosperity of rural dwellers and affect rural space and residential property. Many of these issues will be evident in most countries; other countries may experience one set of pressure problems. The editors hope that the review of housing pressure in the European countryside will reveal both the form, nature and variety of problems now being experienced in different parts of Europe, in addition to outlining policy solutions that are being provided by member states and other agencies in meeting the rural housing challenge now and in the years ahead.

Contributions to the book offer divergent views as to why contrasts between nation states occur, and how such contrasts might be read. Its focus is firmly on the treatment given to particular issues *within* different countries, and consequently on the way local and national bodies respond to accepted challenges. The editors hope that this book will stimulate further interest in the rural housing concerns shared by the UK's constituent parts and its neighbours. And for those approaching the subject for the first time, it will hopefully provide the right level of detail to form an introduction to rural housing issues across the European territory.

Acknowledgements

The editors would like to acknowledge the assistance of all contributors to the book and are grateful for the speed and efficiency shown by authors in making revisions to their chapters following comments provided on initial drafts. We are grateful to Routledge and Caroline Mallinder and Michelle Green in particular, for commissioning the book and providing professional support in progressing the book so smoothly from manuscript to publication.

Finally, we are grateful to Anna Richards and Rui Figueira for their constant support over the months.

Nick Gallent
London

Mark Shucksmith
Aberdeen

Mark Tewdwr-Jones
London

April 2002

Chapter 1
Introduction

Nick Gallent, Mark Shucksmith and Mark Tewdwr-Jones

A substantial amount of literature has been devoted to the subject of European housing policy and practice over the last twenty years (see for example, Winn, 1984; Barlow and Duncan, 1994; McCrone and Stephens, 1995; Balchin, 1996; Oxley and Smith, 1996; Golland, 1998; Gallent and Tewdwr-Jones, 2000). The majority of past studies have negotiated a careful path around the question of what – in practical and more theoretical terms – can be learned from other countries. A further body of work has focused specifically on Eastern Europe (see, for example, Turner *et al.*, 1992; Struyk, 1995; Clapham *et al.*, 1996), examining the housing aspects of a post-communist political and economic transition. All these studies (and others looking at Europe and beyond: for example, Kemeny 1981, 1992; Harloe *et al.*, 1988; van Vliet, 1990; or Doling, 1997), however careful they might be to avoid simple comparison, have established a clear sense of a shared European experience of housing, in terms of its production, regulation and consumption. In practice circles too, there is often a strong desire to draw on overseas experiences as a means of demonstrating to policy makers how home-grown approaches are flawed and might be improved. A recent study of European housing finance, for example (Stephens *et al.*, 2002), has suggested that British social landlords bear a greater cost for private finance than many of their European neighbours. Unsurprisingly, this particular study has generated significant practice interest.

The focus of this book is Western Europe, and more specifically, member states of the European Union, as represented by ten national case studies. It is an edited text drawing together contributions from writers across the European territory: it aims to be both a comprehensive review of issues stretching from the nature of housing pressure to the success of housing policy, and an examination of how housing policy itself is an expression of different values and conditions. At the end of this introductory chapter, we suggest that the ten countries are representative of three broad underlying cultures, and hence three different ways of responding to and managing a range of housing pressures. In other words, we propose a pattern of shared experience across a three-part rather than a one-Europe model. However, the whole of Western Europe, including some countries that found themselves labelled Eastern European after the Second World War, is bound together, to a large extent, by a common sense of history and also by a tradition of sharing ideas. This has been the case for centuries although in terms of political ideology and policy approaches, it was especially true during the latter half of the twentieth century with the arrival of the European Union. It is easy to forget therefore, that economically and socially, these countries may bear limited resemblance. They may sometimes appear to take outwardly similar approaches to a variety of social and economic challenges (Kemeny, 1992), but it is almost invariably the case that the conditions and processes underpinning these challenges are significantly different.

The two key aims noted above can also be thought of as two analytical levels. At the first level, we are providing a comprehensive country-by-country review with individual chapters all following a broadly similar structure. They all have as their starting point the range and type of housing pressure being experienced, and they all end with a review of current policy approaches. At the second level, we use the information provided by the contributors to consider how the strategies and policies they discuss in the latter parts of their chapters are expressions of the values and conditions suggested when they address questions of rural pressure and the relationship between town and country in the earlier parts of their chapters. This second level of analysis is presented in Chapter 13. And understanding how policy links back to national peculiarities enables us to extract broad themes: these form the content of a concluding chapter (Chapter 14). This structure is explained more fully towards the end of this introduction, but Figure 1.1 summarises our general approach.

Much of the remainder of this opening chapter is concerned with the particular issues addressed within the ten case studies, though we also highlight how these issues build into our bigger picture. A brief summary of how this linkage is made is provided in the next section.

Dealing with the detail

The contributing authors commence each of their chapters with an appraisal of the form that housing pressure takes – or rather, what is interpreted as 'pressure'. The rationale here is that policy can only be understood in the light of the pressure or problem that it seeks to address. Some of the authors reveal that such pressure is gauged in terms of the condition or quantity of rural housing: others emphasise the social consequences of wider economic changes affecting the countryside, the impacts these bring to communities, the way in which different consumer interests may clash and the consequent conflicts that can arise.

Level One	An examination of housing pressure and policy within each of the case study chapters (3 to 12). The focus here is on apparent problems and the responses (strategy or policy) instigated by various government or non-government agencies.
Level Two	An analysis of how Level One (i.e. the policy) observations might be understood in the light of cultural and political differences (Chapter 13). Here, we demonstrate how the case study chapters split into three broad types and consider what this typology means in terms of drawing policy comparisons.

1.1 Levels of analysis.
Source: Authors

In presenting separate case studies based around a standard framework, the aim is to create a series of anchors for later comparison. For instance, contributors were asked to consider the relationship between national policy and policy approaches within more peripheral locations, away from built-up areas. In Chapter 13, this is used to establish the degree of division between town and country within political discourse, and also at a deeper cultural level. Likewise, a focus on definitional issues – what constitutes 'rural' or housing 'pressure' – also helps to create a picture of cultural and political contrast or similarity. These front-end issues addressed within each of the case studies lead into questions of strategy and policy and more particularly, who is responding to rural housing pressure and what exactly they are doing. With answers to these types of question, it becomes possible to focus on where 'power' lies (for example, with either the state or private interests) within particular countries and how it is used. So the aim of developing a common structure for the case studies – which is followed to a varying degree by each of the contributors – is to provide a basis for comparison that hopefully moves some way beyond drawing a universal lesson from cursory observation.

One of the simple messages that this book emphasises is that comparisons are both useful and possible. But these often have to be accompanied by heavy caveats and an acceptance that the processes and practices of one country are a product of specific local conditions. Understanding these conditions is a prerequisite to understanding policy that, after all, is merely the expression of deeper social beliefs and attitudes. Allen (Chapter 2) provides an overview of recent thinking in the area of comparative housing studies, pointing out some of the many pitfalls that the unwary researcher faces in this type of analysis.

The remainder of this introduction is divided into three parts. The first is a short note on the original funded research that provided the catalyst for the book. The second runs through the main points of focus within the case studies, giving a brief introduction to each of the issues or key topics discussed by the contributing authors. The third part sets out the structure of the book, explaining how the chapters have been divided and giving a flavour of some of the later content.

The research context

This book is an evolved version of a comparative study of rural housing policy undertaken in 2000–2001. The original study – which was intended to be a review of 'international housing pressure' – was sponsored by Scottish Homes, a government agency in Scotland responsible for housing strategy, policy and the distribution of grant funding to the providers and managers of social housing. This study began life as a tightly structured analysis of 'housing pressure' and responses to housing pressure across a sample of European Union member states (this transect from pressure to policy is retained in this volume), and was intended to inform Scottish Homes' own approach to housing in the countryside. The timescale for the work (just three months) meant that, by the end of the summer 2000, five European case studies had been commissioned and completed; but only two of these were from the European mainland (Spain and the Netherlands) with the remainder representing the Republic of Ireland (ROI), Scotland and Wales. An early contribution from Allen (now expanded and forming Chapter 2 of this volume) was used to frame an analysis of the five national reviews and this revealed what were considered to be critical differences: specifically, a more relaxed approach to regulating housing production in Spain and Ireland, a blurring of urban–rural differences (and hence policy) in the Netherlands and a sharply focused urban–rural debate in both Scotland and Wales. These differences – and the loosely defined associations between particular countries – suggested a potential value in revisiting the work on a bigger scale. Besides addressing the lack of current text books on rural housing issues in Europe, expansion also afforded the opportunity to develop a clearer perspective on rural housing pressure and policy in a comparative sense. The early studies had pointed to clear regulatory differences grounded in the clarity of urban–rural divisions and a cultural resistance to strong state intervention (for example, through land use planning). An obvious question therefore was whether these patterns would hold true on a larger scale, and whether or not a sharper perspective would emerge from an extended study.

The expansion was not intended to simply reinforce a pre-determined view;

its aim was to elaborate on earlier findings and provide a more comprehensive text on housing pressure and policy. Hence new parts of Europe were brought into the study: Sweden and Norway from a hitherto absent Scandinavia; England (the missing part of the British jigsaw); France; and Italy. The selection of countries for the expanded study was driven both by geography and, admittedly, by perceptions of possible differences. Norway and Sweden were to provide the northern European examples, but were also known to reflect particular views towards private interests within the housing market and to have adopted certain regulatory approaches to second homes (Allen *et al.*, 1999; Gallent and Tewdwr-Jones, 2000, 2001). Italy was to join Spain in representing southern Europe and perhaps a less centrally-driven and less coherent approach to housing policy generally and planning regulation more specifically (Alberdí and Levenfeld, 1996; Padovani, 1996). France, together with the Netherlands, would occupy the geographical mid-point, and would also share political similarities. In the Netherlands, we had the blurring of urban–rural differences resulting in a more uniform policy approach. In France, a strong socialist tradition was perceived to have created a similar situation, marked by a history of central planning. And England was considered to be the missing component in the British studies and perhaps the epicentre – particularly within the English South East region – of divisive urban–rural debates, especially in relation to future housing production. The objective of this expansion, therefore, was to provide both a wider geographical coverage and also to test our assumptions regarding a three-Europe model: based on tighter regulation (particularly of private interest and housing consumption), a more informal approach (to the regulation of housing production) and perhaps a more combative approach to negotiating urban–rural divisions within certain countries as a result of prevailing cultural and political conditions.

In the next section, we outline how each of the ten case studies is structured and how their structuring, and the particular questions asked of the contributing authors, is used to inform later analysis along the lines described above.

Case studies: points of focus

The inclusion of the key topics shown in Figure 1.2 (within each of the case studies) was partly driven by the need to gain a comprehensive and logical picture of policy and practice (and hence produce a comprehensive text), and partly to elicit more fundamental information on wider cultural and political conditions. Within the chapters themselves, these topics are frequently broken down into further sub-headings by the contributing authors. Broadly, however, they fit into the three categories shown.

Topic 1	*Rural issues within a national picture*: the first part looks at the emphasis placed on rural (housing) issues, and in what terms 'rural' areas are delimited (population density, environmental factors etc.). This is used to build a picture of the urban–rural interface and the relationship between town and country.
Topic 2	*Defining housing pressure*: definitions of housing pressure – and the related discussions provided in many of the studies – have a similar role to play in building a picture of the wider social (cultural) and political context in which policy is designed and implemented.
Topic 3	*The focus and nature of strategy and policy*: given the contextual issues (Topics 1 and 2), how are particular countries responding to housing pressure? What form do these responses take (specifically rural strategies?) and finally, what degree of success have they experienced?

1.2 Structure of case studies.
Source: Authors

Rural issues within a national picture

Recognising the relationship between the urban and rural in policy terms is an important step towards appreciating more fundamental divisions within (a) society as a whole and (b) prevailing political discourse/debate. The idea that a natural divide exists between the urban and rural is very much a British perspective enshrined in legislation (e.g. the 'Town and Country Planning Acts') and in the geographical breakdown in UK party politics. But it is of course wrong to assume that the same division exists elsewhere in Western Europe (or further afield). For this reason, most of the case study chapters begin by considering how easy or difficult it is to separate rural from national concerns in terms of policy approaches towards housing. What weight, for example, is assigned to rural housing policy tools within national frameworks, and how much specific attention is devoted to rural issues overall? The reader will find that in some of the chapters, it is extremely difficult to detach rural from more general policy concerns. This might be viewed as a policy failure (but perhaps only from a British viewpoint), a result of unsophisticated data aggregation (making it difficult to distinguish urban from rural patterns, as some of the authors suggest) or, on the other hand, proof that some countries deal with urban and rural matters in a more integrated and strategic way than in the UK. It is also probable that a lack of clear dividing lines between town and country in this respect is a product and reflection of particular cultural conditions. Without wishing to give too much away at this stage, the lack of division might be viewed as a measure of greater social coherency, reflecting stronger ties between those living in rural and those living in urban areas (a indication perhaps of the lateness and degree of urbanisation in particular countries). In contrast, a stronger policy division may be the product of a more divided urban–rural culture. These issues are reflected upon in Chapter 13 and the organisation of case study chapters centres upon these key national differences.

Defining 'housing pressure'

The case study chapters are all concerned with defining 'housing pressure', whether in physical, social or economic terms. The definitions offered point to significant variations in attitudes towards rural areas and rural society, the relationship between urban and rural (in cultural, political and policy terms) and, in some instances, the balance between private interest and the needs of local communities. This focus gives some insight into the values that underpin particular policy responses and offers some useful distinctions when considering how countries might be rearranged into broad cultural groupings.

In Britain, it is often assumed that the countryside faces a range of different pressures. These can be economic: the decline of traditional industries and the pressure this exerts on the labour market (manifest in unemployment or rural depopulation of an unskilled workforce). They can also be environmental: the pressure of physical and economic development places a strain on the environment and creates a risk of environmental degradation through unsustainable development practices. The acceptance that this is the case was a driving force behind the creation of the modern British land use planning system. And third, the pressure can also be social: the push and pull of economic forces may cause migration and drive people to or from the countryside and this can take the form of a social exchange where an affluent and skilled population 'hijack' the countryside from a largely unskilled and relatively deprived indigenous population. This is a simplified view of the processes which ultimately contribute to housing pressure: the imperative of environmental protection results in fewer houses being built; a collapsing economy creates a vacuum drawing people from the countryside and leaving only a retired or unemployed population. These processes, alongside changing urban tastes or a desire to abandon urban living (at least for short periods), conspire to create housing pressure that is expressed, in its most basic form, as an inability of local households to compete in the housing market with higher income newcomers. This view of housing pressure in the countryside is broadly accepted as having currency, although its detail is frequently challenged and it is often argued that processes on the ground are far more complex (see Chapter 10 by Hoggart, and Chapter 11 by Shucksmith and Conway).

The interpretation of the processes as 'urban threat' and 'social exchange' may also be an expression of certain values. Only where there are strong divisions between town and country do we see this type of analysis, hence rural housing 'pressure' in Britain is often an 'urban pressure': people moving from towns and cities to the countryside, 'urban sprawl' or an 'urban economy' against which a rural economy cannot compete. A key question is whether this particular interpretation of pressure suggests a divisive urban–rural culture, linking forward to a certain type of regulatory approach. We return to this issue later in this chapter and again in Chapter 13. How pressure is defined is a critical indicator of more fundamental social differences. It may also suggest particular political processes and priorities. In the Netherlands for example (Heins, Chapter 5), there is little sense that a rural society is at threat from urban newcomers, and the whole issue of housing pressure is couched in terms of natural constraints inhibiting the growth of cities. The Dutch example perhaps suggests a weaker division between town and country and an environmental and growth debate that relegates rural community considerations behind more general policy objectives. But this certainly is not the case in Wales (Edwards, Chapter 12), where housing and migration pressure are synonymous. Indeed, here the divisions between town and country are frequently dressed in cultural and Welsh language terms, and issues regarding social equity and individual (housing) rights are prioritised. Strong divisions between town and country (or English and Welsh) emerge in Wales as they do, but in slightly different forms, in both Scotland (Shucksmith and Conway) and England (Hoggart). However, in Sweden, the idea that an urban population threatens intrinsically rural communities has far less currency. Folkesdotter (Chapter 4) points to the lateness of urbanisation in Scandinavia, traditional work and commuting patterns, and strong urban–rural family ties as just some of the factors resulting in a far weaker divide between town and country. This suggests a more coherent and less divided culture and has resulted in policy responses that address issues of social equity that are not based on containing an urban population. That said, parts of Sweden are experiencing certain housing consumption pressures, particularly the west coast peninsulas which have attracted a relatively large number of foreign second home buyers during the last decade (see Folkesdotter, Chapter 4).

In many ways, the first two topics are closely linked and the perceived nature of housing pressure determines how national and rural policy might be either decoupled or treated as one. But coverage of these issues by the case study authors enables us to place particular policies within their proper context. Why this is necessary and how it is achieved are topics examined in Chapters 2 and 13.

The focus and nature of strategy and policy

An objective of the original project was to relate strategy and policies (at partic-ular levels – national, perhaps regional and local) to different types of housing pressure and therefore arrive at some evaluation of the possibility of lifting policy ideas from one country and applying them elsewhere. If, for instance, the Netherlands had a particular means of sourcing additional low-cost housing in some rural communities, could this be replicated in Scotland? Our current objective is not to identify policy lessons, though these may emerge in later analysis. Rather, our concern is with the way in which strategy and policy links back to the cultural and political conditions identified by the authors in the earlier sections of their case study chapters: these links are subsequently used to distinguish policy regimes. At this strategy and policy level, a number of different issues are addressed including the level at which policy is implemented, the involvement of non-governmental organisations in design and implementation, the nature of policy tools (i.e. reliance on land use planning mechanisms or tax measures to exert influence on housing markets) and the success that particular approaches have enjoyed. Policy is viewed as an expression of both cultural and political conditions and of the way in which housing pressure is interpreted, which also has a cultural root. Similarly, the success or failure of policy also says a great deal about the same prevailing conditions.

In Italy (Padovani and Vettoretti, Chapter 7), for example, the state has responded to environmental pressures by developing restrictive planning policy. This policy is implemented by local administrations; but these administrations themselves are tied into a local culture that displays a mistrust of state interven-tion and places far greater emphasis on the family as an agent of social welfare. In the south of the country, in particular, the flouting (and hence failure) of planning law is commonplace: when a family member needs a home, a new dwelling is often erected on family-owned land without recourse to planning offi-cials. The proliferation of illegal housebuilding in Italy is both a measure of the informality of policy control and an indication of the weakness of government agencies relative to the importance of the family (see Chapter 13). It also suggests that the balance of power is with the market (and private individuals) rather than the state in this instance. This contrasts with the situation in northern Europe where policy procedures are more formalised and more regularly adhered to. However, both Gulbrandsen (Chapter 3) and Folkesdotter are careful to point out that a good track-record in policy enforcement is only possible where regu-lations are reasonable and acceptable. Hence, there are examples of policies in Norway governing the occupancy of second homes (termed 'extra houses' by Gulbrandsen) that are not always implemented by local authorities fearful of facing insurmountable enforcement difficulties. However, the reviews of strategy and policy suggest broad policy regimes differentiated by the relative power of the state versus the power of private interests, and perhaps also by underlying attitudes towards state intervention and interference.

Our view is that such cultural factors have produced three distinctive regimes: one that is more regulatory in nature and where power rests more firmly with the state; another that is more informal and prioritises private interest; and one borne of an entrenched urban–rural debate and resulting in a more transient form of power that shifts between competing urban–rural interests.

Structure of the book

The final purpose of this book is to look beyond national and local policy and to consider more fundamental differences and commonalities across the countries of Western Europe. Allen in Chapter 2 initiates the process by setting out a framework of questions for dealing with comparative analysis, using the example of regulatory approaches towards second homes. These questions – aimed at identifying the causes of potential policy differences and similarities – dig beneath the level of policy and aim to provide some justification for extracting European 'themes'. A detailed comparative analysis, drawing on this framework, is presented in Chapter 13, and this precedes a final thematic discussion in Chapter 14.

It is not our intention at this stage to describe in depth the nature of the framework employed in Chapter 13, though some of the detail has been suggested earlier in this introduction. The arrangement of the ten national case study chapters (3 to 12) reflects what we consider to be fundamental divisions, as described briefly in the last section.

Countries arranged within each of the three Parts of the book all share – in very approximate terms – a similar cultural condition. And these different cultural conditions translate into distinct political debates and subsequently into particular policy approaches. Chapter 13 presents the differences in terms of power regimes, considering where political power lies, how it is used and by whom. Here, it is only necessary to note that four of our case study countries are characterised by weak urban–rural differences and by political priorities expressed in terms of universal approaches to housing and planning issues, sometimes manifest as rights governing the housing market irrespective of locational differences. We have deemed these to be cohesive cultures with regulatory regimes (Part One). The next three countries appear to have atomistic cultures, frequently prioritising family over state in terms of welfare provision and in terms of how housing is produced. These cultures emerge as informal regimes where the state may sometimes appear an ineffective regulator of housing production. And finally, the last three chapters all display divisive cultures in which urban–rural divisions are more sharply focused, creating an unstable regime punctuated by conflict and where power is more transient. Again, these divisions are explained more fully once the case study material has been presented. At that stage, there is a clear need to explain how different observations might be interpreted, and perhaps also to show the common themes that emerge from this sample analysis of rural housing in Western Europe.

With this rationale in mind, the following divisions are used within the main body of case study material:

- Part One: Cohesive Cultures, Regulatory Regimes
- Part Two: Atomistic Cultures, Laissez-Faire Regimes
- Part Three: Divisive Cultures, Unstable Regimes

Part One: Cohesive Cultures, Regulatory Regimes: Norway, Sweden, the Netherlands and France have all been placed within the first part of the book. This positioning does not reflect any belief that these countries share a common history or similar policy objectives. The affiliations are far looser than that. We simply suggest that these countries are closer together in terms of shared attitudes towards urban–rural differences, the role of the state in policy intervention and, ultimately, in the way that policy is designed. This part of the book begins with Gulbrandsen's examination of Norway which focuses on the regulation of housing in terms of its occupancy and use through the creation of a suite of universal housing 'rights'. Folkesdotter's appraisal of housing in Sweden has a similar focus, but also looks at Swedish attempts to balance different uses of rural dwellings. Heins' examination of the Netherlands suggests both a weak (and graded) division of rural and urban areas and a more coherent and general policy approach based on national spatial planning. And finally, Auclair and Vanoni's French review concentrates on demographic and economic change, painting a picture of a rural revival mediated by central planning.

Part Two: Atomistic Cultures, Laissez-Faire Regimes: Italy, Spain and the Republic of Ireland are placed together for the same reasons. They all have various 'weaker' state characteristics, manifest in a more informal regulatory regime and in a range of actual contraventions of planning law. This is marked by the informality of the building sector in Spain, illegal housebuilding in Italy and much-publicised sporadic housebuilding in the countryside in Ireland. Padovani and Vettoretto's review of housing in rural Italy suggests a preeminence of general rather than focused policy as well as a traditional reliance on the family as an agent of social welfare (and housing provision). A similar picture emerges in Spain with Valenzuela highlighting the informality of the Spanish housebuilding industry in the countryside. Finnerty, Guerin and O Connell's focus on the Republic of Ireland points to a lack of any tradition of separating rural from urban concerns and makes note of the need to responsibly manage growth in the countryside. It is suggested that planning control has under-performed and failed to prevent low quality developments in many more attractive rural areas.

Part Three: Divisive Cultures, Unstable Regimes: England, Scotland and Wales have the obvious similarity of all being constituent parts of the United Kingdom. It comes as no surprise therefore that they share some common cultural roots, and similar political structures and attitudes – notwithstanding the recent process of devolution. All three countries endure a divisive urban–rural debate, which we believe shapes and underpins political discourse. It has created an unstable regime in which power moves, at different levels, to reflect what are sometimes seen as incompatible 'rural' or 'urban' agendas. However, as well as shared conditions, England, Scotland and Wales also have a number of obvious differences: for instance, urban–rural debates in Wales are, as Edwards suggests, frequently couched in terms of Welsh–English cultural divisions and the survival of the Welsh language in the face of an English (urban) threat. And in Scotland, Shucksmith and Conway argue that the urban–rural debate is complicated by faith in the public sector, which has diminished – to a far greater extent – in both England and Wales in recent years. This third part of the book begins with a contribution from Hoggart dealing more with general principles than local detail. There is, however, a strong link to both the Scottish and Welsh chapters, both of which highlight the types of policy emerging from this broad regime.

This then is the overall structure of the book. As indicated earlier in this chapter, the case studies themselves also provide stand-alone snapshots of current policy and practice within the ten countries examined. Our hope is that the book will have some value and appeal at both this policy level and also more broadly by offering an interpretation across the studies of how the rural housing debate in different parts of Western Europe has developed, and may continue to develop in the future, shaped, of course, by those underlying considerations that have been introduced above and that are examined in greater depth in the final chapters.

Chapter 2
Theories and levels of comparative analysis

Chris Allen

Policy transfer and the rural housing problem

Lesson learning between countries has always been a central feature of the policy-making process. For many years, this has involved civil servants and politicians in the ad hoc conduct of 'fact finding' visits to other countries on the proviso that housing policies used elsewhere might be imported and transposed to solve comparable problems at home. More recently, however, the expansion of supranational levels of government (e.g. the European Union, World Bank and International Monetary Fund), has led to the creation of an institutional structure with the primary purpose of *systematically* 'harmonising' public policy within and between nation states. But, how easy is it to transfer policies – in this case rural housing policies – from one society to another?

There has been a gradual move away from the view that policy transfer is unproblematic (see particularly Harloe, 1985, 1995; Ball *et al.*, 1988; Power, 1993) as postmodern theories that emphasise time and space differences have exerted more influence on comparative housing research (see Kemeny, 1992, 1995; Kemeny and Lowe, 1998; Allen, 1999a,b). Thus, while Kemeny *et al.* accept that the characteristics of capitalism stretch across time and space, they reject the proposition that societies (i.e. spatial locations) are located at different points (i.e. temporal locations) on a linear trajectory of capitalist development. This is because differences between societies are merely attributed to the existence of 'leader' and 'laggard' societies (Donnison, 1967; Wilensky, 1975; Harloe, 1985, 1995; Gould, 1990), so that the transfer of policies from the former to bring the latter 'into line' can be justified.

Concern over this issue of policy transfer is reflected in recent work on second and holiday housebuilding in rural areas. Since the 1970s a number of commentators have been canvassing for *change of dwelling use* (to a second home) and *acquisition of rural property* to be brought under planning control (Bielckus, *et al.*, 1972; Downing and Dower, 1973; Pyne, 1973; Dower, 1977; Dartington, 1977). On this basis, housing policy makers have also advocated the virtues of borrowing the policies successfully used to regulate *change of use* in Sweden (and other parts of Scandinavia) as the panacea for controlling the adverse impacts of the expansion in second housebuilding in Britain. Indeed, a leading figure in the Labour party suggested, in 1990, that a future Labour government would allow

> local authorities [to] restrict the growth of second homes in the affected areas by ensuring that an existing family home would need planning consent for *change of use* before it could be sold as a second home in much the same way as change of use is required to change a home into an office, for example. The procedure would be subject to appeal. *This is the practice in a number of European countries.* There is no question of a ban on second homes.
>
> (Soley, 1990: 39, emphasis added)

In this case, the general view was that specific planning regulations (successfully employed, for example, in Denmark: Gallent and Tewdwr-Jones, 2000) were transferable. Yet, when similar policies (aimed at controlling the use of residential property) were employed in Britain, a number of review studies demonstrated that they did not bring the desired results. For example, Shucksmith (1981, 1990) found that the housing access problems facing some rural communities could not be alleviated by preventing houses from being used as retirement or holiday homes through the use of occupancy conditions. Such conditions merely shunted external demand from new to old stock, causing further price rises in the latter and a parallel reduction in new-build activity as profits in this part of the market were squeezed. This resulted from the fact that there were now fewer buyers permitted to compete for new housing.

The use of planning controls to regulate change of use from primary residence to second home is equally problematic. In Britain, the planning system is principally concerned with material land use change and although planning authorities may sometimes reach decisions on the basis of the type and tenure of housing proposed in a new scheme, they cannot (or should not) concern themselves with the number of days or weeks that owners might choose to stay at home. And this appears to be the benchmark against which second and first homes would be differentiated (Gallent and Tewdwr-Jones, 2001) under such a system. Clearly, this could constitute a serious infringement to the human rights of homeowners.

This of course raises the question as to how certain policies are apparently workable in one place but not in another. The example cited above can be used as a point of entry into this broader question and the remainder of this chapter seeks to provide an answer by:

1   providing an overview of theoretical debates in relation to comparative housing policy research;
2   outlining a methodological framework for undertaking comparison that is sensitive to the differences between countries;
3   outlining a methodological framework for analysing the lessons that can and cannot be learned from other societies, and thus which policies might be successfully transferred; and
4   illustrating an example of comparative research and lesson-learning analysis in action, using the rural housing problems created by the expansion of second housebuilding as an example.

Theoretical debates in comparative housing policy

The convergence thesis is based on the belief that modern societies are all trying to reach the same destination and can therefore learn from each others' experiences (Bell, 1960; Kerr, 1962; Lipset, 1963; Eyden, 1965; Wedderburn, 1965; Zald, 1965 Marshall, 1967, 1970; Mishra, 1973; O'Connor, 1973; Wilensky, 1975). In situations where societies have different characteristics, convergence theory proposes that the societies in question are simply located at different points of historical development. Thus, convergence theory conceives of 'leader' and 'laggard' societies (Donnison, 1967; Wilensky, 1975; Harloe, 1985, 1995; Gould, 1990) and encourages the so-called laggard societies to 'catch up' with the leaders by emulating them (Kemeny, 1981, 1992, 1995; Allen, 1999a,b).

Since the housing problems of other societies are seen to be universal (Marshall, 1970), the housing policies successfully used to address these problems in one society can, the logic follows, be re-packaged and 'borrowed . . . for use in another' (Wolman, 1992: 27). This has been referred to as the process of 'policy diffusion' (Freeman and Tester, 1996), 'policy transfer' (Dolowitz and Marsh, n.d.) and 'lesson drawing' (Rose, 1991). This view has as many opponents as proponents: so why is there no simple route to learning the lessons from other national experiences?

'But societies really are different': the divergence comparative research method

Divergent theorists generally accept the notion that the characteristics of modern societies are similar. However, the proposition that the differences between societies can be accounted for by the fact that they are located at different

('leader', 'laggard') points of historical development, or as ad hoc and unimportant 'variations', is regarded as too simplistic. Conversely, divergent theorists
regard the differences between societies as arising from their unique (economic,
political and cultural) history and, therefore, as important contextual factors that
influence how those societies view rural housing policy.

Divergent theorists have criticised the suggestion that rural housing
problems manifest themselves in common ways because key historical (e.g.
political, cultural etc.) differences emerge between societies over time (Kemeny,
1992, 1995; Doling, 1997; Allen, 1999a,b). Kemeny (1995) has argued that
overlooking these key differences is akin to committing 'the Romeo error'.[1] The
'Romeo error' involves using the taken-for-granted political and cultural assumptions of one's home society, in order to establish the questions that need to
be asked about other societies. Convergence theorists thus identify apparently similar problems in different societies, such as those stemming from
in-migration or, conversely, a localised exodus of population. They then focus
on the *policy instruments* used to tackle these problems elsewhere, so that they
can be borrowed to solve *apparently* comparable problems at home (Kemeny,
1992, 1995; Kemeny and Lowe, 1998; Allen, 1999a,b). That is, comparative
research questions have, then, been framed so as to extract detailed information
about the 'nuts and bolts' details of housing policies used in other countries
(Figure 2.1: question 1, column 2, row c), so that lessons can be learned from
the 'problem solving' experiences of 'foreign' policy makers. Indeed, such was
the purpose of the original Scottish Homes work undertaken by Shucksmith
et al. (2000) that forms the basis of this book.

In using the 'Romeo method', comparative researchers have failed to
analyse the extent to which political (Figure 2.1: row a) and cultural (Figure 2.1:
row b) factors influence the nature of the housing policies and strategies (Figure
2.1: row c) used to address problems that manifest themselves in highly specific
ways in different societies. This being so, researchers have failed to ask themselves whether it is possible to successfully transfer housing policies between
contextually particular societies (Figure 2.1: question 3, column 3, row c) and,
as a result, have inappropriately called for the importation of housing policies
that have had limited (if any) relevance to their own societies.

Divergent comparative research method and rural housing

The critical question here is how might a more sensitive, divergent method be
applied to rural housing problems in Europe? In order to overcome the limitations of the Romeo method, a number of housing researchers have begun to
develop 'divergence' methods for studying comparative housing policy (Kemeny,

1. Investigative focus in 'lesson learning'	2. General research focus for comparative analysis	3. Examples of research questions for the comparative analysis of rural housing
(a) Housing politics	What is the nature and focus of rural housing politics in different societies? e.g. liberal, social democratic	Are there differing social objectives and views of the market?
(b) Housing cultures	What are the cultural conditions and values that underpin rural housing policies? e.g. the nature of 'the countryside', its traditions and the way it is used and who uses it	What is the relationship between town and country? How are town–country distinctions formulated in different places? To what extent is this relationship mediated by issues of consumption and production?
(c) Housing policies	In order to meet particular political objectives, given specific cultural conditions, what rural housing policies are employed?	What policies do different countries employ to regulate their rural housing markets?

2.1 Levels of analysis in comparative research.
Source: Adapted from Allen *et al.*, 1999

1981, 1992, 1995; Barlow and Duncan, 1994; Allen, 1999a,b). Although these divergent methods were not developed in a rural context, they can, of course, be applied here. Each of these perspectives emphasise the methodological importance of examining how the inter-related contexts of rural housing politics and rural housing culture produce rural housing problems and policies that reflect the peculiar history of the society in question.

For example, in an urban context, Kemeny (1992) has argued that dwelling type, density and design policies are heavily influenced by the political history of a country. Thus, countries that have experienced long periods of social demo-cratic political control, such as Sweden, have been shown to be associated with the widespread use of high-density multi-dwelling buildings such as flats. Conversely, countries with a liberal political culture, such as Britain, have been associated with low-density uni-dwelling buildings such as semi-detached, detached, terraced houses (Kemeny, 1981, 1992). Other politically and culturally sensitive comparative research has shown how tenure preferences are determined by the nature of the relationship between 'private' and 'public' housing in differ-ent types of (free/command/social) housing market economies. For example, Kemeny (1995) demonstrates how social market economies 'policy construct' a high prevalence of demand for (low-cost) rental dwellings, whereas liberal cultures 'policy construct' a more intense preference for housebuilding.

Similarly, Allen *et al.* (1999) show how high-density housing policies in social democratic societies, such as Sweden, generate a widespread desire for rural leisure which, given that there is also a high prevalence of low-cost renting (and thus, greater disposable income after housing costs have been accounted for), is expressed in the form of a high demand for second homes in the coun-tryside surrounding urban centres. They also show how the situation is the reverse in liberal societies, such as Britain, with low-density, high-cost ownership housing policies.

On this basis, Allen *et al.* (1999) argue that there are clear historical, polit-ical and cultural reasons as to why Swedish and Danish style planning regulations will not necessarily work in predictable and desirable ways outside their original contexts. In the case of second housebuilding, they argue that the crucial hurdle derives from the institutional separation of 'primary use' and 'secondary use' housing markets in Sweden, which has no parallel in Britain. So, the expansive, stable and focused demand for second housebuilding that has resulted from the 'policy construction' of high-density housing (thus creating a demand for rural tourism) and low-cost rental housing (thus facilitating the channelling of this demand into second housebuilding) has enabled Sweden, for example, to create a separate sector of purpose-built second homes. To this end, the plan-ning regulations relating to *changes in use* and the *acquisition of property* merely represent what could be termed 'second level' measures. These operate, then, within the context of a broader (and 'first level' element of the overall) strategy that is designed to satisfy the demand for second housebuilding through purpose-built development. This being so, planning regulation is merely used as an *interim* measure to regulate demand for second homes in the 'primary use' housing sector while land is released to enable the construction industry to respond to the increased demand for purpose-built second housebuilding. Thus, instead of shifting demand onto 'primary use' housing stock that is not subjected to planning regulation (leading to increased house prices and the exclusion of locals from the housing market, as in Britain), the overall strategy preserves primary use housing stock for rural locals by absorbing, in the medium term, the additional demand for second homes in purpose-built developments of typically 100–200 houses. To this end, house price rises are only ever a temporary phenomenon that wane when the market restructures in a manner that is able to channel demand for residential tourism away from the primary use rural housing market and into purpose-built second home developments.

A broader policy strategy (beyond planning control) would therefore be required to make the Swedish policy instruments work in Britain.[2] Specifically, this would require an institutional separation between 'primary use' and 'secondary use' housing markets so that the demand for second housebuilding could be absorbed by purpose-built developments. However, Allen *et al.* (1999) point out that answering the question about 'what is (politically, culturally etc.) different?' does not take us to the end point of comparative housing policy analysis. A further question then needs to be posed about the wider (cultural and political) context that has been discovered. This asks whether it is possible to transfer this Swedish/Danish separation – between primary and secondary housing markets – to Britain. This again requires an analysis that is culturally sensitive.

In their analysis of this particular rural housing issue, Allen *et al.* point out that these particular European countries have only been able to develop these specific responses to second homes because low-cost rent pooling in high-density urban housing markets has generated an *expansive* and *stable* demand for second homes. Swedish construction companies have therefore been willing to engage in the purpose-built development of second homes because the economic risks that are associated with such ventures are minimal. Conversely, the demand for second homes in Britain has been *more sporadic* (occurring as and when market conditions, such as interest rates, and the disposable incomes of wealthier home-owners allow). This has not provided the conditions in which the demand for second housebuilding could develop, and be maintained, at high *or* stable levels. Reflecting this, they argue that a strategy based on the construction of purpose-built second home complexes would be less likely to work in Britain (as it has in Sweden) because financiers would be reticent to engage in such risk ventures where patterns of demand were both low and unstable.[3]

Conclusions: learning the lessons

In the discussion of comparative housing research presented in this chapter I have argued that while housing problems might appear to be 'basically the same' in modern societies, it can be misleading to merely concentrate analysis on the nuts and bolts of the housing policies used elsewhere. In practice, the net result of this approach to comparative research has been that *too many* 'lesson learners' have returned from 'fact finding' missions with an incomplete understanding of housing problems and policies of other societies.

The framework presented in this chapter has also shown that the nature of *policy problems*, such as those engendered in the expansion of second house-building, are particular to their societies of origin. Accordingly, it was suggested that *policy solutions* to address particular rural housing issues might become meaningless and ultimately fail if imported to, and transposed onto, the wrong societal context. Thus, whereas the 'Romeo error' researcher will simply ask one question, namely, 'what housing and planning policies are used to cure rural ills in other countries?', the comparative researcher – sensitive to the differences between societies – will ask the following sequence:

- What is the wider political and cultural context within which rural housing problems exist?
- Given this wider context, what is the nature of the rural housing problem at hand in that society?
- What housing and planning policies have been formulated to tackle the rural housing problems at hand and how do they fit into the wider picture?
- Is the *wider context* within which these housing and planning policies exist transferable?
- If so, what needs to be done to recreate these wider conditions so that the rural housing and planning policies used elsewhere can be successfully transferred?

Researching the broader political and cultural context within which housing and planning policies exist should not, then, be seen as an irrelevant self-indulgence. Rather, it should be seen as an integral part of the 'lesson learning' exercise. It is only when these broader contexts are recognised as a core element (rather than disregarded as disposable) of comparative investigation that relevant, albeit limited, exercises in policy transference can be conducted. Indeed, as I have argued in this chapter, the policy-transferring endeavour is frequently frustrating because the lessons that can be learned are often limited. Though at least the series of questions listed above gives some indication as to how the series of case studies presented in this book might be better 'read' and therefore better understood. Many of the issues raised in this chapter are revisited in Chapter 13 following the country illustrations of housing pressure and policy development.

Notes

1   Here, Kemeny is referring to the mistaken diagnosis of death in the Shakespearean tragedy *Romeo and Juliet*. In other words, the Romeo error refers to the tendency to uncritically adopt, rather than critically appraise, the common-sense assumptions, which infuse the subject of investigation. In comparative research, these assumptions will be derived from the researcher's country of origin. This leads to a neglect of the manner in which the culture of the country under study might differ significantly from that of the researcher's country of origin.

2   It is interesting to note that this type of market correction (i.e. provide more purpose-built second homes) is now being suggested in Wales, whereas previously only a negative approach to second homes had been contemplated.

3   Has this reality been understood/explored by the current proponents of this form of European solution?

Part One:
Cohesive Cultures, Regulatory Regimes

The next four chapters focus on countries representing what we have termed cohesive cultures, characterised by a less apparent division between urban and rural areas and a policy regime which is both more general in its approach – crossing town and country divisions – and more regulatory. Regulatory regimes are deemed to be those based on stronger central power with local policy often drawing directly on central statute.

In the case of Norway (Chapter 3) market regulation is commonly based on the creation of fundamental property rights. Close to a quarter of Norway's population resides in rural areas; for the most part, housing standards are high and the majority of people own their homes. Compared to other countries in Western Europe, urbanisation in Norway is often characterised as weak and relatively late in arriving. The result is that many people living in towns and cities retain strong family ties with rural communities and inheritance is a common way of acquiring property in the countryside. It has also produced a society less conscious of distinct urban–rural divisions.

Nationally, Gulbrandsen argues that Norwegian housing policy tended to evolve first and foremost within the larger cities, and particularly in Oslo. Here there was a traditional adversity towards private interest and as a result, policy – affecting rent control and construction – tended to deny the scope for private gain. Under these circumstances, home ownership – collective and co-operative, or individual – became the norm and was pegged on a philosophy of preventing anyone from making money by owning another person's home. Gulbrandsen's review of this philosophy helps to explain much of the thinking behind market controls away from Norway's cities: it also illustrates the values underlying the development of policy.

There are two key pressures facing rural Norway: first, pressure to convert farm properties into ordinary residential use and farmland into housing plots; and second, pressure to convert houses from year-round dwellings into recreational dwellings in areas with high landscape/leisure value. The housing market in rural Norway differs considerably from that in towns and built-up areas. First, the market in the countryside is less commercial, with properties changing hands as a result of family connections rather than through real estate agents. Second, the phenomenon of 'extra houses' is a critical part of the rural market, with about 10 per cent of the Norwegian population having an extra house. Again, these are frequently acquired through inheritance. But although market differences are apparent, it is these differences themselves that demonstrate the firm link between town and country: those working in towns often spend much of their time in the countryside. Yet agricultural decline has generated concern over the speed of land use change and the use of some former farmhouses as recreational dwellings. This has prompted a strong regulatory response.

Legislation has been drawn up to prevent particular changes. A Land Consolidation Act, Concessions Act and Allodial Act are used to determine who can acquire farm property, sale prices, physical changes to property and the use of farmhouses and land. The Concessions Act is particularly significant in that it imposes restrictions on real estate transactions. Many transactions cannot be made freely, but require concessions from local government. For example, a transaction involving a parcel of farmland over a certain size would be subject to a concession application, and if the concession were granted, conditions may well be applied. For instance, a buyer might have to live on the farm and engage in agriculture for a stipulated period. Other general obligations may also apply – perhaps relating to permanent occupancy – and are set out in both the Concessions Act and the Allodial Act. Buyers can also apply for dispensation from general obligations. In the housing context, it is dispensation from the residence obligation that is important and many such applications are received from people wishing to use property for recreational and non-permanent purposes.

Though this regulatory strategy is a direct response to the loss of farming land and of permanent residents in some areas, Gulbrandsen's analysis questions whether the priorities legitimising this strategy are correct in the light first, of Norway's limited housing problems, and second, more fundamental social changes. One could argue that the wrong priorities have resulted in a strict regulatory regime that denies the shifting social and economic reality: in this instance, policy may not be a true expression of the mood of the time.

In Chapter 4, attention shifts to Sweden, a country that shares Norway's low population densities and apparent abundance of both countryside and surplus housing. But as in Norway, there are a growing number of housing demand hotspots and these are the product of the fact that more people would like to live in Sweden's countryside than are currently doing so. There is strong demand from the urban population, especially in the light of major transport improvements in recent years. And added to this, many of Sweden's neighbours – particularly Norwegians, Danes and Germans – have been clambering to buy Swedish property in recent years, egged on by low house prices and a favourable exchange rate. Folkesdotter suggests that nearly half a million of Sweden's four million permanent dwellings are today used as holiday homes.

This growth is linked to change in the national economy, spurred on by global process, and manifest in a shrinking agricultural sector. As farming has declined, so too have the traditional values associated with it. Therefore the Swedish countryside is open to new ideas and new ways of living. This is viewed as both good – in the sense that new life is breathed into communities losing population – and bad – in the sense that traditions may be lost. What is clear, however, is that a fundamental social and cultural shift is under way. It is suggested that the agricultural landscape has been reconfigured as a landscape of recreation, marked by the increase in seasonal retreats in remoter areas and weekend cottages closer to urban centres.

For Folkesdotter, these changes are not inherently bad, though they may bring unfortunate consequences: including environmental degradation and a reduction in service viability. Also, higher prices for housing mean higher taxes for locals: and this imbalance (between income and tax) needs some redress. The opportunities for such redress occur at three levels: national, regional and municipal. Government has recently sought to amend tax law and this is welcomed. Plans are also afoot to prevent homes being bought up for holiday use. Folkesdotter is far more reticent about this latter move, claiming such restrictions would be difficult to enforce and might run contrary to European law. She points out that Denmark's longstanding measures to curtail holiday home growth (and foreign property acquisition) may soon be judged illegal by the European Union. So beyond such legislative tools, regional co-operation is seen as an important means of *positively managing* social change, though it appears that municipal inconsistency in the application of management tools (including development control) may well leave some regional strategies in disarray. A key message emerging from Folkesdotter's chapter is that Sweden has tended, in the past, to adopt a fairly centralised approach to dealing with housing market changes. Today, however, significant social upheavals on a regional level are prompting a reappraisal of this strategy.

Chapter 5 starts by painting a familiar picture – familiar at least to British readers – of strong demand for homes in the countryside against a backdrop of restricted supply. Demand levels in the Netherlands are especially high in the 'peri-urban' countryside close to those cities that together form the Ranstad. For those who seek rural homes, the countryside is perceived as the antithesis of the urban: a place of safety, quietness, health and beauty. Given negative experiences of urban living and the concentrated poverty of many Dutch cities, it perhaps appears natural that so many households seek to escape. But escape is only possible for those with higher incomes. The Netherlands is one of the smallest countries in Europe with almost overwhelming population pressure, and therefore housing land is scarce and house prices high. The planning system, in its promotion of urban compaction and environmental protection, adds to this pressure by heavily restricting the release of rural housing sites. What this means is that housing access in the countryside is almost entirely governed by income: planning constraint favours the few and works against the many. But Heins argues that housebuilding in the post-productivist countryside is a positive activity, bringing economic rewards in both the short and longer terms. And restrictions should not necessarily be the same in peripheral and peri-urban rural areas: rather, and for the sake of widening social access, such restrictions should be eased at the edge of the large urban centres. In other words, the time is right to promote a compromise between development constraint and the need to release more housing land. The Netherlands may be small, but the population is growing and a steady supply of new homes is critical. For the Dutch, at least, the answer seems to lie in high-quality edge-development that gives those who aspire to rural living much of what they demand without compromising more sensitive countryside areas.

The Netherlands, largely because of physical factors, has developed a highly regulatory policy regime. However, Heins does point to town and country divisions and the perceptions of significant quality of life gains for those able to move away from the cities. This might suggest a more divisive urban–rural culture. But the Netherlands is placed here in this first part of the book because the view that the countryside is the 'antithesis' of the urban need not be confused with rigid urban–rural dividing lines. While there may well be a desire to escape from some urban areas, the distance between town and country, physically and culturally, is not great and this is reflected in a spatial planning strategy that tends to emphasise city–regional linkages rather than social differences.

The sixth chapter takes us to France; a country which shares many of the characteristics of both Norway and Sweden and the Netherlands. The focus of Auclair and Vanoni's chapter is demographics and particularly the recent population revival witnessed in many parts of the countryside. Since the national census of 1975, it has been clear that rural areas have been experiencing net population increase: a pattern reaffirmed in 1990 and 1999. Seventy-two out of ninety-five rural *departements* experienced positive change leading many commentators to claim a new era of 'rural dynamism'.

But higher demand for housing in the countryside has brought significant supply and access problems in the most pressured areas; and included amongst these is the countryside around Paris, which has been subject to new pressures from commuters. More common rural problems relate to low housing quality, access difficulties facing specific groups (particularly the young) and the social tensions that some ex-urban households appear to bring to rural communities. Auclair and Vanoni argue that four key issues are apparent: these relate to housing quality, selective affordability problems, low-income rural in-migration and holiday homes (which are not a problem per se but, because of the trans-formation of these to permanent residences, are feeding rural population increases). These issues have brought new challenges for the social housing system and for approaches to social support. Government, they argue, is acutely aware of the social problems stemming from new demographic patterns and is attempting to heal regional ills through a selective strategy of assistance to social house-building programmes. The key challenge facing France is how to deal with growth in the countryside and thereby ensure that the benefits of a rural renais-sance are shared more evenly. This challenge is being taken up by a central administration wedded to the idea of strong government and a socialist tradi-tion. So, as in Sweden and Norway, there is a reliance on constitutional power: the conferment of fundamental rights and a powerful planning agenda as the means to ensure greater social equity.

Chapter 3
Norway[1]

Lars Gulbrandsen

Introduction

Between a fifth and a quarter of Norway's population live in rural communities. Settlement has traditionally been dispersed, and the rural building stock has, almost without exception, comprised detached houses or farmhouses constructed from wood. Owner-occupancy has been the norm, not only among farm-owners, but also, in the last century, to an increasing degree among the rural working class. In the past fifty years the rural population has declined considerably, but those who have chosen to remain country dwellers have seen a steady improvement in the standard of dwellings, which is still appreciably better than in the towns. Apart from centrally located areas and areas attractive for holiday and recreational houses, however, the housing stock in rural Norway has low market value.

Hence the housing policy challenge in Norway's rural communities refers neither to poor housing standards nor inadequate housebuilding; nor is it neighbourhoods turning into slums or social segregation. Two types of pressure can be identified. First, pressure to convert farm properties into ordinary residential use and farmland into housing plots in centrally located areas where this type of property has a high residential value. Second, pressure to convert houses from year-round dwellings into recreational dwellings in areas with high recreational value. This pressure is countered by a local development policy designed both to uphold agriculture and preserve local communities by ensuring continued year-round settlement. Both objectives are promoted through legislation in which consideration for the farming sector is at centre-stage, despite the fact that this sector is relatively marginal and frequently located in more peripheral districts. Whereas the housing market in general in Norway has undergone deregulation in the past twenty years, just over 10 per cent of Norwegian housing still remains subject to a regulatory regime anchored in farming that is meeting growing opposition from owner-interests whose frame of reference is a deregulated housing market.

Any meaningful analysis of rural housing is reliant on establishing a working definition of town and country that can be operationalised in available data.

In the second part of this chapter, I briefly describe urbanisation in Norway, which concludes with a definition of sparsely populated areas that provides the best fit with empirical data. In the third part, I provide an overview of the main features of Norwegian housing policy and housebuilding, and in part four describe Norway's present building stock by contrasting the housing stock in sparsely populated areas with the housing stock in towns and built-up areas. In the fifth part I look at the regulatory regime imposed on parts of today's rural housing stock. I discuss how conflict can arise between, on the one hand, the policy objective of preserving the farm sector and year-round settlement and, on the other, individual interests based on financial priorities, local ties and family relationships. Regulation of the general housing market in Norway was removed in the 1980s. This was largely because regulation increasingly conflicted with the interests of a large majority of house owners, without concurrently having clearly favourable effects for weakly placed groups in the market (Gulbrandsen, 1983). In conclusion, I examine the regulation that still applies in rural Norway in terms of its effectiveness and legitimacy.

Town, country and urbanisation

In the past two hundred years Norway has seen much urbanisation. Two centuries ago Norway was an agrarian society with 90 per cent of the population living in rural areas. Urbanisation gathered momentum with the advent of industrialisation in the second half of the nineteenth century. Compared with other countries in Western Europe, however, urbanisation can be characterised as weak, and was relatively late in coming. It was only after the Second World War that urbanisation picked up speed in Norway. The very term 'urbanisation' was little used prior to the 1960s (Rasmussen, 1995), and there is still a strong rural tradition of negativism to urbanisation as a result (Rasmussen, 1988). Large sections of Norway's urban population still have close ties with a rural background in which they were born and grew up. As recently as the period 1970–1990 much of the out-migration of the elderly from the capital, Oslo, was to south-eastern and southern parts of the country that had contributed substantially to in-migration to the city earlier in the century (Myklebost, 1989).

Table 3.1 shows the development in population size and its distribution in town and country over the past two hundred years. In Norway, an administrative distinction is drawn between urban municipalities and rural municipalities. Until 1845 this was the only means of distinguishing between town and country. A hundred years later, urban areas of this type accounted for just over a tenth of the population, and the administrative towns' share of the population had remained unchanged between 1900 and 1946. In the 1950s, the geographer

Table 3.1 Population in Norway and percentage living in sparsely populated areas (1801–1999)

Date	Population (in thousands)	Share living in sparsely populated areas (%)
1801	883.6	91
1835	1290.0	89
1855	1490.0	83
1875	1813.4	76
1900	2240.0	64
1920	2649.8	55
1946	3156.9	50
1960	3591.2	43
1970	3874.1	34
1980	4091.1	30
1990	4247.5	28
1999	4445.3	24

Source: Statistics Norway

Hallstein Myklebost re-examined (1960) the census data from 1875 onwards. He introduced the concept of '*tettsted*' which he defined as a collection of houses with at least 200 inhabitants, where at least 75 per cent of the economically active population were employed outside farming and forestry and where houses were normally separated by less than 50 metres. Myklebost's research has provided the basis for subsequent statistical descriptions of Norwegian urbanisation. Sparsely populated areas have in this way become negatively defined as a residual category in relation to towns and built-up areas, which are more precisely defined.

Centralisation has taken place despite a clear-cut, resolute political objective of preserving the settlement pattern. The trend has been steady and strong, although in-migration to the towns slowed for a few years in the wake of the first EU referendum in 1972 (Rasmussen, 1995). Outlying municipalities in the interior of south-east Norway and in northern Norway have shown the largest drop in population.

Most municipalities have one or more centres with a dense population. Even in rural municipalities a certain portion of the population live in a *tettsted*, and therefore a household cannot be localised to densely or sparsely populated areas based on knowing the name of the municipality of residence. The data I employ to describe today's housing situation are based on the dwelling of the individual household, and this is described in terms of its location in relation to surrounding buildings. The category 'sparsely populated area' is defined as fewer than 200 inhabitants in a cluster. This is much the same classification as was recommended by Hallstein Myklebost in 1960.

Housing policy and housebuilding in Norway

Norwegian housing policy originated in the biggest towns, with conditions in the capital providing a particularly significant basis. Industrialisation and vigorous urbanisation in the second half of the 1800s laid the foundation for a wide-ranging rental market, especially in Oslo. In the 1890s, the city's population and the rate of construction of apartment blocks both gathered pace. In 1920, between 90 and 95 per cent of the city's households were tenants. The share of tenants fell with the size of town. In the next four largest towns the tenancy share was 69 per cent, in the other medium-size towns 58 per cent, while in the country's smallest urban municipalities tenants were in the minority at 45 per cent. In rural municipalities, owner-occupancy was by far the commonest form of tenure. Sixty-seven per cent of households in rural municipalities owned the house they lived in (Gulbrandsen, 1988).

Housing policy in Oslo was clearly adverse to private landlords, both in terms of rental controls and of housing construction organised so as to deny scope to private interests. Both in Oslo and in the other major towns, co-operative housebuilding was at centre-stage. Co-operative housebuilding was organised by co-operative housebuilding associations, usually in conjunction with the local authorities. Housing was organised in housing co-operatives each of whose residents disposed of their flat by owning a share of the local co-operative. In time, however, the participants' ownership of the flats has been extended so that owning or disposing of a dwelling via this form of collective ownership has come more and more to resemble owner-occupancy on an individual basis.

An all-embracing system for financing housing construction was first put in place after the Second World War. In Norway the bulk of new dwellings were financed by the state-owned Housing Bank. This applied to all housing co-operatives, and also to the majority of owner-occupied detached houses. There was also sizeable housing production in rural districts, although another state-owned bank, *Bustadsbanken*, played a part here in the first twenty years after the war (Gulbrandsen, 1998). At the turn of the millennium, dwelling number one million financed by the Housing Bank was completed. A good two-thirds of the houses built after the Second World War were funded principally by loans from the state bank.

Residents became homeowners, either individually or together with others in housing co-operatives. To enable as many as possible to do this, loans were heavily subsidised. The object was to prevent anyone making money by owning other people's dwellings, but neither should they earn money on their own dwelling, for example by selling it. Housing was therefore subject to strict price controls. In the case of owner-occupier dwellings the controls were removed in 1969, although sale prices for Housing Bank-financed owner-occupied dwellings still needed approval from the Housing Bank if the mortgage was to be transferred to the new owner. At the end of the 1960s and the start of the 1970s, it was gradually recognised that the regulatory measures were not working as intended, but a political consensus on the policy implications was lacking (Gulbrandsen, 1983). In the first instance, a majority favoured making regulation even more effective and extensive (Annaniassen, 2002). Indeed in the prevailing political climate it proved possible to achieve a majority in favour of tighter controls on farm properties by incorporating residence and operating requirements in the Allodial Act and the Concessions Act with effect from 1975. Price controls on flats in housing co-operatives were removed in the 1980s, and since then price formation in the housing market has been determined by supply and demand. The regulatory provisions of the Allodial Act and Concessions Act were not removed, however. Thus a form of price regulation has continued for a substantial part of the housing stock in rural Norway. I return to this issue later in the chapter.

Present-day housing stock in urban and rural Norway

The housing stock in present-day Norway can be described using four dwelling characteristics, all of which vary systematically with degree of urbanisation. These are: type of dwelling; size of dwelling; form of tenure; and market value.

There is little in the way of villages in Norway. Apart from house clusters around a courtyard or farmyard that occurred in western and northern Norway up to the second half of the 1800s, the prevailing tradition has been dispersed habitation. In the old agrarian society the predominant type of house was the farmhouse, which in time was supplemented with a steadily increasing element of ordinary detached houses. With growing urbanisation, the prevalence of other types of small houses, such as row houses, increased. Apartment blocks are to be found in most towns, but only to a limited extent outside the biggest towns. In the capital, Oslo, apartment blocks are the predominant building type (Table 3.2).

Detached houses are often large and spacious. Cramped housing is traditionally a city phenomenon, although Norway's first sociologist, Eilert Sundt, observed – in the mid-1800s – some fairly primitive housing conditions in rural areas too (Sundt, 1862, 1975). Table 3.3 collates data from population censuses in 1920 and 1950 with survey data from the 1990s. While housing consumption (judged in terms of space standards) has increased dramatically in both town

Table 3.2 Types of housing by degree of urbanisation

	Three largest towns	Towns/built up areas with more than 2,000 inhabitants	Towns/built up areas with less than 2,000 inhabitants	Sparsely populated areas	Total
% in detached houses	19	52	69	83	52
% in other small houses	27	27	20	10	23
% in apartment blocks	50	11	5	1	20
N:	(2,320)	(4,719)	(830)	(2,133)	(10,002)

Source: Four representative surveys from the period 1993–2001

Note: Percentages do not total 100% as categories 'other types of housing' and 'no answer' are not shown.

Table 3.3 Dwelling by number of rooms in rural areas and in towns/built-up areas

	1920		1950		1993–2001	
	Rural munici- palities %	Urban munici- palities %	Rural munici- palities %	Urban munici- palities %	Sparsely populated %	Urban/ built-up %
One or two rooms	51	57	48	58	5	16
Three rooms	19	18	21	25	12	22
Four rooms	12	11	14	10	28	25
Five rooms	7	5	8	4	22	17
Six or more rooms	11	9	9	3	34	20

Source: Statistics Norway 1923, 1924 and 1957. Surveys 1993–2001

Note: For 'room', kitchen, bathroom, hall etc., are not included.

and country, it should be noted that the increase has been larger in rural areas than in the towns.

The clear-cut negative correlation early in the last century between home-ownership and degree of urbanisation has already been noted. The population census from 1920 showed a broad basis for home ownership in rural Norway.

Table 3.4 Forms of tenure by degree of urbanisation

	Three largest towns	Towns/built up areas with more than 2,000 inhabitants	Towns/built up areas with less than 2,000 inhabitants	Sparsely populated areas	Total
Owner-occupiers, %	41	66	72	80	62
Owners of co-operative flats, %	33	16	5	2	17
Tenants, other, %	26	18	21	18	21
N:	(2,320)	(4,719)	(830)	(2,133)	(10,002)

Source: Four representative surveys from the period 1993–2001

Virtually all farmers (95 per cent) and smallholders (93 per cent) owned their home, but among rural workers too the share was as high as 53 per cent.

Table 3.4 shows the relationship between forms of tenure and degree of urbanisation at the end of the last century. The table is based on data from four nation-wide surveys carried out in the period 1993–2001. The owner-occupier share is lowest in the three largest towns (Oslo, Bergen and Trondheim) and highest in sparsely populated areas. Concurrently, the opposite is the case where the relationship between co-operative ownership and degree of urbanisation is concerned.

Houses' market values vary widely between town and country. House prices are far higher in towns and built-up areas, and the differences have increased over time. There was a general rise in house prices in Norway in the period 1984–1988, thereafter a steady but substantial fall up to 1993, since when prices have been on an upward trend. Table 3.5 shows median values for homeowners' perceptions of the value of their own homes in the period 1993 to 2001. The table documents both higher price perception in towns and built-up areas, and a stronger increase in towns than in rural areas.

Although the towns have grown strongly in the post-war period, and despite the price differences between town and country, new production in rural Norway has also been substantial. At the turn of the last century inhabited dwellings in rural areas showed the same age distribution as dwellings in towns and built-up areas. A quarter were built before 1955, half were built before 1972, while the newest quarter were built from 1982 onwards.

Housing markets function differently in town and country. In sparsely populated areas the house owners usually had the houses built themselves (the

Table 3.5 Median value in NOK thousands for owner-occupiers' perception of value of own house in sparsely populated areas and towns/built-up areas, 1993–2001

	1993	1995	1997	2001
Sparsely populated median	500	600	700	800
Towns/built-up areas median	600	650	800	1,200

Source: Surveys

widespread Norwegian expression 'build a house' is probably a legacy of earlier times when a great many private individuals could rely on their efforts and house-building expertise far more than today). Moreover, it is more common in rural areas than in towns to live in a house that is inherited or obtained through the family (17 per cent compared with 9 per cent in towns and built-up areas). The housing market is significantly more commercialised in towns and built-up areas where 28 per cent have bought their house via a real estate agent compared with 11 per cent in sparsely populated areas.

An especially significant phenomenon in rural Norway is what are known as 'extra houses'; it is fairly common in rural areas to own two houses, and for houses in these areas to be owned by persons living elsewhere. About 10 per cent of Norwegian households own an extra dwelling in addition to the one they live in (Nordvik and Gulbrandsen, 2001). As is seen in Table 3.6, owning an extra dwelling is most common in rural areas. A majority of such dwellings, whether in town or country, are obtained via inheritance. The difference between town and country is that those living in rural areas have their extra dwelling in the locality in which they live whereas those living in towns and built-up areas generally have their extra dwelling elsewhere in the country. For urban dwellers it is probably, in most cases, a question of inheritance of a dwelling in the locality in which they grew up, the extra dwelling being used as a recreational dwelling or perhaps intended for retirement use. In rural areas half the extra dwellings are on the same site as the ordinary house. As mentioned above, it is very common to have a house built oneself, and the prevalence of extra dwellings on the same site probably reflects a widespread tendency and desire to build a new house oneself, even if one has inherited, or will inherit, a house on the same land.

This material simply provides an estimate on a national level of the number of extra dwellings that exist and the number let out or not in use. The latter group is likely to include a large proportion used for recreational purposes. Since there is a lack of information on the geographical location of extra dwellings, it is impossible to provide an estimate of what proportion of dwellings

Table 3.6 Share of households with an extra dwelling and features of extra dwellings, by the degree of urbanisation of the place of residence

	Sparsely populated areas	Towns/ built-up areas
Share owning an extra dwelling, %	17	8
No. of households	(283)	(1,568)
Features of extra dwellings:		
Share in same house/on same site as ordinary dwelling, %	52	8
Share in same municipality as ordinary dwelling, %	79	36
Share not in use, %	51	40
Share temporarily let out, %	24	31
Share obtained via inheritance or through family, %	71	61
Share to be sold in first two years, %	6	12
No. of households with extra dwelling	(48)	(140)

Source: Survey 2001

in outlying areas are no longer inhabited on a permanent basis. Aanesland and Holm (2000) have registered uninhabited farm properties in a small number of outlying municipalities in two counties and found that about 20 per cent of these properties are uninhabitable.

Housing policy challenges in rural communities: agriculture, dwellings and recreational dwellings

Two hundred years ago Norway was an agrarian society. If the population is classified according to the head of household's occupation, 80 per cent were engaged in farming and forestry. Just over a hundred years later, in 1910, the proportion had fallen to 42 per cent: in 1930, the share was 32 per cent. A simultaneous classification of the entire economically active population by occupation placed 29 per cent in farming and forestry. The latter percentage fell to 24 in 1946, to 16 in 1960, to 10 in 1970, to 7 in 1980 and 5 in 1990. In the survey data we are using, farmers are few and far between even in sparsely populated areas. Among households where the interviewee was in the age range 20–70, at least one of the household's two main persons was employed in farming, forestry or fishing in 11 per cent of cases.

The population census from 1960 contained 217,318 farmhouses, representing 20 per cent of the country's housing stock. In the 1990 census farmhouses were not registered, but subsequent sample surveys from 1995 and 1997 arrived at a figure of 8.5 per cent. This corresponds to about 170,000 dwellings. Well over half of the registered farm properties, primarily the smallest, are not in active use but have become pure housing or recreational properties (Sevatdal, 2002). If we assume that the bulk of farm properties are situated in sparsely populated areas, we can, based on the sample surveys, calculate that well over half of the dwellings in sparsely populated areas neither are, nor have been, farmhouses.

Land policy legislation, the Land Consolidation Act, Concessions Act and Allodial Act regulate (a) ownership, by determining who is entitled to take over farm properties, (b) sales prices, (c) the size of property units and by the same token how the property structure is to evolve and (d) the use of farmhouses and land. The rules are primarily applicable in cases of transfer of ownership (Sevatdal, 2002).

Up until September 2001, the lower limit for what was defined as farm property was, with some reservations, a minimum of 5 decares of farmland. In this way a large number of houses in rural Norway were subject to agriculturally based price controls. Both the Allodial Act and the Concessions Act are applicable here.

The Allodial Act gives the family the right to own the land, and determines a line of inheritance such that the owner is not free to dispose of his property independently of his heirs. An allodial right is accumulated after 20 years' ownership, and a condition is that the property can be utilised for farm operation. In 2001 the minimum area was raised from 10 to 20 decares of farmland or 100 decares of productive forest. When a property is transferred under the provisions of the Allodial Act the price is fixed by appraisement (*odelstakst*) in which the property's return from farm operation is central to the price fixed. Upon division of a deceased's estate, the heir with the highest priority is entitled to take over the entire property undivided (right of primogeniture) in accordance with an appraisement (*åsetestakst*). This appraisement is determined such that the person who takes over is financially able to hold onto the property. The *åsetestakst* is usually 25 per cent lower, and never higher, than the *odelstakst* (Sevatdal, 2002).

The market for farm properties appears to be fairly closed. Figures in Table 3.7 show that transfers in the form of gifts or by distribution of estates (inheritance) are far more common in this market than in the ordinary housing market.

The Concessions Act is general in nature. As a general rule a concession is required in order to acquire real estate property (Concessions Act of 31 May

Table 3.7 Registered transactions by property type in Norway, 2001

	Sale on open market %	Gift %	Certificate of undivided possession of estate %	Adminis- tration/ division of estate %	Number
Housing property with building	69	4	7	14	(87,054)
Recreational property with building	46	16	11	18	(14,055)
Farm/fishery property with building	27	27	10	25	(7,365)

Source: Statistics Norway

Note: Forced sales and unstated or other forms of transfer are not included in the table, but are included in the bases for the percentages.

1974). The object of the Act is to secure an effective protection of the farming sector's productive land (Falkanger, 2000) and of a regime of farm owner- ship and utilisation that is most beneficial for society. The object clause of the Act refers specifically to consideration for the agricultural sector, the need for land for development purposes, nature conservation and outdoor recreation interests, and a trend in property prices that is not deemed socially regressive. An amendment in April 2001 added a further explicit consideration: the settle- ment pattern.

The Act contains important exceptions associated with the nature of the property or buyer's status. For example, a concession is not required to acquire a single site of up to two decares for a house or recreational property within the same municipality provided the buyer or his immediate family do not already own such a site there. Neither is a concession required to acquire built-on prop- erties of up to 20 decares in size, regardless of the number of properties involved; this limit had been 5 decares until September 2001. Nor is a concession required to sell or transfer property to someone closely related by blood or marriage. A concession is not needed if the acquirer takes over the property under the provisions of the Allodial Act.

If a concession is granted, conditions may be attached to the acquisition. An undertaking to reside on and operate the property must be given in order to take over a farm property without a concession. The person taking over the property must settle there and operate the property for at least five years. If the acquirer has taken over the property under the provisions of the Allodial

Act, the obligation to reside on and operate the property is extended to 10 years. This obligation was incorporated in both the Allodial Act and the Concessions Act as recently as 1975. As from 1995 the obligation to operate the property can be met by leasing out the land, but in the case of acquisition pursuant to the Allodial Act the acquirer must meet the obligation himself (Aanesland and Holm, 2000). In 1999 more than 30 per cent of farmland in operation was leased land. To meet the residential requirements the acquirer and his household must either report a change of address that is approved by the national population register, or, if the acquirer's family lives elsewhere, the acquirer must spend the night on the property during at least 50 per cent of the mandatory residence period, after first notifying the municipal authorities how he intends to organise the practicalities.

Dispensation from the obligation to reside at and operate the property can be applied for. In the housing context it is, above all, dispensation from the residence obligation that is important. The amendment of 2001 added the interest of population settlement patterns to the act in order to give municipalities an opportunity to follow a more restrictive practice in areas of falling population. Since 1997 the individual municipality has been authorised to decide all applications for exemption from the residence and operation obligation under the Concessions Act and the Allodial Act. In the period 1997–1999, a total of 3,297 cases were decided by municipalities in the first instance (Report to the Storting No. 35 (1999–2000)). The bulk of these cases came under the Allodial Act (86 per cent), and the vast majority of these applications – 91 per cent – were granted. In the same period, 339 cases were decided by the county agricultural committee or the county governor. In the next half of the cases – 44 per cent – the decision was changed.

The number of farm properties between 5 and 20 decares that were de-regulated by raising the area limit in 2001 is estimated at just under 15,000 (Sevatdal, 2002). However, given the trend towards a less regulated market for farm properties, the return on farming and forestry will determine prices for such properties provided they do not offer alternative uses as housing or recreational properties.

The area of limit of 20 decares may however be suspended to prevent dwellings being converted into recreational properties. The freedom from concession in respect of properties below the minimum size can be restricted by municipal decision in the case of properties previously used as dwellings (the so-called zero limit regulations imposing an extended concession requirement for built-on properties). This is designed to prevent year-round dwellings being bought up with a view to recreational use. However, in cases where these regulations have been introduced (zero limit for concessions), freedom from concession applies where the buyer intends to use the property as his permanent residence. In contrast to farm properties, the residence obligation for dwellings subject to the concession requirement can also be met by letting the dwelling to others.

The zero limit does not prevent a year-round dwelling from becoming a recreational property provided the acquirer is a close relative. To plug this loophole a number of municipalities have, with ministry consent, made regulations with a basis in the Building and Planning Act to the effect that it is forbidden to change the use of a year-round dwelling to a recreational dwelling without the municipality's approval. In cases where this rule is applicable it will, for example, not be possible to inherit a childhood home for subsequent use as a holiday or recreational dwelling. Here, too, the residence requirement can be met by letting. This problem applies above all in relation to small towns and attractive holiday areas along the coast. There are no direct price controls, but the market price of a house in a small town on the south coast will in many cases increase many times over if the buyer is not required to live in it and can use a previous year-round dwelling as a recreational home. Seventy-six municipalities have introduced some form of residence requirement. A total of 578 cases were dealt with under the Concession Act's 'zero limit' rules in the period 1996–1999. However, only 4.7 per cent ended in rejection (Report No. 35 to the Storting (1999–2000)).

Conclusions

Strengthening the farming sector and safeguarding the dispersed settlement patterns were central considerations when regulation of farm properties was tightened in 1974. Has this met with success, and to what extent will further success be secured with the rules imposing residence and operating obligations?

A serious objection to the regulation of the housing and property market – that was phased out during the 1980s – was its evident ineffectiveness (NOU 1981: 5; Gulbrandsen, 1983). The same doubts about effectiveness can be raised in relation to the controls still operating. It seems clear that municipal control, for example of whether a new owner whose family lives elsewhere actually spends nights in the property for at least half of the period of the residence requirement is, to put it mildly, a difficult, if not virtually impossible project. There is a very strong likelihood that local oversight will become enmeshed in disagreement and conflict. The modest number of rejections may be an indication that genuine control opportunities are absent, or are only possible through over-zealous inspections motivated by considerations other than a desire to strengthen local population settlement on a year-round basis.

The large number of dispensations may also be a sign that there is little will in most localities to impose a strict practice in regard to the residence requirement. This is largely because the agricultural significance of the obligation to operate a property appears to be taken care of via the leasing out of farmland. It should also be recalled that many potential cases that would otherwise have been dealt with in due course have not reached the authorities because a large number of owners had taken steps to complete their sales before the change in the law took effect in 1975. About 75,000 properties changed hands in 1973; in 1974 the number jumped to about 112,000 only to fall back to a normal level of 72,000 in 1975 (Gulbrandsen, 1989).

Regulation will usually entail value transfers from seller to buyer. Aanesland and Holm (2000) point out that owners of farm properties close to built-up areas, and in areas where holiday properties are in great demand, are affected in a very different way than owners in peripheral areas where there is little demand for holiday homes. They suggest that market prices in outlying districts will, to a far greater degree, resemble the maximum legal price. They also point out that the residence requirement has probably not been conducive to maintenance of the housing stock in outlying districts. Their survey of a small number of municipalities showed that a large proportion of uninhabited farm and housing properties were, in practice, perceived to be uninhabitable. In four out of six surveyed municipalities this proportion was between 55 and 100 per cent, while the share was just over 20 per cent and just under 40 per cent in the two last municipalities.

Judging from the relatively new housing stock in outlying districts, the will to invest has been substantial. Though housebuilding has been subsidised by loans from the State Housing Bank, there has also been a great deal of private effort and investment. Where older housing stock is concerned, however, regulation (especially the residence obligation) has weakened the will to invest and engage in necessary maintenance. In the somewhat longer term, maintaining the large housing capital present in outlying districts will be a problem, especially in areas whose recreational value is limited. A number of earlier dwellings are probably being kept as recreational homes, not least for sentimental reasons based on childhood experience or family ties. However, urbanisation means that a steadily decreasing portion of coming generations will have ties with a rural childhood.

Increasing the area limit from 5 to 20 decares in the autumn of 2001 is an important step towards a less regulated market for dwellings whose value in present-day society is primarily of a residential and recreational nature. However, the degree of restriction faced by owners in municipalities that practise a zero limit compared to those in other municipalities may grow significantly. Since this decision is assigned to the individual municipality, differing local political majorities could have dramatic effects in terms of the market value of very similar properties on either side of a municipal boundary. This will be perceived as arbitrarily unequal treatment that could impair the legitimacy of the rules. Moreover, legitimacy is not strengthened by the absence of controls on all other property transactions.

Given the large measure of dispensations, and the limited possibilities for effective controls, the rules' effectiveness is also greatly reduced. The maintenance of settlement patterns by coercive measures, which encroach on property rights and run contrary to wider social and economic trends, will bring lasting problems. Not least because the prevailing trend is for the movement of labour away from primary production to other sectors, alongside a simultaneous movement of young people to the largest towns and built-up areas where they are more inclined to settle.

Note

1   My thanks to colleagues at NOVA for worthwhile comments and above all, to Åsmund Langsether.

Chapter 4
Sweden

Gärd Folkesdotter

Introduction

Sweden is small, cold and sparsely populated with an average of 20 inhabitants per square kilometre. In comparison to some other countries in Europe, almost the whole of Sweden might appear rural. However, certain parts of the country are more rural than others: a fact revealed by the ongoing debate over the growing imbalance between a few more densely populated urban areas or regions and the rest of Sweden. Stockholm, Gothenburg and some university towns have experienced recent population growth, but the majority of Sweden's 289 municipalities have lost people. Only 81 had any increase in 1998 and these municipalities were primarily situated in the metropolitan areas (Johansson, M., 2001).

This situation causes different problems in different regions; there is a growing housing shortage in Stockholm and some other cities and a surplus of housing with vacant flats in many other municipalities. Municipal housing companies have even torn down buildings containing relatively modern flats – built after the Second World War – as neither politicians nor planners see a need for such properties in the future.

The cost of housing increased during the 1990s and few new dwellings were built, especially rented flats. In 1991 there was a change of government, housing subsidies were cut, planning and housing allocations were deregulated and housing production became heavily dependent on market forces. Tax reform was introduced, and this was to a large extent 'paid for' by the housing sector through increased taxes on construction, housing maintenance and management and smaller tax deductions on housing loans (Hedman, 2001: 76). The effects were dramatic; low levels of housing construction and higher housing costs. Today, these costs account on average for 31 per cent of disposable income per household (Hedman, 2001: 77).

Also on the agenda has been the increasing segregation of ethnic immigrant groups; in several housing areas the percentage of Swedes (born in Sweden by Swedish parents) has decreased and Swedish-speaking children have become a minority in many schools. Sweden has long been a net receiver of immigrants;

today the country has about one million first-generation immigrants. Including second-generation immigrants, close to one-fifth of the population has a non-Swedish background (Andersson, 2001: 11). Immigrants from countries outside Europe and North America often end up in rented housing developments in areas where unemployment and dependency on social assistance is extremely high (Lundström, 2001: 82). Social exclusion amongst these groups is an increasingly important and worrying feature of Swedish society.

Finally, sustainable development has, for a long time, been a catchword in Swedish politics. The National Board of Housing, Building and Planning – the Swedish government agency for planning, the management of land and water resources, urban development, building and housing – has formulated strategies for sustainable development (*Planering för hållbar utveckling*, 2000) but these seem to focus more on urban areas, though there is some discussion about circulation of food and waste between urban areas and surrounding countryside. The general picture then is one of a sparsely populated country containing a handful of key urban centres. These centres have attracted much attention in recent years as the cost of housing has risen along with the concentration of relative poverty. Rural areas, however, face their own challenges and these form the subject of the remainder of this chapter.

Housing pressure in the countryside

Considering the falling population in large parts of Sweden, it is easy to understand why there is no general pressure for permanent housing in the countryside or rural areas. There are, however, more people wanting to live in rural areas than doing so. Both SIFO (*Svenska institutet för opinionsundersökningar*, a privately owned Swedish institute for opinion polls) surveys and studies of population movement patterns conducted by the National Rural Agency – a governmental agency working for living conditions and development for residents of sparsely populated and rural communities – show that it is mainly people between 30 and 64 years of age who dream of living in the country (Gustafsson, 2001: 95). The same tendency is revealed in earlier studies (Ayala, 1980; Folkesdotter, 1986) while other studies and statistics show an increase of population in rural communities within commuting distances from metropolises (Gustafsson, 2001: 95).

Holiday homes are frequently portrayed as a key issue in the Swedish countryside. Regarding such properties, the last decade has seen an increasing interest from other European nationals; Danes and Germans have been buying holiday homes in the south of Sweden and Norwegians on the west coast. There are a large number of second homes in Sweden, about half a million (Müller, 1999), which is quite significant compared to a population of 8.8 million and a housing stock comprising a little over 4 million permanent dwellings. Second homes were often built and used as first homes before conversion into second home use. Newly built second homes are often of a high standard and may be used as first homes without upgrading. The stock of second homes is indeed a key feature of the rural housing market and one that is central to understanding the pressure that the Swedish countryside and small communities face.

What is rural?

'Rural' is a term here used to denote sparsely populated areas, in natural or agricultural landscapes. The economically active population in rural areas and rural communities in Sweden is no longer dominated by people working in agriculture, forestry, fishing and the like. The majority living in sparsely populated and rural communities make their living from manufacturing, trade and communications, and care-related professions. The biggest changes in employment among rural dwellers from 1994 to 1998 have occurred in business services, a fast growing sector, and in care, where the numbers have fallen considerably. These changes are also seen in the employment structure of residents in densely populated areas (Gustafsson, 2001: 94).

Maria Gustafsson at the Swedish National Rural Agency (*glesbygdsverket*) has defined 'rural communities' as being 'areas outside localities that have a population of over 3,000 inhabitants' (Gustafsson, 2001: 94) where a quarter of the Swedish population lives. Jan Amcoff discusses the issue of 'what is urban/what is rural' in the second chapter of his recent thesis (Amcoff, 2000), making numerous references to work in human geography and rural sociology: much of this work focuses on whether 'urban–rural' can be seen as a dichotomy or a continuum. Amongst others he considers the work of Halfacree (1995) and his construction of the typically rural area:

> Physically, such a village should have a small population, probably less than 1,000 people; it should be relatively compact and set in attractive countryside; it should have a few basic shops and a pub; and there should be little evidence of new development, especially housing estates. Socially, the inhabitants of the village should be mixed in age and social class; they should work locally, ideally within the village; social activities should be rather 'traditional', quite well-developed and not bear the mark of being introduced by outsiders; and a communitarianism rather than sectarianism should be the prominent village ethos, although this sense of community should be organic rather than self-consciously introduced.
>
> (Halfacree 1995: 14, quoted in Amcoff 2000: 27)

It would be difficult to find a village fitting Halfacree's description in Sweden today. And even in the past, many villages had either one or no shop and certainly no pubs. Today, few people in villages work close to where they live, and villages are often spread out, not compact. It is evident, then, that the majority of researchers working with rural issues use definitions of 'rural' or 'countryside' related to population density. Jan Amcoff, for example, has used a definition of rural areas (*landsbygd*) as those 'outside localities with 1,000 inhabitants or more'. The countryside is understood as 'the living milieu outside the built-up cities and localities (urban places)'. Different terms and definitions have certainly been employed in different studies (e.g. 'urban area', 'sparsely populated area' and 'countryside') and many of these terms, and their use, are examined by Folkesdotter (1986).

Dieter Müller (1999) is another commentator with an acute interest in this issue of definition. With regards to his study of German second homes in Sweden, he does not find it suitable to use the standard Swedish definitions of urban or of urbanised countryside:

> Settlements that have more than 200 inhabitants are considered urban in Sweden, but in Germany people would consider this a village. Thus even the so called urbanized countryside, referring to areas more than 30 km away from the nearest town at least 10,000 inhabitants but not more than 30 km away from a local center with 2,000–10,000 inhabitants (Johannison *et al.* 1989) would definitely be considered as extremely rural. Areas outside the nearby commuting hinterlands, i.e. the countryside at least 30 km away from an urban center with more than 10,000 inhabitants, should form an arena that can satisfy the demand for secluded second home living in a rural environment for a reasonable price.
>
> (Müller, 1999: 56–57)

Perhaps the main point here is that density-based definitions might prove useful for the purpose of delimiting rural areas within one country and for a certain period. Such definitions are relatively easy to apply but other qualities may be more interesting. What might be considered 'rural' or 'urban' in Sweden may not attract the same label in Germany, England or Spain. Yet for this discussion, it is necessary to use the vernacular and suitable definition(s) of rural areas within the country in question though it would be good for comparisons to use the same definition(s) in several countries.

A recreational landscape?

Amcoff's recent (2000) study of movement patterns into the Swedish countryside had two primary aims: first, to describe population changes in relation to growth in the housing stock; and second, to seek an explanation for these changes. Data from east central Sweden provided the backbone of the study, though a wider analysis across the entire country was also undertaken. Amcoff's work shows that the population outside built-up localities, and particularly close to the larger urban centres, rose (but not continuously) between 1970 and 1995. This growth was attributed mainly to the influx of families with children who, in many instances, converted existing second homes into permanent residences. During this period, the actual dwelling stock grew at a faster rate than the population. But, Amcoff argues that:

> A British-inspired possible explanation based on the attractive force of the middle-class image of the rural idyll is rejected on empirical grounds. The same goes for an explanation in terms of low-budget detached housing. Explanations emphasising the reduced geographical restrictions on rural living (e.g. improved commuting possibilities) seem to fit the empirical data better.
>
> (Amcoff, 2000: abstract)

However, closer parallels with Britain's rural stereotype can be found elsewhere. In another study of counterurbanisation also in east central Sweden, but which drew on empirical data from household interviews, the reasons for moving to the countryside were analysed in terms of the values and previous experiences of the migrants. The concepts of 'freedom', 'peace and quiet', 'sense of community' and 'independence' were found to be important factors resulting in a move to the countryside; as were previous contacts with relatives in the countryside (see Heins in Chapter 5) and ownership of a second home that could be upgraded to a permanent dwelling. But on the other hand, people's motivations tended to relate to personal utility and benefit and not to the expectation of joining some idealised 'community' (Stenbacka, 2001). In a review of past literature by Folkesdotter, it is suggested that in remoter, more sparsely populated areas at least, many in-migrants are returning to their native community (Folkesdotter, 1986).

This influx of people has certainly affected the way people live their lives in the countryside. This has been demonstrated recently in an interview-based study of two communities – Falköping and Tidaholm – facing depopulation:

> With the mix of life styles it is evident that these life styles will influence each other and that new ways of living eventually will develop. 'Modern people' moving out from the cities bring with them a mobile way of living accustomed as they are to working in various places and to spending leisure activities in a variety of places. Traditionally

people in the countryside live in the places where their farms are situated and where they have grown up, their social life often being restricted to the area.

(Nordström and Mårtensson, 2001: 40, summary in English)

However, despite higher mobility, villages in the area still seemed to be characterised more by tradition and history than by any new influence. Those originating in the area sometimes find it difficult to understand or accept the interests of newcomers in what they consider to be 'their' environment. Newcomers to the area are often seen as 'outsiders' for many decades (ibid.: 47) and it is clear that people continue to live quite different lifestyles, displaying little in the way of common culture. As well as different backgrounds, they are living in the area for different reasons and Nordström and Mårtensson concluded that women, in particular, found it difficult to reconcile traditional rural roles with urban experiences and values (ibid.: 48). However, lifestyles related to agriculture may also differ (Borgström and Ekman, 1992). But largely, when agriculture's influence wanes there appears to be more room for other groups and lifestyles. In 1996, only 2.3 per cent of the economically active population worked in farming, forestry and fishing. Nowadays, the rural landscape is one of recreation not production and this has resulted in an influx of people. Yet in the past, because of the harshness of farming life, many people wanted to leave the countryside in favour of the cities (Rundblad, 1951).

Returning to an issue raised earlier, this transition to a recreational landscape has been marked by an increase in second home purchasing. Müller (1999) provides an analysis of such purchasing by German buyers between 1991 and 1996. Müller's study says much about how the rural landscape is perceived and about its changing function. The first part of his study focuses on the considerations seen as important by purchasers prior to acquiring a second home. The second part concentrates on the selection process and the third on the repercussions second homes bring to rural communities. On the issue of repercussions, he looks at the extent tourism in general, and second homes in particular, affect local development and the relationship 'cottagers' share with the local population. One conclusion is that second homes have come to symbolise a more internationalised and integrated Europe. Of the 15,500 cottages in the Müller study, 11,500 were owned by people from other Nordic countries and Germany: the biggest single group of owners were Danes together owning 2,291 properties (ibid.: 104). But it is the rise in the number of German second home buyers, not just in Sweden but across many parts of Europe, that has become a real phenomenon in the housing market.

The dramatic increase of German property acquisition in Sweden started in 1992. The overall size of Sweden's second home stock is subject to much debate though it is generally accepted that the 'true' figure is somewhere between 500,000 and 700,000 units. Müller's analysis relies on the UMCOBASE data which suggest that there were precisely 498,943 cottages in Sweden in 1996 (Müller, 1999: 97). Between 1991 and 1996, about 4,000 Germans bought cottages in Sweden. By 2001, there were a total of 5,500 German-owned second homes in Sweden: a figure big enough to cause adverse publicity, but tiny in comparison to levels of German second home ownership elsewhere. Germans own about 300,000 second homes in Spain, 100,000 in France, 80,000 in Italy and 65,000 in Portugal (Müller, 1999: 49, from figures provided by the *Deutsche und Schweizerische Schutzgemeinschaft für Auslandsgrundbesitz*, published in *Spiegel spezial* 1997(2): 115). In Müller's interview survey, 15 of the 91 German cottagers (who were categorised according to the schema set out in Table 4.1) stated that they had previously considered buying property in Denmark, but were prevented from doing so by legal constraints. Sweden offered the next best opportunity, offering '*die Ruhe*', or 'calmness' that so eluded them in urban Germany.

It is certainly not unreasonable to suggest that Sweden's once largely agricultural countryside and coastal communities has undergone a transition and emerged as a 'recreational landscape'. This transition has been marked by second home purchasing, particularly amongst foreign nationals: though any erosion of traditional values is only indirectly linked to this urban encroachment. Rather, its more direct cause is the decline and waning influence of agriculture, forestry and fishery. The countryside has certainly changed. On the up-side, there appears today to be more room for different lifestyles and values. But what of the down-side, and the potential problems stemming from the higher housing costs mentioned earlier, and the new sources of housing demand described above?

Table 4.1 Types of German second home buyers in Sweden

The devoted fans of Sweden	Heavily devoted to Sweden, sometimes having friends and relatives in the country
The dedicated cottagers	Interested in owning a second home where they could escape from urban life and Germany
The coincidental and impulse cottagers	Became aware of the opportunity to buy a second home, surprised by the low prices and the rather uncomplicated procedure.

Source: Author (after Müller, 1999)

New pressure points?

Housing supply is *not* the key issue facing the majority of municipalities. It was mentioned earlier that in some instances, selective demolition of 'older' properties – comprising flats with central heating, modern bathrooms and kitchens – has been undertaken by municipal housing companies despite the protestations of residents. This is not a strategy – aimed at increasing housing quality – that might be employed were there a supply problem. The same 'surplus' housing issue is also evident in the countryside. Changes in farming practice mean that landholdings are frequently amalgamated leaving many farm buildings (including dwellings and outhouses) redundant. In some instances, the only hope for these buildings is that they will be bought up by wealthy buyers (Rimsén, 2001a) able to afford the upkeep of substantial wooden dwellings of 600 square metres, and with fifty windows.

A more acute problem in many rural municipalities stems from the closure and deterioration of commercial and public services and infrastructure (Gustafsson, 2001: 97). The number of rural schools and foodstores has fallen dramatically over the past few years and many post offices have shut down. This loss of services is partially due to the seasonality of rural living and also due to oversupply in the past. Yet while some services are simply no longer required, there are huge and growing pressures on others. Some areas with swollen summer (or winter) populations – especially on the archipelagos – have difficulties in handling the seasonal surge in sewage waste water and on many islands, supplying large enough quantities of fresh water is a real problem. Big-city pressure is evident in the water quality on the Stockholm archipelago, for example, where salt water penetration into wells and difficulties in hygienically disposing of waste water have been increasingly common. Sewage from private houses is often insufficiently purified and causing growing concern (Fehler *et al.*, 2001: 99).

Another problem facing local people in the old fishing villages located on these same archipelagos close to the built-up centres of Stockholm and Gothenburg is the recent and significant increase in property tax, which makes it difficult for people to manage their housing costs. This problem results from the general increase in property prices experienced in these areas and therefore the re-allocation of properties into higher tax bands. House price rises have been significant: a consequence of new market pressures. In Fjällbacka, for example, a community near the Norwegian border in the municipality of Tanum in the province of Bohuslän, around half of all properties are used as holiday homes. One local politician, interviewed for a newspaper, saw this increase in holiday use as a threat to the viability of the local school and other essential services (Nilsson, 2000). Similar concerns were voiced by another politician in Strömstad, a west coast municipality, when defending a large-scale development project in Kebal. It was argued that the development should go ahead because locals were being priced out of the market for traditional fishermen's houses on the Koster Archipelago: 'There, they are pushing out fishing lads and their families, making their living from the sea. In Kebal, no local people have to move' (Johansson, L., 2001, *Dagens Nyheter*, 24 June, Section Bostad: 14).

But while some locals may not welcome the intrusion of Norwegians, those people moving into the area for the summer months, or permanently, are often overjoyed to have acquired a holiday home in such a magnificent location, and for so small a cost to them:

> 'The whole Koster archipelago is open to us . . . [It's] a place of dreams to us Norwegians', say Svein and Aud Løken, summing up, reckoning to be there when their vacation starts, in their own cabin with a pier of their own. . . .
>
> (Johansson, L., 2001, *Dagens Nyheter*, 24 June,
> Section Bostad: 14)

At times, the influx of people into these areas can be at odds with Sweden's longstanding interest in protecting its many areas of outstanding natural beauty. Broad legislation and particular policy has often aimed to restrict new housebuilding in certain places. For example, the Shore Act (*Strandlagen*) enacted in 1952 gave special protection to the banks and shorelines of rivers and lakes, and these measures were later incorporated into more comprehensive environmental law. The aim – then as now – was to secure the public use of shorelines for bathing and other forms of outdoor recreation. It built on the ancient right of public access – or *allemansrätt* – that allows people to walk on and use, in other ways, open land as long as they do no harm. But this right is repealed on land close to buildings and development and therefore where development pressure is great, there is a demonstrable erosion of the *allemansrätt*. It is also the case that foreign purchasers do not always have the same understanding or respect of such ancient rights and traditions, and moves by some incomers to prevent open access has been a source of much conflict.

Therefore, and despite the abundance of housing in many areas, the combination of environmental and market pressures in particular places has caused a considerable amount of local concern. How government at regional and national levels has made various attempts to vent this mounting pressure is examined in the next two sections.

Policy and strategy at the national level

Property tax levels in Sweden are closely related to market prices: if the average price paid for property in a given area increases, then a higher tax burden is felt by all. This can mean that less well-off homeowners living in a popular area (with strong market pressure) may face the problem of rising taxes. It is hoped that the government will act to ease the pressure on homeowners. Property taxes may very well become an issue in campaigns before the general election scheduled for 2002. Tabled proposals currently include an across-the-board decrease in the general tax rate: from 1.5 to 1.2 per cent of assessed property value. Another change, targeted more specifically at lower income groups, will see no one paying more than 5 per cent of their personal/household income in property tax.

These measures are aimed at helping those living within more pressured parts of the countryside, usually in close proximity to major urban centres. For those in remoter areas, government's objective is to improve housing quality and service standards. The Swedish National Rural Agency – a governmental organisation – has been established with a remit to work towards better living conditions and development opportunities for residents of sparsely populated areas. The intention is that this national body should co-ordinate and facilitate the strategies of different local agencies, particularly in the woodland inner regions and the more remote archipelagos.

But back in the more pressured areas, perhaps the critical issue – mentioned earlier – is that of external housing demand. In a recent article for one of Sweden's biggest newspapers, the head of the Swedish National Rural Agency, Pia Enochsson, claimed that many more attractive rural areas risk the total loss of their permanent populations as homes are bought up by wealthy incomers and turned into holiday cottages (Enochsson, *Dagens Nyheter*, 5 July 2001, Section A: 4). She sees three possible ways of handling this situation. The first is to do nothing and simply accept the current changes, though this would mean the end of many archipelago communities. The second option is to adopt new legislation that would make it more *difficult and complex* to turn permanent dwellings into holiday homes. Third, a more direct approach could be taken, banning the use of new housing for recreation. Enochsson has announced that the Swedish National Rural Agency favours new research into the use of permits to control the transfer of dwellings into second home use. New or alterered legislation might require buyers to declare whether or not they are intending to live in a property on a permanent basis. Further amendments to the *Real Estate Purchasing* and *Planning and Building Acts* (*jordförvärvslagen, plan-och bygglagen*) among others are also proposed and would lead to an effective ban on the conversion of permanent to holiday homes.

In my view, such conversion would be very difficult to regulate or control. Neither current nor past attempts to control holiday homes have been particularly successful. Responsibility for implementing planning policy lies with the municipalities (with the exception of those areas designated as specially protected areas of natural and/or cultural interest) which tend to have quite modest financial and staff resources. The policing of such new policies would require massive resourcing, removing the majority of municipal staff from other tasks. Foreign buyers must make applications to purchase property in Sweden at the current time, though very few of these applications are ever rejected (Müller, 1999: 102). Over the border in Denmark, a far stricter system of control is in place. People without permanent residence status in Denmark were usually not allowed to purchase a second home in the country and this legislation was accepted in the Danish–EC negotiations in 1972, when Denmark tried to limit the German second home purchases along the Danish coast. Germans often go to Denmark on holidays and Danes may have felt and still feel a risk of being overwhelmed by Germans. The German occupation of Denmark during the Second World War may have contributed to uneasy feelings. However, as a result of a more recent EU Council Directive this solution is seen as a temporary solution: 'Existing national legislation regulating purchases of secondary residences may be upheld until the Council adopts further provisions in this area (88/361/ EC, Article 6.4, cited in Müller, 1999: 102, from *Justitiedepartementet*, 1991, Appendix II).

The only country that maintained its national restrictive legislation on foreign second home purchases was and still is Denmark. In the future, even the Danish limitations can be expected to be abolished (Müller, 1999: 103). Given this precedent, it also seems unlikely that Danish-style controls will be introduced in Sweden.

Regional strategies and co-operation

Such difficulties sometimes mean that a softer approach to specific regional problems is necessary, without recourse to primary legislation. For example, three country administrative boards – Uppsala, Stockholm and Södermanland – located on the east coast, and stretching 150 kilometres north and 100 kilometres south of Stockholm, have recently prepared a joint programme on *Environmental and Resource Management*. The programme encourages cross-border co-operation and aims towards achieving more sustainable patterns of development, often attempting to deal with those impacts resulting from new housing pressures. Fehler *et al.* (2001) have listed some of the key objectives of the programme focusing on the basis for sustainable development in the archipelago:

- *Archipelago water must be clean.* The water must not contain high levels of plant nutrients, nor should the water contain toxic elements in such amounts that plants, animals and ultimately human beings would be harmed.
- *The environmental values of the water beds and their ecological function should not be depleted.* The waterbeds cannot be long-term misused or used as tipping places for polluted substances.
- *A well-cultivated cultural landscape is an indispensable ingredient in the environmental and cultural values of the archipelago.* Residing farmers and fishermen are needed, property owners and users must take responsibility for land and water resources. Old buildings must be preserved and used carefully.
- *Large sections of the coastal and archipelagic regions, which are presently undeveloped or have sparse habitation, must be preserved in this state.* Large sections of uninhabited regions need adequate protection against gradual exploitation.
- *It is necessary to have a conscious approach towards the ongoing shoreline displacement, siltation and redistribution of land and water that current land elevation continues to cause.* Along the entire coast, land elevation is reshaping the coastline. New shore pastures and cultivable land appear. With the increasing number and size of pleasure boats, requests for dredging the areas near piers and in shallow inlets have grown. Knowledge about the biological values under the surface is often inadequate, making it difficult to assess the effects of many minor dredgings.
- *Democracy and sustainable development.* The development and preservation of the archipelago is a question for its citizens. The knowledge capital must include local experiences of opportunities and threats in everyday life. New enterprises, using local resources, should base their activities on sound and deep knowledge of the conditions governing archipelagic life.

These are fairly lofty intentions, but provide a framework around which these municipalities can come together. It is a shared vision and a recognition that some action must be taken in the face of massive development pressures with well documented environmental impacts. Such programmes are likely to attract EU support. The EU has stated its intention to develop a common strategy for the planning and management of coastal regions and the region described above is to be included in the Interreg III initiative, which aims to support cross-border collaboration (Fehler *et al.*, 2001: 102).

Rural housing and local action

Despite these national debates and regional plans, local action remains critically important in relation to housing issues within the municipalities. Planning and building regulations, though sometimes weak, are administered at this level but the approaches towards housing issues can differ significantly from one municipality to another. In those areas losing population, there is often a tendency to allow new housing immediately on the shoreline: it is only those municipalities with high development pressure who are eager to protect shores and woods from such encroachment. This huge variation in attitude has been a source of much recent concern.

The Swedish Environmental Protection Agency, for example, has claimed that many municipalities are too generous in their interpretation of the 'special reasons' clauses permitting them to allow building near waterfronts. In fact, although legislation indicates that these reasons should always be specified prior to permission being granted, this often does not happen (Rimsén, 2001b). Part of the problem lies in the fact that it is county councils that should decide these matters, but many have delegated power to the municipalites, which are far more parochial in their outlook. An investigation by *Dagens Nyheter* (the largest newspaper in Sweden) has suggested that where county councils have taken responsibility for deciding special permissions – mainly on the west and south coasts – restrictions have been much more tightly enforced. It is only where there is a strong tradition of delegation – on the east coast – that problems of inconsistent application have arisen (Johnson, 2001).

The government certainly wants to see more consistent application of development controls and has asked the Swedish Environmental Protection Agency to propose ways to strengthen the protection of waterfronts. However, it is also argued – in government circles – that a more relaxed approach should be taken in more sparsely populated areas in order to facilitate balanced regional development (Johnson, 2001). So the debate is very much a circular one, with government wishing to promote greater consistency in development control while giving some counties and municipalities the discretion to allow some waterfront development. It certainly appears that government runs the risk of contradicting the aims of some regional strategies, which seek to block further development in remoter areas (see *Regional strategies* on pp. 54–6).

The future

It is, as always, dangerous to make predictions, though there are some obvious trends. Migration into Stockholm and other metropolitan regions looks set to continue, though in-migrants will be drawn from a gradually ageing population with fewer younger households. Adjacent to these urban centres, it seems likely that many former holiday homes will be transferred to permanent use, though this process will be reversed in remoter depopulated regions, where the number of holiday homes will grow. Foreign property acquisition will continue with cottages, crofts and farms being sold to buyers from abroad, attracted by relatively low house prices and a favourable exchange rate.

Improvements in transport infrastructure – both roads and railways – are likely to have an impact on many regions. The *extension* of commuting, rather than holiday home buying, looks set to become the key issue for many rural municipalities. Or rather, many more households will choose a 'double residency' lifestyle with homes closer to work and homes further afield which they retreat to at the weekends (Johansson, M., 2001).

Sweden faces a growing number of exogenous challenges. The process of globalisation, alongside immediate developments across Europe and within

4.1 Rågårdsvik – a small fishing village on the Swedish west coast. Many of the houses are only used in the summer, 1985: Erik Nordin.

4.2 An old croft in Hålsingland, parcelled off at the beginning of the last century and now used as a second home, 1982: Gård Folkesdotter.

4.3 Hermansö – an old fishing village on the west coast. The buildings on the waterfront were originally used for fishing equipment. Most of the houses in the village are now second homes, 1976: Gärd Folkesdotter.

Sweden's neighbours, is driving forward economic changes that are reflected in the country's spatial structure (Böhme, 2001). The enlargement of the EU, for example, will most certainly affect agricultural policy and rural communities. But being a member state of the EU, Sweden will not be able to ward off extraneous pressure simply by erecting new legislative barriers. In the case of property acquisition, it seems likely that transfers may not be stemmed.

Chapter 5
The Netherlands

Saskia Heins

Housing in the Netherlands: the national picture

Central government intervention has traditionally been the driving force behind housing policy and strategy in the Netherlands. While other countries might have developed a less interventionist approach, with a greater role for local agencies and the private sector, central planning has been at the heart of Dutch housing policy. But this situation is slowly changing and there has, in recent years, been a discernible shift towards local responsibility and the market. If the European approach to housing is seen as being less comprehensively and intensely public sector-led, then the Netherlands is slowly but surely becoming more 'European'. This change has grown, perhaps paradoxically, from the success enjoyed by this highly centralised approach. An apparent end to past housing shortages, the availability of relatively inexpensive housing for lower income groups (at least in the cities), and the greater importance attached to high-quality living environments amongst housing consumers have resulted in a shift in the focus of housing policy. Strong leadership in mass provision is no longer needed and so the role of government is today more about maintaining and managing the status quo than additional delivery. It also retains an important monitoring role (Ministry of Housing, Physical Planning and Environment, 1997, 2001).

The legacy of state involvement in Dutch housing is a large social rented sector, which accounts for some 36 per cent of the country's total housing stock and an owner-occupied stock, which – at 52 per cent – is small relative to levels of home ownership elsewhere in Europe (Ministry of Housing, Physical Planning and Environment, 1999). During the last few years, however, national government has taken the view that there is too little home ownership in the Netherlands and is now vigorously promoting ownership over renting. The result of this strategy is that the social rented sector is shrinking: it is losing large numbers of middle income groups and those remaining in the sector tend to be less well off, unable or unwilling to make the jump to home ownership. Hence the sector is becoming associated with concentrated poverty and social polarisation. But because social renting developed at a faster rate in the cities, it is the urban centres that have been most affected by this process, though rural communities – with their 20 per cent, on average, social housing – have not been immune from the effects of this tenure-biased policy. Other processes have been at work in the countryside and critical amongst these are population loss and ageing, and the renewed interest in the countryside displayed by the Netherlands' urban population. These are some of the issues addressed within this chapter.

Defining 'rural areas'

There has been a great deal of discussion surrounding the definition of rural areas. The Council for Rural Areas (1997) for example, does not see 'rural' as necessarily meaning outlying parts of the Netherlands but as counterparts of urban centres: urban and rural areas are closely linked and cannot exist in isolation; rather they enjoy a symbiotic relationship. In this vision, the 'rural' is present almost everywhere albeit in different forms and in various 'blends' with adjacent urban areas. For example even small green and watery enclaves within towns might be considered 'rural', as might larger, similar areas at the edge of a city. The notion of 'rural' space does not merely encompass wide expanses of open land some distance from towns and cities, though these are of course important. These areas themselves also differ dramatically in *form* and *use*: both 'natural' and man-made landscapes can be labelled rural and while some rural land is under agriculture or forestry, other areas are dominated by wetlands and recreational use. This broad definition owes much to Dutch history and the fact that the country has little in the way of remote wilderness but retains a desire to identify its rural roots.

As in other parts of Europe, the Netherlands is subject to an advanced process of increasing spatial disconnection of work–residential location and increasing levels of mobility have, in general, led to the disappearance of the sharp functional, economic and socio-cultural distinction between urban and rural areas. Morphological differences, however, remain. Quietness, open space and greenery can be seen as intrinsic qualities of a rural landscape and as distinguishing characteristics between urban and rural places. Hence, from an urban point of view, the countryside derives its importance and value from these distinguishing features: it retains scarce qualities, which are under increasing pressure as a result of urban expansion.

However, any definition of the rural is also dependent on who is trying to define it and for what purpose. Different people experience the rural in different ways. Closely related to this point is the necessary distinction between 'the rural' and 'the countryside'. These concepts are no longer synonymous as rural residential environments need not necessarily be located in what is traditionally thought of as the countryside: such environments can of course be found in the countryside, but they can also be created in or near urban agglomerations.

Furthermore, there is perhaps a critical difference between 'peripheral' and 'peri-urban' rural areas. The latter are characterised by relatively high rates of growth, high levels of prosperity and an abundance of younger people. They also play an important role in providing open-air day-recreation opportunities for those residing in nearby urban centres. The former peripheral areas, on the other hand, are located some distance from city–region housing and labour markets and are not subject to the same suburbanisation pressures. So some rural areas are locked within the urban sphere of influence and share a close bond – economically and culturally – with the nearest big centre or centres: they become, to all intents and purposes, the 'city's countryside'. The urbanisation of peri-urban rural areas in the Netherlands is viewed as a direct threat to landscape quality and ecological integrity. It has been a driving force behind the restrictive spatial planning policies of the Dutch government, which in turn are responsible for constraining the supply of new homes in the countryside.

This distinction of rural types is critical, as is the government's planning strategy. For this reason, much of the discussion that follows will concentrate on these principal issues:

- supply constraints within the Dutch housing market;
- increasing levels of demand for ever-more scarce rural homes; and
- the spatial planning policies affecting rural areas.

The diminishing supply of rural homes

The Dutch countryside has been transformed from an agricultural productivist landscape to one dominated by multifunctional consumption and described as 'postmodern'. Consumption activities such as recreation and tourism, nature conservation, landscape protection and housebuilding have been introduced and continuously extended. This rural commodification process is recognised throughout much of the urbanised western world and is both immense and irreversible. Rural areas themselves – as a result of their special (non-urban) qualities – have become marketable commodities and the demand for a slice of the rural is rising.

This demand is most apparent in the housing market where the supply of rural homes always seems to fall short of expectations. Although housing can be considered as an economically rewarding function for much of the countryside (Van Dam and Buckers, 1998), spatial policy in the highly urbanised Netherlands has sought to put a cap on further urbanisation and housebuilding.

With a total surface area of about 4.15 million hectares, the Netherlands ranks among the smaller countries of Western Europe: coming between Denmark, which is marginally bigger, and the slightly smaller Belgium. But with a population that now stands at 15.5 million, the Netherlands is one of the most densely populated countries on the planet: and density is especially high in the 'Randstad', the western Dutch conurbation combining the cities of Amsterdam, Den Haag, Rotterdam and Utrecht.

Limited land area and huge population density creates an almost permanent pressure on rural areas. They are used for living, working, recreation, transportation and also provide opportunities for new forms of economic production. At the same time, however, there is a desire to ensure that natural assets and unique landscapes are safeguarded for future generations. The balance, therefore, between necessary use and adequate protection is particularly fine and difficult to achieve in a Dutch context. This is certainly true in the area of housebuilding. Government, as was noted earlier, plays a central role in controlling the rural housing market through the use of planning policy that imposes significant restrictions on the building of new dwellings. The resultant supply shortfall means that house prices, particularly in the peri-urban rural areas are universally high and constantly climbing. Planning restriction also means that when new houses are built, these are almost invariably aimed at the high end of the market. Hence rural living is becoming an increasingly elitist activity; a viable option only for wealthier households. It also means that the housing needs of existing rural communities frequently remain unmet, and those on lower incomes have little chance of securing a rural home. The government's switch away from social housebuilding and its increasing reliance on market provision, of course, compounds this problem.

On the demand side

From the 1960s onwards, there was clear evidence of a trend towards population decentralisation, though this process was confined mainly to the Randstad. However a decade later new flows had emerged with people beginning to move to remoter (peripheral) parts of the country. But by the 1980s, it appeared that these movements had been only a temporary phenomenon and rural population growth began to lag someway behind growth in the cities. In the peripheral rural areas, population loss became the norm: young people left, the population structure became skewed in favour of older people and levels of natural population increase consequently declined. However, this phenomenon was also short-lived and by the 1990s a new period of positive urban–rural migration had arrived (Van Dam, 2000) and is continuing, abated only by housebuilding constraints.

Numerous reports point to a significant demand for rural living in the Netherlands (see for example, Elbersen, 2001; Van Dam *et al.*, 2002; Ministry of Housing, Physical Planning and Environment 1997, 2001). Nevertheless, just 5 per cent of all household moves in the Netherlands are from urban to rural municipalities and this is due largely to limitations on new housing supply (Van Dam and Heins, 2000).

But why is demand so strong? There is a clear preference amongst many Dutch households for greener residential environments, away from the various problems associated with urban living. Though, more specifically, motivations often fall into distinct categories: they can relate to work or education, or to personal household (e.g. health) or residential factors (e.g. more space or perceived higher quality of life). Residential factors appear to be particularly important in the Netherlands. Many potential urban–rural movers claim to be seeking a sanctuary away from the noise and drabness of urban living: the characteristics they apparently want are quietness, greenery and closeness to nature. They are driven on by a particular conception of the countryside and what it has to offer, and in the Netherlands – as in the United Kingdom – those who reject cities often have a highly romanticised view of rural areas.

The hope in the Netherlands is that these qualities can be recreated (or created if they never existed in reality) away from 'the countryside'. This possibility stems from the point made earlier: that concepts of the 'rural' and the 'countryside' are in fact different. Rural residential environments are not confined to the countryside but might also be found or created in suburban or urban locations. In other words, the characteristics that are demanded by some sections of the urban population could be realised closer to home. The key question, then, is whether demand could be diverted to such pseudo-countryside residential environments. Some research has pointed to a significant demand for development that attempts to combine rural with urban attributes: people want to live 'rural' but enjoy the convenience of living close to work and urban facilities. The pseudo-countryside is nothing new but harks back to Howard's Garden Cities concept: giving people the best of both worlds. The strategy would go some way to safeguarding the Netherlands' limited supply of open countryside (Van Dam *et al.*, 2002) assuming that homes in the pseudo-countryside were built at sufficiently high density to avoid further sprawl and that people could accept the apparent contradiction of higher-density rural living.

The shape of rural pressures: a more complex picture

The supply and demand factors responsible for the patterns described above do not affect all households equally. Rather, these factors work selectively bringing different experiences and outcomes for different groups. This is the conclusion reached by a number of researchers – including Atzema and Van Dam 1996; Van Dam; 2000, Van Dam and Heins; 2000 and Elbersen 2001 – who argue that age, income and wealth shape people's residential experiences. Retirement, for example, unties households from their place of former employment: they become free to move further afield in search of homes. Those with higher disposable incomes (or greater accumulated wealth) have far more choice in the housing market. And the choices of households with (i.e. older) and without children (i.e. younger) will differ for reasons related to need – the need or desire, for example, to raise children in what is perceived to be a safer and cleaner rural environment. This is of course the widely accepted view of how migration patterns and residential choices are formed.

However, work by Van Dam *et al.* (2002) has shown that age, income and lifecycle are not always dominant factors in determining such residential choices. Rather, residential and recreational histories seem to be more critical. Those who have lived in the countryside previously and perhaps have some particular tie with a certain community have a greater propensity to move from an urban centre. The same is true of households who have, in the past, made frequent visits to the countryside. So while older and richer people, or those with children, may express a strong demand for rural homes, this pattern is refined further by past experiences. Hence, there are a wide variety of household types seeking homes in the countryside though only a lucky few can translate this desire into reality. Rural property is highly sought after and increasingly scarce: a government demand study conducted in 1998 showed that in order to meet this demand an additional 400,000 rural homes would need to be provided between 2000 and 2010 (Table 5.1).

Table 5.1 Current stock and future housing demand in the Netherlands

Type of residential environment	Stock in 1998 (1,000s)	Demand in 2000 (1,000s)	Demand in 2010 (1,000s)	Increase in demand 2000–2010 (1,000s)
City centre	380	748	877	129
Outside centre	2,300	1,524	1,576	52
Village	2,300	2,226	2,357	131
Edge	580	1,003	1,111	108
Rural	830	1,054	1,245	191
Total	6,400	6,556	7,166	610

Source: Ministry of Housing, Physical Planning and Environment, 1997

Despite these figures, very little past effort has been devoted to understanding why people move from one type of area to another. More recently, the general importance of place has been recognised by the Ministry of Housing, Physical Planning and the Environment (1997, 2001). In the past, it was assumed that as long as homes of the right type and quality were provided, these would absorb demand irrespective of their location: the recognition now, however, is that people demand good location, safe neighbourhoods, appropriate amenities and facilities and reasonable levels of accessibility. The government has recognised, in short, that a home is only as good or desirable as these extraneous qualities allow it to be.

The apparent preferences for rural over urban living provides some clues as to the type of future development that will seemingly attract and retain people. There is evidence that movers are seeking additional living space: they prefer detached houses and farmhouses above apartments and semi-detached houses. They are also looking for private exterior space, especially gardens. And they want space beyond the confines of their own property – or, in other words, low density is preferred above higher density developments. Furthermore, the presence of typical rural characteristics such as peace and quiet, greenness, landscape, nature and open space are considered important. Nearby facilities and services are less important on this hit list of desirable attributes with the exception of shops. Obviously, the visual characteristics of the environment play a more important role than the presence of, or accessibility to, facilities and services (Heins *et al.*, 2002).

There is a political pressure, of course, to give people at least some of the things they demand. Population increases are generally considered to be a positive economic indicator revealing broad satisfaction with local quality of life: and the converse is true where population is declining. In many rural areas, all available indicators point to a high quality of life for local residents and various studies have related this to low population densities (725 square metres per person, compared with 161 square metres in the Netherlands as a whole – giving existing residents those qualities that potential in-migrants aspire to). Others have made the connection between general quality of life and a far lower fear of crime in the countryside (Strijker, 2000).

What all this adds up to is a perception of the countryside as a better place to live: rural areas are seen to have comparative advantage not just for residents but also for companies seeking to relocate away from the cities. The migration of some businesses has enabled young people to remain in the countryside, though it also created a new wave of in-migration heaping further pressure on the housing market. But there is a recognition, of course, that countryside qualities cannot be recreated everywhere and are therefore finite and scarce. Hence, new conflicts have arisen relating, in particular, to property rights (the rights, for instance, of local people to secure homes in their local areas) and more general access to housing and land. These conflicts are both tangible – initiated when migrants or second home buyers force up house prices – and subjective, arising from contrasting perceptions as to the legitimate use of the countryside – as playground for an ex-urban elite or as a place where people can live and work (European Commission, 2000).

In recognition of people's desire to live in the countryside, and based on an appreciation of particular rural qualities, the strategy of government has been to absorb additional rural housing pressure where possible while meeting expectations in other ways where necessary. How this is being achieved is examined in the next part of this chapter.

Managing the pressure

The Dutch authorities are active in spatial planning at all administrative levels. The Ministry of Housing, Spatial Planning and the Environment has prime responsibility for national planning policy and also for the integration of this policy into the European framework. Below this upper tier, the *provinces* set out their own policies within regional spatial plans while the *municipalities* draw up local plans in which the rules guiding development and land use change are established. There is a requirement of course for conformity across these various tiers.

The current national framework is set out in the *Fourth National Policy Document on Spatial Planning* (VINEX). This document establishes the principle of urban compaction: the aim being to halt urban sprawl and thereby safeguard open space. The preoccupation of planning at the present time is to ensure that all new dwellings are located on so-called 'VINEX sites': these are sites specifically identified within the VINEX document and in the case of rural development, are adjacent to existing urban centres. The intention is to prevent new clusters of rural development from springing up, but to ensure instead that necessary housebuilding in the countryside (and on greenfield sites) takes the form of limited encroachments. The VINEX works to a planning horizon of 2015.

But there are already clear signs that limited and tightly controlled rural encroachments will be insufficient to satisfy demand over the longer term. Therefore, policy planners and commentators alike are looking ahead to the *Fifth National Policy Document on Spatial Planning* and its likely contents. In general, it seems unlikely that there will be substantive changes to planning policy: urban compaction, for example, will remain the prime objective. But given the shortfall in rural housing supply relative to demand, there are indications that the next Spatial Planning Document will seek to increase rural supply in a number of more innovative ways. It has been suggested that the conversion of agricultural buildings and disused military installations might be permitted. This would represent an extension of the Ministry of Agriculture, Nature Management and Fisheries' recent *Ruimte voor Ruimte* (Space for Space) strategy which has provided generous subsidies, especially in the south of the country, for farmers withdrawing from agriculture and converting old buildings into new homes. This is one means of increasing housing supply and reducing agricultural over-production, but questions must be raised as to where young people will find jobs if the majority of farms close and the old productivist landscape is wholly replaced by one of middle-class consumption.

Conclusions

The Netherlands is a small country facing almost overwhelming population pressure. Those who experience the problems of high-density living first hand are often drawn to the countryside's apparent tranquillity and open spaces. It seems to hold the promise of a much higher quality of life. But it is clear that much of the countryside is unable to absorb current demand pressure: land supply is limited, house prices are soaring and the planning system is striving to manage land use change in a sustainable way. And this means restricting further housebuilding in rural areas. But policy cannot suppress aspirations; rather it must seek to satisfy these in new ways. Hence, the concept of the 'pseudo'-countryside has arisen: developments that try to deliver much of what people want but through environmentally sensitive means and higher quality. Limited rural encroachments give some people the opportunity to move away from cities, particularly those on higher incomes. But still, this is not enough and even incidental building initiatives (e.g. the reuse of non-residential buildings for residential purposes) will be insignificant against the weight of current and future demand.

There is a clear moral argument for opening up the countryside to a considerable amount of extra development. At the beginning of this chapter, it was noted that the promotion of home ownership has created acute social polarisation in the cities: those with the means to do so have abandoned the social rented sector and this sector, which once dominated urban areas, is rapidly becoming a focus of deprivation. Housing scarcity in the countryside, on the other hand, means that only the rich can afford a rural home. Hence, there is a clear division between the affluent countryside with its high quality of life, and the cities with their crime, pollution, overcrowding and deprivation. Surely more people, with a variety of backgrounds, must be handed the opportunity of moving from the cities: though this must be balanced with policies aimed at addressing the current urban malaise. Nobody wants to see total urban abandonment or further hollowing out of inner city areas; but restrictions on rural housebuilding have simply been too severe. There are several arguments to support the case for the easing of these restrictions.

First, and from an economic perspective, getting people into the country-side and building new homes has clear economic benefits. Many of the old rural industries are finished and people are surely the lifeblood of any area. Second, the obsession with environmental protection is obscuring the fact that the Dutch countryside could absorb further growth in some locations. Though of course a balance must be struck: rural residents value what the countryside already offers and this must not be sacrificed to development pressure. But on the other hand, it may be the case that some space reductions (higher density building) can be worked into developments without undermining what people already aspire to: and, of course, this means that more people could enjoy the countryside. One clear argument is that personal space might be reduced, while public open space – available for entire community enjoyment – is increased. Third, the greatest demand for rural living is not in the remoter, more environmentally sensitive parts of the country, but close to existing urban areas. The VINEX recognises

5.1 Detached house in low-lying countryside: S. Heins.

5.2 Typical old farmhouse: S. Heins.

this pressure and seeks to release sites to satisfy demand. But the solution to this housing pressure will not be found by simply releasing greenfield land. There is a need to understand what people value most in their residential environments and what they might be willing to do without.

The concept of the 'pseudo-countryside' encapsulates this balance, reducing planning constraint (in edge locations) but offsetting this with better quality development. It seeks to replicate the most prized aspects of the rural lifestyle, but in a higher density setting: above all, it is about compromise.

Chapter 6
France

Elizabeth Auclair and Didier Vanoni

Introduction

In 1999, France had a population of 58 million people, occupying a land area
of some 544,000 square kilometres. While the average population density is close
to 100 inhabitants per square kilometre, this average figure masks significant
geographical variations – from 729 in the most densely populated urban areas,
to 17 in some remoter parts of the French countryside. More than 75 per cent
of the population live in areas defined as urban and during the last fifty years, in
line with other European countries, France has undergone a transition from
being a predominantly rural to an urban society. This has been marked by the
development of big cities and their suburban hinterlands. However, many indicators reveal, today, a revival of the countryside, and the appeal of rural living is
demonstrated by the recent growth of many smaller communities. This renewed
vibrancy provides the backcloth for this chapter. Though before focusing on the
countryside in more detail, a general account of housing issues affecting France
at the current time is offered in the next section.

Housing trends

The key housing question facing France today is not one of supply or absolute
quantity, but relates to more detailed concerns over stock distribution and the
adjustment of supply to demand in particular regions. There are also important
issues being raised over the quality of much of the country's housing stock. But
perhaps the principal issue is a social rather than a physical one and concerns
access and affordability. Many rural people, especially the young who typically
seek smaller dwellings, find it extremely difficult to gain access to housing. But
such difficulties vary in scale across the country. In the Paris region, for example,
access problems are especially acute, though less pronounced elsewhere. It is also
the case that the pressures facing towns and adjacent countryside differ in scale,
though the practice of distinguishing urban and non-urban problems is less
common in France than it might be elsewhere. Rather, there is an assumption

that the two are interdependent and that the problems facing the countryside represent the flip side of problems facing nearby towns or cities. So less effort has been made on identifying distinctly 'rural problems'.

The history of French housing can be divided into several periods. Immediately following the Second World War, the focus was on the replacement of destroyed dwellings. By 1950, the ratio of dwellings to people was about 1 to 3: or 14 million units against a population of 40 million. The critical issue at this time was the need for new housing.[1] This was in part due to high levels of in-migration from France's former colonies following the end of the Algerian war and also a result of simultaneous natural population increase. But towns gained a great deal more population from these processes than the countryside, which was losing people at an alarming rate. During '*Les trente glorieuses*' – the thirty years of growth between 1945 and 1975 – and especially during the 1960s and 1970s, government launched a number of key housing policies. Public sector agencies used state subsidy to embark on a huge programme of housebuilding. At the peak of this period, almost half a million dwellings per year were being added to France's housing stock, the majority of which were built by these public agencies and often in the form of apartment blocks. High-rise estates sprang up on the edges of many towns where costs were substantially lower. In more recent years, however, a large number of these estates have been a focus of social and economic difficulties and in an effort to address such difficulties, government has promoted an array of remedial measures known collectively as the '*Politique de la ville*'.

Public sector housebuilding declined in the aftermath of France's economic crisis of the mid-1970s. And this coincided with other important changes. Critical amongst these were the apparently changing aspirations of the French population: urban in-migration began to slow markedly while many existing city-dwellers initiated an urban exodus and headed for the countryside. Government policy also took a new direction with the promotion of home ownership. The feeling at the time was that home ownership should be attainable irrespective of household income and therefore government began offering those on more modest incomes cheap loans. The first of these were the 'PAP' loans – or '*prêt à l'accession a la propriété*'. These were followed later by other similar loans: e.g. the '*prêt à taux zero*'. At the same time, government was claiming to have learned the lessons from failed high-rise buildings and began to promote the construction of lower density single dwelling houses. By the beginning of the 1980s, such dwellings accounted for more than two-thirds of housing completions and by 1999, 56 per cent of the French housing stock comprised individual houses. But stock type varies across the country and there are, for obvious reasons, far more low-density individual dwelling houses in rural regions. For example, in the

Vendee Departement on the Atlantic coast, nearly 87 per cent of dwellings are of this type, though the figure falls to 41 per cent on the French Riviera where apartment blocks dominate.

This move away from higher density apartment blocks has led to the creation, all across the country, of new lower density estates on the outskirts of numerous towns. Similar estates have been locked onto smaller villages but at a reduced scale. This form of urban development remains prevalent today despite moves to promote higher densities and more compact cities, and despite all the problems associated with low-density suburban living. But transport and infrastructural difficulties aside, it is also the case that the cost of home ownership has proven to be too great a burden for many households. Problems have been experienced in repaying government loans, in maintaining properties and in meeting the high transport costs associated with suburban living. In short, home ownership for many households has proven to be a far from ideal means of meeting housing needs.

In broader terms, housing conditions have greatly improved for the majority of French households. The number of dwellings available rose from 13 million in 1946 to 23 million in 1996: an increase of 80 per cent compared with a population rise of only 45 per cent. The average floor space of dwellings has also increased dramatically since the end of the Second World War, while levels of overcrowding have plummeted. Average floor space in 1970 was 68 square metres: by 1996 the figure was 88 square metres. And over the last thirty years, the number of persons per dwelling has dropped from 3.2 to 2.5: over the same period, the number of rooms per dwelling increased from 3.2 to 4.0. At the very least, the personal space available to individuals has risen significantly, particularly in less densely populated rural regions.

France's countryside

Despite our earlier suggestion that policy has not sought to overtly emphasise urban–rural differences, the countryside (including agricultural, forestry and 'natural' lands) represents a significant part of the French landmass: 93 per cent or 54 million hectares in total. Such rural areas have a population density that averages just under 35 persons per square kilometre. To some groups, these areas are viewed as a critical focus for environmental protection and regional planning; but to others, such 'wide open spaces' require little in the way of policy intervention and should be left to their own devices. There is also a commonly held belief that housing and social difficulties are mainly urban problems and have not touched the countryside to anything like the same degree.

However, the countryside has played a key political role for many years. Public policy, for instance, has been strongly conditioned by the needs and demands of farming, though the countryside itself has become less dependent on the agricultural economy in recent times. New economic strengths have emerged including tourism, marked by the increase in the number of holiday homes. The overall character of the countryside has also altered, particularly with the advent of 'interstitial' urbanisation between key centres and the movement of hitherto 'urban' activities – including certain types of business – into rural areas. These changes have brought with them new challenges, and not least amongst these is the challenge of defining exactly what is meant by 'rural' as opposed to urban space.

Delimiting rural France

In economic terms, the separation of rural from urban areas seems neither practicable nor sensible. The interdependence of the two is demonstrated by the fact that 2.6 million people leave rural and semi-rural areas each day and commute to city-based jobs. Often what is rural is simply viewed as that which is not obviously urban, in economic and physical character. The search for a definitive guide to urban and rural space is a relatively new endeavour in France. In 1996, INSEE (*Institut National des Statistiques et des Études Économiques*) revised the way in which it defined rural areas. Previously, rural communities were those with fewer than 2,000 inhabitants: the replacement system was designed to allow for a greater diversity of circumstances. All local communities were subdivided into two groups: those under urban influence and those with a rural dominance. The breakdown continues below this level and four types of rural area are identified.

- 'Under weak urban influence': located in the periphery of a city and have 20 per cent of their populations working in a nearby town.
- 'Rural centres': offer between 2,000 and 5,000 jobs and the number of jobs is equal or greater than the resident population.
- 'Communities at the periphery of rural centres': have 20 per cent or more of their populations working in a 'Rural centre'.
- 'Remote rural local communities': rural areas not falling into any of the previous three categories.

Using this classification, it can be shown that the rural population in 1999 (13.6 million persons) was about the same as the rural population in 1962, meaning that the ebbs and flows of in-migration and out-migration appear to have cancelled themselves out over this period. During the last forty years, there has been no net change in France's rural population total. However, there are important regional and local variations and these provide the focus of the next section.

Rural demographics since 1962

Although the rural population appears stable (in absolute terms) the actual proportion of people living in the countryside has declined: from 29.3 per cent in 1962 to 23.3 per cent in 1999. This is a result of greater population growth in France's larger towns and cities and, in more recent years, a huge expansion within suburban areas. These patterns are shown in Table 6.1. It was noted earlier that depopulation affected many rural communities during the last century. This process created significant pressures in the rural economy as people migrated to seek a greater diversity of job opportunities in the cities. This pressure was particularly acute in the agricultural sector, which lost 70 per cent of its workforce (3.5 million persons) between 1945 and 1975. The decline in the number of agricultural workers is continuing unabated today as between 30,000 and 40,000 people leave the sector each year. This loss is in part a result of ongoing mechanisation – affecting, in particular, large-scale farming ventures around Paris and many vineyards – and in part due to the loss of young people who no longer remain to take over family farms. This desertion by the young is especially pronounced in the French interior.

The rural population has also undergone a massive transformation in terms of its social configuration. Fewer than 20 per cent of current jobs are in agriculture while service sector industries are thriving, in much the same way as they are in the cities. The balance of agricultural and service sector employment in different rural areas accounts for significant variations in social and economic well-being. Against an index value of 100, average income in the Champagne-Ardennes region is 193, compared to just 40 in Limousin. Where the loss of

Table 6.1 The population of France 1962 to 1999

	Population (millions of inhabitants)				Population (%)			
	Urban centres	Sub-urban communities	Rural areas	Total France	Urban centres	Sub-urban communities	Rural areas	Total France
1962	27.146	5.666	13.613	46.425	58.5	12.2	29.3	100
1968	30.381	5.859	13.473	49.712	61.1	11.8	27.1	100
1975	32.878	6.537	13.177	52.592	62.5	12.4	25.1	100
1982	33.357	7.715	13.263	54.335	61.4	14.2	24.4	100
1990	34.372	8.862	13.381	56.615	60.7	15.7	23.6	100
1999	35.217	9.674	13.628	58.519	60.2	16.5	23.3	100

Source: INSEE. *Recensement général de la population*, 1999

agricultural employment has not been balanced by new job opportunities, household incomes have plummeted.

Since the mid-1970s and the wider economic downturn, increasing levels of unemployment in the cities have decreased their appeal to potential migrants. For this reason, people have stayed put and some rural areas have experienced renewed population growth. The 1975 census revealed that a turning point had indeed been reached and the rural population was on a clear upward trajectory. This trend has been reaffirmed by successive national censuses since that date with the last two censuses (1990 and 1999) showing that rural areas have gained 247,000 persons during the last twenty years, but this pattern has not been uniformly felt. Between 1990 and 1999, rural areas gained an additional 410,000 people but lost 163,000. Much of this loss is a reflection of the ageing population structure within many parts of the countryside. But that said, 13,950 communities experienced positive change and the majority (72 out of 95) of rural *Departements* saw net increases with the arrival of newcomers who often express very different needs and tastes from the older population that they effectively replaced. However, in the so-called 'empty triangle' ('*la diagonale du vide*') stretching from the north-east to the south-west of the country, population levels are still declining and socio-economic indicators continue to reveal acute disadvantage compared to those rural areas experiencing a renaissance in recent years.

The general picture, however, is a positive one and many observers point to a new vibrancy and dynamism that seems to have taken hold in many parts of the French countryside, produced not so much by the pull of rural living but by the problems facing urban society.

The consequences of rural dynamism

So-called 'secondary suburban areas' and 'interstitial urbanisation areas' (between major centres) with their well-developed transport infrastructure have experi-

Table 6.2 Change in total dwelling stock

	Rural under weak influence	Rural centres	Periphery of rural centres	Rural isolated	Urban centres	Suburban communities
1968–1975	+3.7	+12.2	+2.1	+1.4	+15.2	+16.0
1975–1981	+9.9	+9.5	+9.8	+4.8	+9.4	+23.6
1982–1990	+10.0	+7.4	+10.0	+4.6	+8.3	+19.3
1991–1999	+9.0	+8.0	+8.0	+5.0	+11.0	+15.0

Source: INSEE, *Recensement général de la population*, 1999

enced the steepest growth. Half of all the recent population increase is concentrated in communities located in the periphery of 17 key urban areas: included amongst these are Paris, Nantes, Toulouse, Montpellier, Nîmes, Perpignan and Bastia. These regions form a semicircle and are home to approximately half of France's rural population. In the areas away from these centres, growth is much slower, confirming perhaps the interdependence of rural and urban areas.

In the past, it was rural areas that were feeding urban growth: today, this situation has been reversed and the tide has apparently turned in favour of the countryside. There is a clear need to reflect this relationship and dependency in planning and especially housing policy, given the consequences for the housing market in areas that are either gaining or losing population. Hence policy has focused on managing growth around the key urban centres and on dealing with decline in the three areas that continue to lose population: Limousin, Midi-Pyrennées and Auvergne.

Population change and the housing challenge

What do these changes mean in terms of housing need, demand and access? There are different challenges from one region to another and there is no single problem to be addressed. Growth brings with it demand pressure but this pressure has not been judged as significantly high outside the Paris region: the supply of housing in the countryside usually matches demand and average housing costs are typically low. However, even 'typically low' costs can be too high for certain categories of household: and there is evidence that younger people do experience difficulty in securing homes of the right type and cost.

It is also the case that low population densities in some areas result in poor transport, employment and service opportunities. Remoteness and the weakness of local job markets are key problems facing many households, particularly those who need to work and need to travel. For these reasons, the countryside is often portrayed as a focus of social exclusion. This is certainly true for indigenous younger people who seek work and homes in their community of birth. But public policy has also focused on what can be done to assist new types of households moving to rural areas with a wide variety of needs and expectations. It is not only wealthy people who move to the countryside but also the socially disadvantaged who seek a higher quality of life away from cities. The availability of relatively cheap housing allows them to make this move: but once installed in new communities, the types of services required in these communities may alter dramatically.

The broader policy challenge facing the French government has two elements: first, meeting the housing (and related) needs of a new type of rural

Table 6.3 Housing characteristics in France

Date of construction	Rural under weak urban influence	Rural centres	Periphery of urban centres	Rural isolated	France
Before 1915	39.8	23.7	46.0	44.5	23.0
1915 to 1948	10.8	13.8	12.4	12.0	13.7
1949 to 1974	21.1	33.1	15.2	20.1	35.0
Since 1975	28.3	29.4	26.4	23.4	28.3
Total	100	100	100	100	100
Level of comfort:					
Without at least one of these elements: interior toilet, bath or shower, central heating	32.8	19.3	41.5	39.2	20.2
With interior toilet, bath or shower and central heating	67.2	80.7	58.5	60.8	79.8
Total	100	100	100	100	100
Type of housing:					
Individual housing	90.4	68.9	95.6	98.6	55.8
Apartments	9.6	31.1	4.4	1.4	44.2
Total	100	100	100	100	100

Source: INSEE, *Enquête Logement*, 1996

population comprising a mix of income groups and second, developing policy that reflects the differing needs of remoter and interstitial rural communities. Below this level of broad challenge is a range of key housing issues: these are examined in the next section.

Issues of housing quality

France's rural housing stock comprises a large proportion of older dwellings built before 1915 (from 23.7 per cent to 46 per cent according to the rural area, against 23 per cent for the whole of France) and while quality in the main rural centres is comparable to that in larger towns and cities, much rural housing is of a lower quality and lacking in one or more basic amenity (Table 6.3).

The proportion of dwellings lacking at least one main element of comfort (interior toilet, bath or shower, or central heating) is quite high in rural areas, and can reach 41.5 per cent of the housing stock.

Quite naturally, rural areas offer a very large majority of individual homes (between 68.9 per cent and 98.5 per cent of the housing stock according to the area). This situation seems to contribute to the attractiveness of rural areas especially for urban families living in apartments and wishing for more space.

Affordability

Rural housing is generally cheap and broadly affordable, a situation that differs markedly from that described by Hoggart in England (see Chapter 10 in this volume). Indeed, decisions to move to the countryside are frequently driven by the knowledge that cheap housing is readily available outside major urban centres. Such housing also offers occupants far more space and the demand for detached properties, with gardens, has now reached unprecedented levels. People are willing to commute further and incur far higher transport costs in order to acquire cheaper housing and a great deal more space. Rural living offers many people the chance to own their homes, releasing them from the high rents that many face in bigger urban centres.

But although living in the countryside might seem like a positive and more affordable option, it is not always an expression of preference. Large homes in the cities are expensive and people with growing families often have no other option but to move to less central locations given the lack of large and affordable apartments in urban areas. So around many large cities, the trend towards rural living is merely part of an economic decentralisation that can have negative repercussions for less well off households and, particularly for younger people trying to secure accommodation in their home communities. This type of process and pressure is especially pronounced around Paris, and mirrors the situation in the English Home Counties.

But away from such hotspots, it is generally the case that the cost of acquiring rural property is fairly low. Greater cost is incurred however, when households attempt to bring fairly low quality homes up to 'urban' standards. For richer commuters, this is rarely a problem, but for those households with more modest incomes, the cost of essential repairs and improvement often means that rural living is far less affordable than it at first seemed. The more general problems facing such households are examined in the next section.

Low-income rural migrants

Recent work by Vanoni *et al.* (1998) has revealed that some areas have rapidly developed into pockets of disadvantage, populated by socially excluded households on relatively low incomes. Those moving to the countryside in search of cheaper housing often find themselves in homes that lack central heating, hot water or proper sewerage. They also gravitate to areas where there are few jobs or social opportunities and rapidly become trapped, unable to move back to towns even if they wished to do so. These problems are compounded when new migrants lose touch with former family and social networks and then find themselves increasingly isolated in their new 'homes'.

The significance of such problems is extremely difficult to quantify and the national picture of this type of migration and disadvantage is rather sketchy.[2] However data concerned with the migration of those who subsequently seek welfare benefit (in their new *Departement*) reveals that France's remoter rural areas – including Ardèche, Aveyron, Gers and Hautes Alpes – are particularly susceptible to this phenomenon. They also reveal that the types of social problem that were hitherto associated with inner urban areas (Burgel, 1993) are being exported to the remotest parts of the country, with significant implications for both housing and wider social policy (Séchet (1996) provides a more comprehensive overview of these problems). The urban dimension of this problem has concerned government for some years, but its rural manifestation has received far less attention. But as in other countries, there is a recognition that rural housing deprivation assumes a very different form to urban deprivation. For example, various statistics put the number of homeless people in France (SDF or *Sans Domicile Fixe*) at somewhere between 200,000 and 600,000 but the vast majority of those sleeping rough are located in large urban centres. Members of the rural population classed as 'SDF' (a small proportion of the above estimates) are so classified because their housing situation tends to be precarious rather than desperate, living temporarily with friends, in short-term hostels or squatting. And many people enduring such difficulties suffer additional social and personal problems, commonly in relation to their mental health.

Holiday homes

Housing pressure is often viewed as the transportation of hitherto urban problems to rural settings. Issues of housing supply appear to take a back seat to these wider concerns. In this context, the issue of holiday homes – that feature so prominently elsewhere in Europe – appears less important in France. However, such properties do play an important role in the countryside and this comes as little surprise given that France claims to have more holiday homes than any other country in the European Union – rising from 600,000 in 1962 to 2.9 million in 1999 (INSEE, *Recensement général de la population*, 1999). In some regions, the numbers of holiday homes are so great that they have a significant impact on the local and regional economy. In Lozere Departement, for instance, one dwelling in every three is a holiday home and these bring a huge and guaranteed influx of visitors to the area each year. In recent years, growth in the number of such properties has been levelling off and many former holiday homes are being permanently occupied. This is, to some extent, a result of major infrastructure and transport improvements, which have encouraged some owners to turn their backs on city homes and live full-time in the countryside and commute over greater distances. Other former city-based professionals now choose to work from home, though growth in this phenomenon does not seem quite as pronounced as was originally expected. Additional factors leading to the conversion of holiday to permanent homes includes the tendency for some households to abandon expensive urban living and others to settle permanently in their holiday home on reaching retirement age. This transformation of seasonal homes is yet another process resulting in the apparent repopulation of the French countryside. The abundance of relatively inexpensive rural property means that this added demand on the rural housing stock is rarely viewed as problematic.

Facing the housing challenge

Despite a tradition of strong public intervention in various spheres of French life – via social, economic and planning policy – the housing sector remains very much market oriented. Regional strategies play an important role in guiding new housebuilding but these, in addition to national policies, rarely make a distinction between 'rural' and 'urban' priorities. Policy itself is implemented at the local level by either the Departements or by the municipalities. The main tools used at these levels are focused on either physical/supply issues or social concerns.

Housing supply, construction and planning

French construction and planning strategies tend to be generic in the sense that apparently urban tools are applied equally in non-urban settings. The urbanism legislation ('*Code de l'urbanisme*') for example defines at the national level the general rules for land use and construction, as well as for protection of agricultural land and open spaces. It is then up to the local communities (urban and rural) to define their orientations: they are charged with the preparation of the municipal plans. These plans, formally known as *'Plan d'Occupation du Sol'* (POS) have, following the Housing and Urban Planning Act of 2000, been re-labelled the *'Plan Local d'Urbanisme'* (PLU). They provide a framework for organising land use change and fix the limits of 'urbanisation' and future construction. It is interesting to note that the title itself suggests that physical development is an urban activity and in some way 'anti-rural': the title also points to the fact that planning is viewed as an urban activity and is not retailored for rural settings.

It is generally the case that planning has few intentionally rural aspects. However, the state itself does play a key role in delivering new housing in the countryside: it achieves this through the promotion of a broad social housing sector and via the *'Agence Nationale pour l'Amélioration de l'Habitat'* (ANAH). The social housing sector is responsible for supplying more than 25 per cent of all new homes: and although the major element of its recent building programme has focused on urban and suburban areas, there has been an increase in its activity in the more pressured rural areas (although fewer than 5 per cent rural of dwellings *nationally* are social sector provided).

There are various reasons why social provision is increasing in the countryside. First, it has been claimed that such provision is part of a conscious effort to move certain disadvantaged households away from troubled urban areas to places where their needs can be better catered for (Vanoni, 1999): they are offered other forms of social assistance as part of this relocation package. These measures often address households who do not only meet financial problems but who seem to accumulate several 'behaviour handicaps' which makes it difficult for these families to settle in collective housing estates. The solution of access to a single-family home can appear as a means to avoid neighbourhood problems and to offer a dwelling adapted to specific ways of life.

Second, it has also been the strategy of government to build small social housing estates (of between 5 and 40 dwellings) aimed specifically at young people who are experiencing difficulty in meeting market housing costs in the more pressured rural areas. Effort is being made to ensure that such estates blend in with existing architecture, are integrated within current settlements, and are not obvious add-ons that end up as concentrations of social exclusion.

Another key tool is aimed not at increasing supply, but at maintaining the quality of existing housing stock. Through direct subsidies and loans, the ANAH provides homeowners with the means to improve their homes either for their own use or for private letting. But this loan system brings greater benefits to more affluent households than those struggling to meet the costs of home repairs: receipt of loan assistance is dependent on homeowners being able to match-fund repairs (Vanoni, 1999) so works against those on low incomes who are unable to do so. Well-off homeowners who invest in improvements may even qualify for tax breaks: another benefit that will not accrue to the less well-off.

Dealing with the social aspects of housing problems

Many social problems – some of which are mentioned above – afflict rural as well as urban French society: social exclusion (and the challenge of integration), indebtedness, drug-abuse and mental health problems are all commonplace. Several pieces of legislation since 1990 have together sought to promote *'Le Droit au Logement'* (Housing Rights – mentioned in the *Loi Besson* Act (1990) and the *Loi d'Orientation pour la Ville* Act (1991)) with the aim of supporting disadvantaged households through a variety of means. The *Fonds Solidarité Logement* (FSL or Housing Solidarity Fund) for example, provides local administrations with the means to help disadvantaged or indebted households to either remain in their own homes or gain access to a home in the first place. In instances where people suffer acute social problems, funds are available for the provision of 'very social or integration housing'. The PLAI fund (*'logement d'integration'*) aims at giving access to households in difficulty to a dwelling adapted to their specific needs, such as a big apartment for large families, or a house with a garden for those who want to stock various material, etc. Added to this, these households are accompanied by social workers who help them manage correctly their dwelling (maintenance, correct use and regular pay out of the rent). None of these are measures designed for specifically rural problems, but they receive equal support and commitment in whichever setting, rural or urban.

The same is true of one final housing strategy designed with socially disadvantaged households in mind. Since 1990, all Departements must have in place a '*Plan Départemental d'Action en Faveur du Logement des Personnes Défavorisées*' (a housing plan for the disadvantaged). These plans must identify the broad problems facing an area, stress local concerns, fix priorities, outline the necessary response and assign responsibilities and funding. These are essentially housing plans with a broad social remit and intended as a basis for tackling area-based social problems in an integrated way. This departmental plan is a procedure, which adds more means to the existing measures, in order to help the local actors develop access to housing. It can be an exceptional loan for a debt problem related to housing, or for paying the various taxes needed to get access to a dwelling. Implemented twelve years ago, this procedure that aims at limiting the number of homeless households, can be considered as one of the major social policies contributing to the housing rights as defined by law.

Conclusions

The changing fortunes of the French countryside are linked closely to recent trends in urban society. The one-way flow of people from rural to urban areas has recently been subject to a partial reversal and the countryside (in general) has witnessed a net increase in population. This national picture, however, masks important regional variations and some remoter parts of the countryside have continued to lose people at an alarming rate. These patterns – explored at some length in this chapter – are at the heart of what many people consider to be a renaissance of the French countryside: a transition from near stagnation 20 years ago to renewed vibrancy. But this renaissance has not benefited everyone: there are still significant pockets of disadvantage and some households have found themselves excluded from this newly found prosperity.

Some of the strategies put in place to deal with these problems have been discussed above: but their success has been curtailed by two factors. First, there has been a clear reluctance among many rural administrations and other agencies to build new social housing, fearing that such a move will simply act as a green light for lower-income households, attracting a new wave of poverty into the countryside. This fear is heightened by the fact that many small rural communities have few resources and believe that importing new social problems will bankrupt them. Second, there is the classic problem of economies of scale: the main providers of social housing prefer to concentrate new housebuilding in larger urban centres rather than scattering small schemes in several different places. In France, this problem is compounded by a lack of local building contractors in many remoter rural areas, which increases the costs incurred by providing agencies that must import the necessary construction expertise (Vanoni, 1999). It is more generally the case that social housing providers have weak operational networks away from the semicircle of key urban centres mentioned earlier. But this reluctance to build social housing in rural areas, is not so much related to technical or financial questions, as to the management difficulties that appear once the households are settled in. Thus, it is more difficult to cope with management problems (such as the high costs of running houses) in rural areas where the housing is dispersed.

The government is committed however to ensuring that the countryside's renewed vibrancy benefits as many people as possible and has set about developing a regionally-delivered strategy for encouraging local agencies to build more homes and invest in social support schemes. The *Loi Solidarité et Renouvellement Urbain* (SRU) of 2000, for example provides a framework for the regional and national distribution of additional social housing with the aim of breaking down current patterns of social segregation. The SRU provides further incentives for areas with a poor track record in social housing provision to add more homes (over the next fifteen years) to their current stock: at the same time, resources are shifted away from those areas that already have significant amounts of social housing. The regional planning act of 1998 (*Loi d'Orientation pour l'Aménagement et le Développement Durable du Territoire* – or LOADDT) complements the SRU providing incentives for local groups to join forces and implement local development projects in which housing is the central concern.

While it might be too early to gauge the success or wider consequences of these strategies, it is clear that conscious efforts are being made to respond to France's recent and dramatic demographic changes. It is recognised that changes have brought with them huge implications for the way the rural population – new and old – is housed and also a commitment to ensure that new housing supply is meshed with adequate and wider social support.

Notes

1   It also must be stressed that during the years that preceded the Second World War, the construction rate was very low.
2   Part of the study was based on an analysis of official data collected in 1995 and 1996 and was concerned with the percentage of persons benefiting from minimum income help (RMI).

Part Two:
Atomistic Cultures, Laissez-Faire Regimes

The next part of this book examines three countries that are each characterised first by what we have termed 'atomistic cultures' and secondly by 'laissez-faire' policy regimes. To a greater or lesser extent, Italy, Spain and the Republic of Ireland all share a particular view of state intervention and the role of informal networks in meeting family or wider social objectives. The importance attached to family (as an 'agent of social welfare' according to Padovani and Vettoretto) and either the informality of some policy or the outright rejection of regulation, are key cultural and political aspects of life in these countries.

In Chapter 7, Padovani and Vettoretto argue that in the period since the Second World War, the Italian population has found itself reasonably well housed. But beneath the surface, a range of problems and challenges remain. Income inequality and the proliferation of illegal housebuilding mean that many areas are subject to acute social and housing imbalances. And pockets of disadvantage follow broad geographical lines, with the north-centre enjoying relative prosperity compared with the less developed south. These broad regional differences are usually emphasised above more localised town and country disparities, and indeed there have been few attempts to distinguish particular rural concerns from those affecting the country in general.

Fifty years ago, the idea of a rural area was synonymous with poverty and with antiquated agrarian practices. By the 1970s, they were often viewed as more heterogeneous areas where new ideas and ways of living were taking hold. Today, the same areas are seen as the stage for an entirely new social and economic praxis. But Padovani and Vettoretto also argue strongly that not all areas labelled rural are the same. Rather, there are fringe locations subject to growing demand and less susceptible to illegal development, and 'diffused cities' (the urbanised countryside) where new industries vie for position and where immigrant workers often find themselves poorly housed. There are also tourism areas where there might be housing supply problems if it were not for incredibly lax planning control. And in some regions, there are areas untouched by new economic prosperity and where depopulation and deprivation remain catchwords for everyday life. Throughout these different rural areas, the authors point to two principal concerns:

- the pre-eminence of general – rather than focused – policy and a reliance on the family as an agent of social welfare (and housing provision); and
- the proliferation of illegal housebuilding, which has resulted in a ready supply of houses, but of questionable quality and accompanied by adverse environmental impacts.

In this context, it is suggested that the biggest challenge faced by rural communities stems from a recent shift away from general (to targeted and urban-focused) policy and a political commitment to clean up the planning system. The first move will see families – which have hitherto benefited from general housing policy and been given free-reign to provide intra- and intergenerational social support – replaced as the key agent of housing provision. Support for the family is likely to fall off and this will hit rural areas, with their strong family networks, particularly badly. The second move will mean that rural communities and the informal economy become more exposed to labour and housing pressures. Housing supply shortfalls, which have, hitherto, been absent across many areas, may suddenly emerge.

The authors of Chapter 7 conclude that targeted support and a commitment to sustainable urban–rural quality are essential: the challenge is to ensure that it is not the poor and disadvantaged who bear the cost of Italy's new social and environmental agenda. It will also be important that future policy is an expression not only of the values of a changing society in the north and central parts of the country, but also the south of the country where a more 'atomistic' and family-oriented society has been the mainstay of social support for generations.

In Chapter 8, Valenzuela argues that rural housing issues in Spain have been relegated behind a more dominant urban agenda. But the countryside has been subject to important shifts in recent years, driven by agricultural decline and manifest in population change. Change but not loss: new economic opportunities have brought with them new people. An ex-urban population – comprising permanent residents and second home owners – has come to dominate many parts of the Spanish countryside. But rural housing remains relatively abundant and cheap, so access and unequal market competition are not *always* the key concerns facing small communities (and divisive conflict is often avoided). Instead, the key issues are economic diversity, exactly who this diversity benefits, and housing quality. A secondary issue relates to the geography of rural disadvantage: it tends to be remoter communities that have fared worst as a result of economic change, while those located close to cities have been buffeted by urban investment. The young are also particularly susceptible to the pressure of an unstable local economy. This means that conflicts can arise where there 'is a coincidence of agricultural revival or economic diversification and a simultaneous increase in urban tourism-based housing demand'. Competition for better quality housing, rather than housing per se, is the key focus of such conflict.

Valenzuela suggests that regional governments have tended to develop dual-track housing policy, assigning equal attention to local housing and to urban or tourism-based use. Across both tracks, the focus has been on promoting new economic forms, encouraging new supply (or greater quality) and bringing about wider infrastructure improvements. Below this regional level, various local strategies for dealing with housing concerns can be identified and these are frequently more informal, relying on self-build and the involvement of small local housing providers. It is also the case that families will extend their homes as a response to changing needs. The level of illegal building is lower than in Italy, but the same informality in housing production (and more relaxed approach to regulation) can be found in many parts of the Spanish countryside. These approaches, stretching from regional strategies to local actions, are judged to be reasonably successful by Valenzuela. But the issue for the future is whether the dual-track approach, for dealing with both indigenous and imported challenges, can be sustained and if housing conflict can be contained in the face of immigration pressures and heightening demand for rural homes from the urban population. The real question facing Spain is whether there is enough housing, of the right quality, to keep everyone satisfied over the long term.

Within a context of strong economic growth, Finnerty, Guerin and O Connell explore Ireland's existing, current and possibly future housing and more general socio-economic challenges. There is no tradition in Ireland of separating rural from urban concerns and the problems facing urban hinterlands and remoter parts of the country are frequently conflated. But recent growth – marked by unprecedented demand for homes and a consequently huge programme of residential new-build – has brought with it a desire to measure impacts and counteract, if necessary, unwanted side-effects.

Ireland is dominated by owner-occupation (80 per cent), and has relatively weak private rental and social housing sectors. House prices have soared in recent years, especially around Dublin and other urban centres. A culture of ownership, together with a lack of real alternatives and burgeoning housing demand, has created significant affordability and access problems for many of the one-third of Irish households deemed poor. The failure to adequately respond to these problems has been blamed on an under-performing planning system, land hoarding by some developers, insufficient investment in social housing, and (of particular importance), property speculation either of a general nature or manifest in second home purchasing.

Finnerty, Guerin and O Connell argue that existing demand pressures – of various types including general speculation, over-spill and second or holiday homes – are at the heart of Ireland's housing crisis. And this crisis reaches a zenith in the countryside where local residents are particularly disadvantaged as a result of low wealth and limited income, and where the greatest potential for further demand pressure exists. Responding to such problems is therefore a matter of urgency. The lack of direct focus on access and affordability is noted at both the development agency and national policy levels. Some movement towards solutions is evident, however, at the local level where plans are being drafted and implemented that aim to curb sporadic housebuilding and vent the pressure of second home demand. But such moves are controversial given Ireland's 'clientelist' political culture, its promotion of private interests and its reliance on market solutions. They run contrary to the tradition of a more relaxed approach to regulation, and what many see as underperformance in planning is merely an expression of Irish attitudes towards government intervention.

Chapter 7
Italy

Liliana Padovani and Luciano Vettoretto

The broad picture

During the four decades following the Second World War, housing conditions in Italy improved significantly and, by 1991, Italy had attained what many consider a reasonable level of housing resources. The last census revealed that there were a total of 1.26 dwellings for each household and almost two rooms for every inhabitant; the vast majority of dwellings were equipped with at least basic facilities (Table 7.1). The state of disrepair of the older stock had been taken care of and by the late 1990s, 61 per cent of total investments in housing took the form of rehabilitation.

Table 7.1 Housing selected indicators, Italy, 1951–1991

	1951	1961	1971	1981	1991
Total dwellings					
rooms per inhabitant	0.79	0.94	1.18	1.53	1.83
dwellings per household	0.97	1.03	1.09	1.18	1.26
dwellings per 1,000 inhabitants	240	281	322	388	441
Occupied dwellings (principal dwellings)					
persons per room	1.4	1.2	1.0	0.8	0.7
dwelling size (rooms per dwelling)	3.3	3.3	3.7	4.2	4.3
household size	4.0	3.7	3.4	3.0	2.9
dwellings per 1,000 inhabitants	226	257	283	310	348
% of dwellings without bathroom	89.6	71.1	35.5	13.7	4.1
% owner-occupied	40.0	45.8	50.8	58.9	68.0
% social rented sector				4.8	4.9
Secondary homes (non-permanent dwellings, vacant)					
% of secondary homes on total dwellings	5.7	8.3	12.2	20.0	21.1

Sources: *Census of Population and Housing*, Istat (National Institute of Statistics)

High levels of new housebuilding and an orientation of public policies in favour of developing and improving the housing stock have been critical to these achievements. Intense housebuilding was a key feature of the first three post-war decades and contributed to the improvements experienced by a considerable number of households (see Figure 7.1 for general indicators of population increases in the latter half of the twentieth century). A growing number of people became homeowners and a remarkable proportion of households now has more than one house at their disposal (10 per cent of households have a 'second home' of some kind).

Despite this broad picture of success, specific problems facing particular areas or social groups persist. There are housing shortages, for example, and these are evidenced by acute overcrowding and patterns of house sharing.[1] New patterns of economic change are also bringing with them new social problems, particularly the polarisation of more vulnerable social groups. Immigrants[2] may find themselves confronted with serious problems of housing access while a decline in private rental opportunities is having a disproportionate impact on elderly people, one-parent families and those forming new households. Spatial and social exclusion is most visible in the least prosperous urban areas where decay seems to go hand-in-hand with deprivation. If the ones mentioned constitute a range of unresolved housing problems expressed by lower income households, at the other end of the spectrum, greater prosperity may result in a shortfall in housing of a high enough quality to meet consumer demand and expectations.

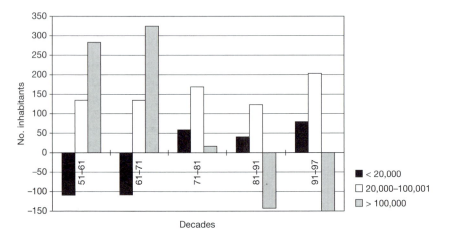

7.1 Average year population increase (1,000 units) per types of communes: urban > 20,000, non urban < 20,000 inhabitants.

Source: *Elaborations on census and housebuilding statistics*, Istat

From this last point of view, the challenge for Italian housing policy today is twofold: first, to deal with the new problems stemming from low quality suburban housing development (in particular high-rise public and private estates) that characterised much of the 1960s and 1970s. And second, to provide basic facilities and infrastructure to those illegal developments – outside the planning framework – that sprang up in the 1970s and 1980s. Self-promoted illegal house-building has figured prominently in Italy for decades. In 1984, it was estimated that 2.7 million (12.3 per cent of the stock) illegal dwellings had been built since 1971. Additions to this total fell rapidly in the 1990s when only 23,000 to 30,000 such dwellings were being built annually compared to 200,000 twenty years earlier.[3] But this is still 12 to 13 per cent of all new housebuilding. In the past, much of this non-regulated development was suburban in form and particularly significant in central and southern parts of the country. It also took place in some rural areas, either as second homes, mostly along the coast and particularly in the south, or as primary residences. Hence rural areas as well have, to varying extents, been affected by these forms of self-promoted, totally or partially illegal housing and have to set up policies to contrast these practices of housing provision.

As we can see from this outline, Italian housing is characterised by a widening rift between a well-housed majority – enjoying the benefits of a high-quality urban environment – and a growing minority of households faced with poor housing and deteriorating living conditions. This division is reflected in household income inequalities[4] and follows a broad geographical pattern, splitting the more prosperous north-centre from the considerably poorer south.[5] But as elsewhere in Europe, this general picture is complicated by another scale of advantage and disadvantage locally: there are pockets of prosperity in the south, just as there are pockets of poverty in the north.

In the following paragraphs we will consider the more direct implication of this broad national picture on housing issues in rural areas.

Rural Italy: the physical and social dimensions

Italy has a reputation as an urbanised and continually urbanising society. The processes that have led to the concentration of a sizeable part of the population into densely settled areas continue, if at a lower intensity, today. Density figures[6] point to the country's urban tradition (Figure 7.2), with a few large-scale metropolises (such as Milan, Rome, Naples, Turin) and a dense network of medium and small cities.

Although this pattern of urban living was well established in the run up to the Second World War, it was further accentuated in the period between 1951

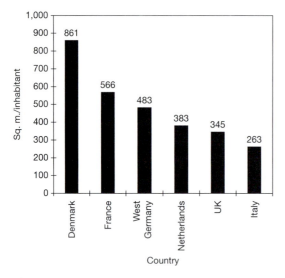

7.2 Urbanised area per inhabitant in some European countries – 1981.
Source: Leone (1996)[7]

and 1971 when the proportion of total population resident in 'inhabited centres'[8] rose from 76 to 87 per cent. At the same time, the proportion residing in 'hamlets' (*nuclei abitati*) fell from 8 to 4 per cent and the overall population in 'scattered' rural areas from 16 to 9 per cent.

These figures suggested that rural areas were either shrinking or fewer people were choosing, or able, to live away from cities. However, the concentration trend slowed after 1971 and the proportion of people residing in hamlets or scattered areas levelled off in the following decade. The alteration in urban population growth and the territorial redistribution of inhabitants and activities that occurred in the 1970s and 1980s had their effects on rural areas. Using one 'physical/environmental' definition of rural areas (that considers the ratio of urbanised land against green areas, and draws in population density (Merlo, 1997)), one can see that by 1991 roughly one-quarter of the Italian population lived in rural communes. These were defined as areas where 95 per cent of their territory was not 'urbanised': a further quarter lived in communes that could be considered rather more rural than urban (with green areas constituting at least 75 per cent of land area) (Table 7.2). The latter areas are viewed as more transitional and these patterns seem to be borne out by recent analyses of social morphology showing that about 20 per cent of the population resides in low-density areas characterised by the coexistence of small firms and rural economy (Vettoretto, 1996). Thus, alongside the more dense urban settlements, one finds

Table 7.2 Urban and rural communes, according to the urbanised surface and density[9]

		Communes (n)	Surface (1,000 ha)	Population 1991 (1,000 inhab.)	Population 1991 (%)
Very rural, non-urbanised surface	> 95%	4,890	20,971	12,774	22.5
Rural (low density), non-urbanised surface	> 75% < 95%	1,557	4,301	7,505	13.2
Rural (high density), non-urbanised surface	> 75% < 95.6%	582	1,249	4,798	8.4
Urban (medium density) non-urbanised surface	< 75%	509	789	5,830	10.3
Urban		562	2,823	25,871	45.6
Total		8,100	30,133	56,778	100.0

Source: *Sociologia del verde*, Merlo (1997)

many open spaces and hybrid situations or 'rururban' settlement, where different forms of urban spread may coexist. The overall situation breaks down into the following:

- A network of compact traditional urban settlements comprising large and medium sized centres.
- A historically established network of small centres with large non-built-up spaces.
- A phenomenon, in recent decades, which has seen these small centres become a framework of low density settlement characterised by distinct patterns of economic activity and housing types. In other words, and in the absence of swathes of open countryside, Italy's rural areas comprise low-density intermediate landscapes that are clearly not urban but nor are they rural in the strict sense. An area where new housing types, some innovative small firms (from industry to agriculture), or traditional activities may coexist producing a variety of 'rururban' landscapes.

There is also a social dimension to the way in which rural areas are defined. Between 1951 and 1991, agricultural activity plummeted from 44 to 7 per cent.

In the earlier part of this period, this decline was offset by the growth of industrial activity. In the latter part of the same period, and particularly during the 1980s, the service sector began to play a dominant role. Many would view this transition as a modernising process in which rural areas prepared themselves for a new role in a very different kind of society. This process had three distinct phases, in which the concept of rural assumes different meanings:

1   'Rural' as synonymous with poverty and deprivation, lacking modernisation and lagging behind in economic, social and cultural terms. This phase sees notions of the rural linked very tightly to changes, or a lack of movement, in agriculture (1950s and 1960s).
2   'Rural' as socially and economically heterogeneous low-density areas, where local societies seem able to merge cultural/social tradition with more modern ideas and integrate agriculture with small industry (1970s and 1980s).
3   'Rural' as the space for new social praxis (i.e. new forms of housing, tourism and leisure activities) (1980s and 1990s).

Agriculture and the notion of 'rurality' are no longer conflated and rural areas have become associated with a broader range of both economic and social activities. This transformation raises a number of questions with regard to housing and housing policy. In the next section, we attempt to link social and economic processes with rural housing outcomes.

Changing rural space and housing

The following schema (Table 7.3) outlines the main social and economic changes in Italy alongside their impact on rural areas, and particularly on matters relating to housing.

Table 7.3 summarises a number of trends that are now explored in a little more detail. In the immediate post-war years, Italy – like most southern European countries – began the process of 'catching up' in terms of industrialisation and urbanisation. This meant that Italy experienced, in a relatively short period of time, the processes that had affected many other countries since the Industrial Revolution. There was massive migration from south to north (Figure 7.3): human and material resources crowded into urban systems of the north-west while the south and part of the north-east were experiencing a situation of decline and relative poverty. This pattern of growth resulted in huge pressures on the urban housing stock, that could only partially be satisfied by public sector provision. At the same time, in rural areas housing needs and problems were

Table 7.3 Housing stock and rurality in Italy since 1950s

Period	Processes	Rural housing outcomes
1950–1960	**Rural as a synonym for poverty and social deprivation:** Fordist development. Urbanisation and development of the metropolitan areas in the north. Neglect of the rural areas and accentuation of rural poverty and deprivation including regional and territorial imbalance. These were the years of large-scale internal migration leading to loss and depletion of the human resources in rural areas.	Serious disrepair in the housing stock, lack of basic facilities, and critically poor services and infrastructures. During this period, many people residing in the south or in rural areas chose to work in the more prosperous cities of the north or abroad. Part of the remits sent home by the emigrants were spent on housing in the place of origin, but not on modernising old stock. Rather, savings were spent on building new housing outside the traditional centres. No investments for the maintenance or refurbishment of traditional buildings, old city centres and the fixed social capital. This period sees an increasing gap between housing conditions in rural and urban areas as well as the first signs of a second home boom in very selected areas.
1970–first half of the 1980s	**Rural as 'small-scale businesses in low-density areas' development:** Marked by recession, a restructuring of the economy, a halt in urban growth, and the growth of peripheral systems of small firms in central and north-east Italy (concepts of industrial districts and endogenous development). The redistribution of population and the beginning of population decline in urban areas (first in the cities of the north, then those of the south) led to the re-population of peripheral areas (in particular in the centre-north). Marked also by the return of emigrants, many of whom are retired.	Development of housing in low-density areas. Process of individual houses provision (legal and illegal housing and self-promotion). Growth in the number of second homes (50 per cent of the total housing stock increase in the decade 1971–1981 was due to the development of non-occupied dwellings). Gradual convergence in standards of housing quality in urban and non-urban areas.
Second half of the 1980s–1990s.	**The rural as the locus of new forms and types of housing:** Increase in weight of service industries within urban economies; redevelopment of the old industrial areas; growth of industrial districts in the south; 'soft' forms of local development ('soft' tourism, quality agriculture and crafts, small, high technology firms). Slowing of population growth, transformation of the family and immigration from developing countries. Growth and diffusion of public services and private-sector service industries. Growing concern over pollution, traffic congestion and crime in urban areas.	Consolidation of the processes of largely self-promoted owner-occupied house building in low-density areas. Differentiation in types of housing, in forms of tourism. Slowdown in second-home production and evolution of the sector. New populations added to the local ones, producing a growing demand for quality and regulation. Further reduction in the differences in housing and living standards between urban and rural areas.

Source: Authors

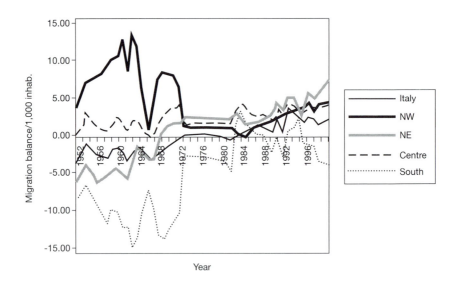

7.3 Migration balance per large geographical regions, per 1,000 inhabitants
Source: Elaboration on Istat data

neglected which produced a pattern of scarce housing resources (Figure 7.4) and low housing quality (marked by the absence of basic amenities – Figure 7.5). While the public sector focused its resources on meeting housing needs in urban areas, private sector housing was completely absent in rural areas where the only solution was self-help and the reliance on money flowing back from emigrant workers who had joined the exodus to the north-west or abroad.

The 1970s and early 1980s brought with them an inversion in these development and migratory trends. There were the first signs of important changes in the structure of the national economy and the most striking feature of this change was the growth of small businesses and firms in central and north-east Italy: regions that had hitherto been predominantly rural.[10] The flow of population reversed (Cencini *et al.*, 1983) with the occurrence of urban sprawl at the fringes of metropolises and large urban areas, but also new forms of population growth in small communes in peripheral non-urban areas. This increase was fed from a variety of household profiles: returning emigrants; young families seizing the new local economic opportunities; newcomers from the still disadvantaged interior and mountainous areas, attracted to these new loci of growth (Figures 7.1 and 7.3).

But these new peripheral growth areas not only drew in businesses and permanent settlers, but also a variety of temporary, mostly holiday, homes.

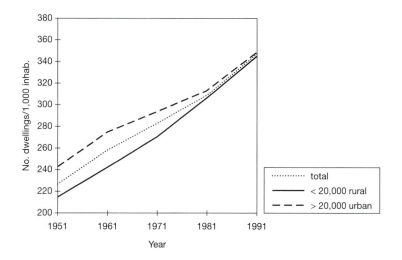

7.4 Occupied dwellings per 1,000 inhabitants.
Source: Istat Census and *Libro Bianco sulla Casa*, Ministry of Public works, Rome, 1986

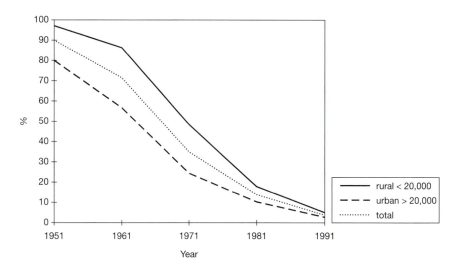

7.5 Percentage of occupied dwellings without bathrooms.
Source: Istat Census and *Libro Bianco sulla Casa*, Ministry of Public Works, Rome, 1986

Roughly half of all new housebuilding in these areas during the 1970s comprised homes that were not permanently occupied. This phenomenon had as much to do with people's desire to maintain links with their places of birth (which for those emigrated to the cities of the north, still remained an important aspect of their self-identity) as with the greater value now being placed on environmental assets for tourism development. From a purely housing perspective, this period was characterised by far more building in low-density rural areas (Figure 7.6) and a convergence of housing standards across urban and rural areas (in terms of rooms per inhabitant, general quality and reductions in house sharing: Figures 7.4 and 7.5). The general increase in housebuilding also brought with it a rise in the number of owner-occupiers, often as a result of traditional local practices of self-provision. Ownership often hinged on the use of 'family' savings (rather than mortgage credit) and informal labour (rather than the use of private contractors).

In the most recent phase, the trends of the previous period have been confirmed with qualitative changes reconfiguring urban areas as well the 'diffuse city'[11] and rural areas continuing along the path towards low-density development and lines between rural and urban becoming less clear-cut. In those rural areas with high-quality environments and/or significant historical/cultural resources, there has also been a differentiation of tourist activity with a 'soft' or 'intelligent' tourism focused around place-identity, traditional produces and crafts, and which respects local heritage and landscape. Second homes are peripheral to this more 'intelligent' tourism and have been subject to two trends: first a general slowdown in production (Figure 7.6) and second, a substantial change in the social profiles of those buying properties for this purpose. These trends

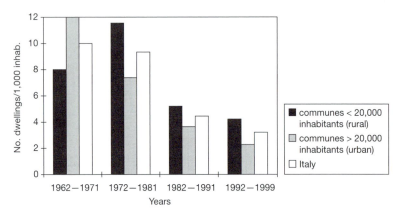

7.6 Average numbers of dwelling completions per year per 1,000 inhabitants.
Source: Elaboration of census data and housebuilding statistics

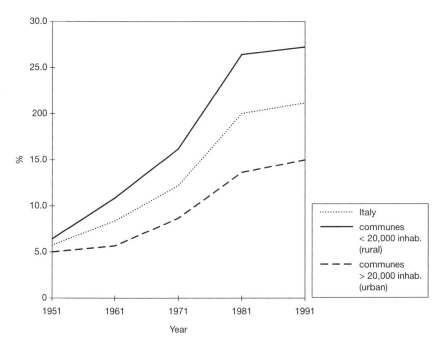

7.7 Percentage of second homes of total housing stock in urban and non-urban communes.
Source: Elaboration of census data and housebuilding statistics

reflect shifting attitudes towards the countryside. These have been characterised by greater emphasis on environmentally-compatible lifestyles – manifest in new ways of building, respect for local traditions, interest in innovative forms of farming – as well as the rediscovery of local cultural traditions and people's apparent need to forge closer links with what they consider their rural roots. To conclude, the question, in this phase, is the rise of new housing and environmental perceptions, preferences and behaviours, that seem to imply an often original demand for land regulation, whose impacts on the housing market are still difficult to recognise.

Different rural places, different pressures

The processes highlighted above have led to social and economic differentiation between rural areas and hence different housing problems and pressures. But given the lack of national analyses, any discussion of the nature of such differences must rely on indirectly related sources or limited local studies.[12] Some insights can be gleaned from inquiries conducted by the Central Institute of

Statistics (Istat, 1998 and 1999) which – with regard to rural areas – have shown the following:

- people gravitate towards smaller communes based on personal assessments of environmental quality and because they perceive rural areas to be safer than the big cities;
- but there is no evidence to suggest that those leaving larger centres are doing so only because of 'push' factors: i.e. higher housing costs, eviction from the rental sector, pollution. Rather, 'pull' factors are more significant: i.e. to have a larger house, more space, to be able to enjoy green areas or even to live closer to work in an increasingly diffused city;
- however, housing costs in these outlying areas are thought to be high and rising, which is an indication of one potential housing pressure.

These general observations broadly apply to all rural areas. The distinguishing features across what might be considered a 'rural continuum' and the different form of housing pressure that may be identified in each type of rural context, are as follows:

- Low-density housing and economic development (distinct from classical suburban development) at the fringe of metropolitan areas. This occurred from the 1980s onwards and has given rise to a blurring of urban/rural boundaries. These areas may – on some indicators – qualify as 'urban'. But their low-density brand of settlement is coupled with plentiful open space and heterogeneous land uses with agriculture being interwoven with leisure art-crafts and small businesses. There is a prevalence of one-family houses (detached) and traditional self-build practices (which commonly lead to two-family dwellings) are less frequent. Here, the formal housing market and construction industry dominates. There is a clustering of higher income social groups with many people working in the new economy. Some split their time between rural retreat and city home. These groups of affluent consumption are still a minority, yet their purchasing power may mean that house prices, as well as the quality of services, rise in the future to the detriment of local economically weaker groups.
- In the central region, the north-east and sometimes in the south of the country, low-density settlements with more urban characteristics can be identified. These are linked to diffused small or medium sized manufacturing firms (sometimes organised into industrial districts). Such low-density areas may take the form of 'diffused cities'[13] (if they are more urban) or 'urbanised countryside'[14] (if the pendulum swings the other way). Like

the metropolitan fringes, these areas have a mix of land uses, considerable amounts of greenery, a dominance of one-family houses, high levels of consumption and high incomes. But unlike the fringes, housing practices tend to be family-centred. People build their own homes and there is far less consideration of the public good (in either environmental or social terms) which can mean a general decline in quality of life.[15] Direct housing pressure is limited thanks to relatively high levels of earning and the inherent flexibility in the housing market derived from a tradition of self-promotion, self-help, a tradition of parental support,[16] and flexibility in supply resulting from weak regulation in land use. However, the needs of immigrants – required by manufacturing industries – tend not to be satisfied either by the local market or by public policies.

- In areas of tourism development, there are several types of housing pressure. (1) In the established tourist areas, with hotels and second homes serving mainly high income groups,[17] pressure is generated by affluent visitors who drive up not only the cost of houses, but all consumption goods. (2) In areas of more recent (seasonal) tourism development, primarily in the low-density coastal areas of the south where illegal building has been rife, there are few comparable pressures. Here, planning regulations have little impact on housing supply and hence the cost of homes. Rather, the effect is to erode environmental quality and degrade those very things that tourists value so highly. (3) Finally, there are the quality, non-seasonal areas of 'soft' tourism, hitherto untouched by traditional tourism and retaining much in the way of local identity, culture and environmental quality. Here, the tendency is for incomers to acquire old – or at least traditional style – homes.[18] Those gravitating to these areas are typically well educated and tend to spend a considerable part of the year there. But although some old buildings have been refurbished or transformed into second homes, the impact on the housing market has been small and in these areas at least, the local population has gained more than it has lost from the influx of visitors.

- In areas of 'intensive' agriculture or the development of 'agro-industrial' systems – including quality vineyards or floral market gardens – or 'extensive' agriculture[19] (Garofoli, 1991) there is little evidence of housing demand or supply pressures. And this is despite the presence of tourism activity.

- Finally, some areas continue to experience acute social deprivation and depopulation, including parts of the Italian Alps or the Apennines – with little in the way of tourism income – and the inland areas of the South (Garofoli, 1991). These areas are characterised by large numbers of older people, general population decline, and deteriorating housing conditions, which reflect the inability of people to maintain their homes, due to age and low income. Here, the housing challenge is not one of increasing supply and opportunity but, in the short term, of giving people the means to improve their living conditions. In the longer term, the challenge is to reverse the fortunes of such areas and create conditions of economic and social stability.

Policy and strategy

With some difficulty – given the lack of available information[20] – the above sections have sought to outline the pressures affecting different parts of 'rural' Italy. Because of the variety of pressures apparent and the lack of priority assigned to rural housing, it is not easy to identify either specific policies or broad strategies designed to directly tackle rural housing pressures. Inertia at both the local and national levels is, in part, due to the cultural role of housing in Italy and, in part, to the way housing issues have been defined in public policies. Acquiring a home is a family and private concern before it is a public issue: hence the importance of self-promotion, the relegation of planning control and the apparent acceptance of illegal housebuilding. Notwithstanding these 'cultural' matters, it is possible to identify policies that even if not strictly housing related, have had an impact of Italy's housing system and housing conditions within the different types of rural area outlined earlier.

At least until the early 1990s, housing policy centred on the family and a variety of indirect forms of support to promote housebuilding rather than tackling area-based problems. Public policy has been characterised by a general ignorance of those problems listed in the previous section but has, in an indirect way, contributed to broad improvements via general policy. For example, the promotion of home ownership did contribute to raising housing quality in rural areas. But the untargeted support of ownership has resulted in a failure to understand or adequately respond to a range of environmental and social problems. In this section, the intention is to consider the impact of general policy tools on rural areas. We begin with social housing provision.

Social housing provision

There have been very few attempts to tailor social housing provision to the needs of rural communities. Perhaps the only specifically 'rural' tool dates back to the 1978 Housing Act[21] when a quota of funds was set aside to subsidise the construction, extension or conversion of rural buildings for housing use. Thirty

Four major areas of public action:

1 The institutional system set up to programme, organise and implement social housing provision. Within this domain three main schemes of social housing have been developed: (a) Provision and management of a fully subsidised form of housing: the social rental sector or *edilizia sovvenzionata*.[22] In terms of stock, the Italian social rented sector is very small, just 1 million dwellings (5 per cent of total occupied dwellings), largely located in urban areas, but also to be found in smaller non-urban centres. It is worth noting that its total size has remained largely unchanged since the 1950s. This is despite the injection of public funding into this sector. In the 40 years from 1951 to 1991 some 1,299,000 social rented dwellings were delivered through new housebuilding or rehabilitation. But this did not increase the size of the stock because in the same period an equal number of dwellings were sold to tenants, either under standard provisions contained in the Housing Financing Act, or through specific legislation governing privatisation. (b) Provision of financial support (partially subsidised sector) to promote home ownership among less affluent groups – the so-called '*edilizia agevolata*'.[23] (c) Promotion of special schemes of public-private partnerships to develop housing programmes open to a larger range of social groups than the private market. This last scheme is called: *edilizia convenzionata*, 'convenzione' being the term for the agreement that needs to be signed by the local authority and the developers involved.[24] It is difficult to quantify the outcome of these two last programmes of action; some reasonable estimates consider them to account for two to three times as many dwellings as the social rental sector.

2 The body of norms and procedures that come into play when making *land* available for residential development. This release of land for development depends on the limits imposed by the *piano regolatore* (local land use plan), the acquisition of a building permit, which can be onerous; and, in some cases, on an implementation plan. Special powers are available (since 1962, Act no. 167) for local authorities to develop special land use plans and to acquire land in order to implement social housing schemes.[25]

3 A third area of public action is *rent control*. Since the end of the Second World War different forms of rent control have been introduced and abrogated in Italy. If the declared intent was to respond to special housing emergencies or mitigate problematic trends in the private rented market, the result was that on various occasions some sections of the private rented stock became an important source of low-rent housing for low-income families. Such rent controls have not been applied in rural communes.

4 A fourth area is *taxation and/or tax relief*. Some forms of tax relief are targeted at subsidised housing. A second type of tax relief benefits individuals entering home-ownership or buying their first house. Encouraging access to home-ownership was the aim of Italian governments from the early 1950s to the early 1990s, and tax exemption was used as an important measure to this end (tax relief on mortgage interest payments, etc.). Another form of indirect incentive to take up home-ownership has been the broadly unobtrusive housing taxation system.

7.8 Main forms of public action in housing in Italy.
Source: Authors

billion lire were set aside in 1978 and another 20 billion four years later.[26] But this amounted to just 3.3 per cent of the total sum destined for subsidised housing (*edilizia agevolata*) in the period 1978 to 1987. By 1997, the set aside sum (in total 90 billion lire) had been used to lever 430 billion lire of additional private investment into these subsidised schemes. This meant that during the last 20 years, the provisions of the 1978 Act resulted in 14,000 to 15,000 units being added to the rural housing stock.[27] Though modest in numeric terms, the strategy was designed to complement agricultural policies co-ordinated within regional plans for agricultural development[28] and was part of a wider effort to stabilise communities and entire regions.

As for Italian housing policies in general, one specific feature[29] that emerges is the presence of a generally weak social rented sector and a policy bias strongly in favour of home ownership. For a variety of reasons, Italian governments have not instituted policies aimed at promoting a sizeable social rented sector, but have given explicit support to families seeking to buy first or even second homes. That is not to say that public resources have not been allocated for housing, but rather that they have been used in ways other than to promote *direct* housing provision for social renting (Padovani, 1984, 1996).

The public sector has been devoting both resources and effort to housing the Italian population (see Figure 7.8), though this does not appear to be reflected in the current size of the social rented sector. However, the goal has not been to create a vast rental safety net, but to promote vertical social mobility. The way that social housing over the last forty years has been sold off – half on a redeem contract and half to sitting tenants – reveals that even fully subsidised public housing was conceived as simply another means to increase levels of house-building amongst low-income groups. The family rather than the state was to be the safety net and giving the family ownership of a home was seen as a way to shift social responsibility away from a welfare system that was particularly weak in the immediate post-war period. It was also assumed that a housing strategy strongly oriented towards ownership would channel resources to a 'household sector' that would henceforth mobilise its 'own resources' (mutual aid, labour, expertise and family finance) to meet present and future generations' needs. Similarly, 'secure' housing would provide a platform for other forms of family-based welfare – including care for aged parents, for children, support through periods of unemployment, homelessness or illness and so forth.

Even if public funds for housing tended to be concentrated in urban areas, where needs were judged to be higher, this approach to housing policy – with its strong bias in favour of housebuilding – was in fact congenial to the needs and *modus operandi* of public and private actors in the smaller non-urban municipalities. Moreover, the emphasis on general distribution of funds[30] – a characteristic of Italian government policies until the 1980s – coupled with the leverage that authorities can apply at the regional level, has meant that smaller communes have indeed benefited from this type of funding. It can be argued, therefore, that until the 1980s at least, this general approach did bode well for rural areas. But all this changed in the 1990s when, for the first time, housing problems were seen to have a specific urban slant and thought to affect certain social groups more than others. In response, public action was reoriented towards the larger cities and away from areas of low-density settlement.

In conclusion, public policy – and social provision – worked relatively well for rural areas when it was untargeted. But when the tools were 'refined', it was rural areas that lost out. But this analysis focuses predominantly on national policy and ignores issues of local and regional implementation. There is no way to know whether local practices led authorities to deal more specifically with the pressures identified in earlier sections. The fact is that almost no research has been undertaken at this level in rural Italy, though these are surely concerns that merit further study.

Housing and land use regulation

Housing regulations, and particularly those policies governing the release of land for residential development, have played a key role in improving rural housing conditions. Since the Second World War, various instruments for the control of land use change and the maintenance of building standards have been introduced. Even small towns now have a land use plan in which the rules determining the form that permitted development will take are set out. The entire system was overhauled in 1977 when it was decided that the infrastructure costs associated with new development should be borne by the developer rather than the state, theoretically making development that much more difficult and expensive. However, the critical issue is that the actual implementation of these rules has been – and continues to be – rather weak with a significant amount of development going ahead contrary to, rather than in conformity with, planning regulations. In Italy, public policies in general – and particularly those in rural communes – have been marked by a laissez-faire attitude, offering the maximum of direct and indirect incentives to promote housebuilding or rehabilitation, and the minimum of controls on the release of land for housing development and on the process of housebuilding itself. This orientation not only reduced the cost of the house, but also allowed families to organise their resources (which were scant in market terms but sufficient within a family-centred programme) and to produce housing packages that can satisfy the family components' present and future needs.[31] Thus, significant additions to the housing stock in recent years have occurred outside the structured housing market, either by way of direct connection between end-users (families), small landowners and local contractors, or through different forms – both formal and informal, legal and illegal – of self-promotion. Families have acted 'alongside' the state and the market as important agents of housing provision (Padovani, 1988 and Tosi, 1987): a response perhaps to housing been posed as a 'family issue' rather than a problem to be addressed by public policy and the welfare state.

But this model, which marshalled investments in housing construction and was somehow able to bring improvements in the housing conditions of a considerable number of people, at the same time, generated significant social and environmental problems. In the 1990s, debates over the proper form of spatial planning and a greater emphasis on environmental quality (in part a result of European legislation) led to a reappraisal of regulation and a new perspective on the 'achievements' of past policy. In particular, attitudes towards illegal settlement hardened. On the one hand, attention focused on how illegal building had caused severe environmental damage (with environmental quality now assigned far greater value) and on the other, it was noted that housing quality in such settlements was unacceptable. In the context of sustainability, it was suggested that future generations would bear the full environmental and social costs of today's illegal developments.

Policies in other sectors

The last concerns mentioned above require not only a housing response but a more general strategy for dealing with rural development on the one hand, and environmental protection on the other. In other words, an integrated territorial approach is needed that encompasses both social and physical challenges. Such approaches have, at various times, been sponsored by the European Union and include the Community Initiative Leader and the Objective One Integrated programmes. Other initiatives have been taken forward by the Italian government and include various integrated programmes for urban, environmental or territorial renewal, or more localised projects focused on specific issues during the 1990s. These include the Territorial pacts for industry, and for agriculture and tourism. Their scope and impacts are discussed by Padovani, 1998 and by Laino and Padovani, 2000.

Conclusions

A housing policy based on generalised support and subsidy appeared to bring fairly favourable results at least until the 1980s. But the drawbacks of this policy, and the *de facto* support for a family-centred strategy, are today judged to outweigh its benefits. Assessments of success are often measured against priorities at a particular point in time: and these priorities have apparently moved on at pace. New priorities as well as contextual changes bring up new challenges to public policies in rural areas.

In the first place there has certainly been a weakening of the role of the family as the core agent in the supply of welfare services, housing included. A drop in Italy's birth rate and a reduction in the size of families have come at a time when the number of those falling below the poverty line has soared. Poverty is also more prevalent in specific regions and these factors would seem to invalidate the aspatial strategy of channelling social support via the family: very few resources to pool for intra-familiar transfers will be available in these areas. Indeed, the trend compromises the family's role 'as a clearing-house for the pooling of social and material resources and for their (intra- and inter-generational) redistribution among its members according to need' (Castles and Ferrera, 1996: 181). These trends and the switch in policy focus towards more (socially and spatially) targeted aims may cause particularly severe difficulties in rural areas, which are more exposed not only because the family there has traditionally played a more important role, but also because of the convergence, in terms of housing and quality of life standards, between urban and rural areas. The latter will put a further burden on housing policies in rural areas and their capacity to cope with the higher standards of quality required, on the one hand, and with the weaker role of the family and kinship networks in welfare provision, on the other. In other terms, a weaker family may find it difficult to face the increase of costs induced by the search for higher quality (sustainable building and better services) that will imply new public subsidies.

Some rural families may suffer, but so too will the countryside's immigrant workforce. In the second of the rural types described above – the 'diffused cities' or the 'urbanised countryside' – the housing market, and sometimes local government policy, tends to exclude immigrants mainly because of racial bias and the emergence of anti-tax and anti-welfare sentiments affecting a large sector of the local electorate.[32] In neither the public nor the private sector are the needs of immigrants taken into account: this failure of policy stems from an institutional reluctance to integrate immigrants and recognise at least their vital contribution to the development of local small industry if not their potential contribution to Italy's cultural resource. More often than not, immigration is seen as a challenge to law and order rather than an opportunity. The situation originates tensions and sometimes conflicts between immigrants and some components of the local population as well as between industry, that in a situation of full employment needs manpower from abroad, and local authorities.

Behind those problems facing both traditional family structures and immigrants are the recent attempts to stem the tide of illegal settlement. While such moves are couched in environmental and quality terms, they pose a direct threat to both economically strong (sometimes at the border of legality) and economically weaker groups, the first unwilling, the second unable to bear the higher costs resulting from government's desire to see more sustainable and closely regulated patterns of development. Moreover, because of the links between illegal housing and informal production, any policy aimed at halting this kind of development may have far-reaching consequences within the rural economy. In conclusion, the rise of more sustainable and environmentally concerned housing preferences and behaviours, that seem to imply also a new demand for land regulation, is likely to produce impacts on housing markets that need to be further explored and evaluated.

7.9 'Dacia' style house – low-density developments at the fringes of built-up areas (Lombardy): E. Marini.

7.10 Scattered housing in the south of Italy (Province of Lecce): Paolo de Stefano.

7.11 Low-density housing in rural Lombardy: E. Marini.

A key challenge therefore is how to prioritise environmental concerns without causing major difficulties for weaker social groups. Indeed, environmental improvement, under the current system, does bring costs which may badly impact on the less well off and, moreover, on those residing in rural areas where the family and informal patterns of housing provision have traditionally been so important. The necessary realignment of public and private praxis was progressed by previous governments – and particularly the last administration based on the 'Olive Tree' coalition. But much work remains to be done if a sustainable balance is to be achieved. There are already signs that people are ready to live in different ways, judging in particular from the positive local response to recent European policies aimed at promoting integrated local projects that combine social with environmental agendas. Future success is likely to depend on gentle persuasion: possibly through the discouragement of illegal development coupled with a commitment to supporting self-promotion strategies within the confines of planning law.

Notes

1   In 1991, according to census figures some 700,000 to 900,000 households were experiencing severe overcrowding or house sharing. Some 800,000 households had been affected by eviction orders from the private rented sector in the ten years between 1982 and 1992.

2   Immigration from developing countries constitutes a relatively new phenomenon in Italy.

3   Since the 1980s and particularly in the 1990s, a sequence of Acts were adopted to legalise these dwellings (the so called 'Condono edilizio') and a more strict control on housebuilding activity was exerted.

4   Revenue distribution placed Italy, in 1994, amongst the countries with the highest income inequalities, just after Portugal, Greece and Spain (Eurostats, 1994).

5   In spite of development policies implemented in southern Italy, the gap between the centre-north and the south has not been reduced. As an indication of this, one could quote the Istat figures (*Note Rapide*, 4 July 2000) which show that in 1999 the percentage of households below the poverty line totalled 11 per cent in the south, 1.4 per cent in the north and 2.6 per cent in central Italy.

6   In a European comparison, Italy presents the lowest percentage of one-family dwellings (32 per cent compared with 54 per cent for the EU15) and the lowest value of urbanised area per inhabitant.

7   Istat calculates the urbanised area by starting with 'non-productive territorial area' and then subtracting the area of internal waterways, lakes and infertile mountain

land – and thus obtains the area occupied by buildings and roads. In the 1991 census, this came out as 2.215 million hectares (7.3 per cent of the national territory, which measures 30.1279 million hectares) (Leone, 1996).

8   The Istat definition sees an 'inhabited centre' (*centri abitati*) as a nucleus of urban life in the form of a compact settlement, with public spaces and services, an autonomous social life and the ability to attract people in from the surrounding territory.

9   Satellite information reveals that, in 1991, about 90 per cent of the national territory was made up of green areas, and that agricultural land made up around 57 per cent of the territory (Merlo, 1997). The average value for the ratio between green areas and total territorial area was around 87 per cent.

10   This subject is discussed in various works, of which the following have been influential: Bagnasco (1977), Bagnasco (1988); Becattini (1989); Bodo and Viesti (1997); Dematteis (1983); Fuà and Zacchia (1983); Garofoli (1991).

11   A phenomenon to be found in the more evolved types of 'industrial district'.

12   Official statistics do not provide a specific breakdown of information concerning the size and extent of housing in rural areas. One has to rely on proxies; in particular on the size of population as determining whether a location is rural or not. However, the annual Istat surveys do provide information on housing and socio-economic conditions within small communes that are not included within metropolitan areas. Relevant information is mainly available from an array of secondary sources: local research on the forms of diffuse industrialisation, urbanisation, local development and the transformation of the countryside and the agrarian economy. Most quantitative studies in Italy focused on rural transformations are essentially concerned with the analysis of demographic changes, while analyses of social and housing transformations are fragmented. Note also that the last national research concerning housing in all the various types of settlement dates from the late 1980s. There has been no national research on this matter in the last twenty years.

13   In Italy, 'the diffused city' indicates a low-density settlement, generally the result of the development of areas of small businesses, which over the course of time has acquired levels of services comparable to those in the traditional city.

14   'Urbanised countryside' indicates a mixture of urban and rural, but with farming still playing a sizeable role in the local economy. The term is normally associated with the presence of light and traditional industries.

15   A small survey carried out in the mid-1980s in a Veneto town looked at those households that had become owner-occupiers in the previous ten years. It revealed a wide divergence between the level of satisfaction with the actual home and the level of satisfaction with the external environment (the latter had been eroded by a perceived lack of safety, no social spaces and a generally low-quality environment).

16   From the Istat Annual Report of 1998, it emerged that about 12 per cent of married couples went to live with their parents immediately after marriage while waiting to get their own home. In the regions of north and central Italy, one of the main reasons why young people aged between 18 and 34 continue to live with their families is the difficulty in finding accommodation. Unfortunately, this information is not broken down according to the population size of the towns concerned.

17   For example, Cortina, certain areas of Trentino and the Sudtirol and parts of the Ligurian riviera.

18   For example, the hills of Tuscany and Umbria.

19   Such as those areas in the Po valley dominated by the cultivation of rice or maize.

20   As has emerged from the above sections, the question of housing in rural areas has not been at the centre of either researchers' or policy-makers' attention.

21   Art. 26: rural housing, Housing Act n. 457/1978. The ten-year plan.

22   Public funds, granted primarily by central government, are made available to local public bodies and to local authorities, enabling them to provide social housing for rent either through new building or rehabilitation. The dwellings must conform to standards established by national and regional laws, and building costs must not exceed limits fixed by the state. Renting is the initial form of tenure of these dwellings, though a large part of this stock has been privatised.

23   Various forms of grants and loans (the most common being low-interest loans and mortgage assistance) are provided to finance new housebuilding or rehabilitation of dwellings, which have to conform to a set of rules (such as limits in the size and price). Family revenues dictate both initial access to these loans and the subsidised interest rate.

24   The *convenzione* defines the relationships between, on the one hand, the local authority which can supply land at lower than market prices and offer economic incentives (such as lower urban development fees, or exemption from the payment of some components of the building permits' cost) and, on the other hand, developers willing to provide dwellings, subject to a set of constraints (such as limits in selling prices, forms of tenure, profile of users).

25   Special powers have been available (since 1962, Act no. 167) for local authorities to develop and adopt land use plans for social housing (PEEP, *Piani per l'Edilizia Economica Popolare*).

26   Law 94/82, art 21. Quinquies, *Gazzetta Ufficiale* n.84, 6 March 1982.

27   Estimates produced by the authors using as source of information the Acts that made these funds available.

28   Delibera CIPE, 20 July 1979, in Aniacap (1992).

29   Also a characteristic of southern European countries such as Spain, Portugal and Greece.

30   Which confirms that government action was not designed to answer the needs of specific local situations.

31   See A. Tosi's 1994 criticisms of the institutional definition of 'needs' Chapter III pp. 83–109.

32   In the regions of the north-east, the League Movement (anti-state, anti-welfare and closed to foreigners) has gained much support.

Chapter 8
Spain

Manuel Valenzuela

Introduction

In policy and planning circles at least, the issue of rural housing in Spain occupies a marginal position. Past neglect perhaps reflects a lack of private sector interest in the rural housing market: there are extremely few national construction industry players working on rural schemes and housebuilding in the countryside is, instead, dominated by small local promoters and developers. In some areas, even self-build adds more units to the local housing stock than formal sector constructors.

A lack of general awareness of rural issues is compounded by the fact that information on rural housing is difficult to get hold of. National Housing Plans, for instance, rarely differentiate between rural and non-rural concerns and there are no specific policy regulations relating to housing in the countryside. The characteristics of dwellings (and issues of housing quality) are, however, examined within specifically rural settings, though quality is judged against standard parameters that are applied irrespective of the (urban or rural) location of homes. But despite this dearth of information, it is generally acknowledged that housing outside the urban centres is subject to a particular set of processes and changes. First, the way in which the stock is used has changed drastically in recent years, reflecting a reduction in agrarian activity. Second, demographic changes are driving other processes (and creating new demands) such as the increase in new residents or seasonal visitors (including second home users) who do not establish a permanent relationship with the countryside.

The latest data (gathered in the 1991 Spanish Population and Housing Census) shows that Spain's rural areas are dominated by owner-occupied housing, typically of between 61 to 90 square metres in size (three bedrooms). Rural housing quality is usually judged to be between 'regular' and 'good'. But perhaps the most significant fact revealed in official statistics is that the cost of housing in the countryside is generally very low. This is a result – at least in part – of the reduced cost of labour, construction materials and land away from Spain's cities. And so, with low prices, reasonable quality levels and no apparent shortfall in supply, it might appear that there is very little else to be said on the issue of rural housing in Spain. But this is far from the truth, as this chapter will demonstrate (MOPU, 1983).

Defining rural Spain

Spanish local government is organised into municipalities: a municipality is considered 'rural' if it meets the criteria set out by the Spanish National Statistics Institute (INE). Rural areas are defined as those having fewer than 2,000 inhabitants. Municipalities with between 2,000 and 10,000 inhabitants are regarded as being 'semi-urban' while those with more than 10,000 residents are deemed to be 'urban'. This strictly quantitative measure sometimes suggests that areas with otherwise 'rural' characteristics are in fact semi-urban or completely urban. For instance, in parts of southern Spain, some municipalities with more than 20,000 inhabitants have economies almost entirely based on agriculture. On the other hand, there are also low-density (under 2,000 inhabitants) municipalities, which have 'urban' type economies based on industrial production or the tertiary sector. It is difficult to pigeonhole areas purely on the basis on population size. A better indicator of rurality might involve the combination of population data with information on the position of agrarian activities within the local economy and labour structure. For instance, rural areas might have 25 per cent of their economic activity defined as being agricultural. This alternative view of what constitutes a rural area is mentioned here because agriculture has a critical link with the demand for rural housing. Technological innovation, for example, has made agriculture less labour-intensive and a lower proportion of the population work in farming today than did so in the past: therefore demand from those engaged in farming is reduced.

So the definition used in this discussion is based on the notion that a municipality's relative rurality will be determined by the size of settlements, economic dependency on the agricultural sector and – additionally – the degree of concentration or dispersal of people and buildings.

Patterns of change in rural Spain

The economic decline and depopulation of Spain's rural areas have brought profound impacts to the housing market. The process of depopulation reached its zenith in the 1960s and 1970s (although it is still apparent today) and resulted in absolute losses of population in a number of regions – including inner Aragón, the mountainous areas of Castilla and Leon, Extremadura and La Gomera Island. The extent of depopulation has varied from one place to another, though the agricultural zones (cereal areas in the inner regions of Spain), mountainous regions and the less accessible areas (bordering Portugal and inner Aragón) have been hit especially hard. However, rural areas dominated by intensive agricultural production (coastal orchards and the inner fertile plains) have fared a great deal better. There has been a kind of 'natural selection' at play leading to the eradication of small settlements and landscapes dominated by dispersed farmsteads: Castilla and Leon, and Pirineos have been subject to unprecedented levels of depopulation. History has shown that this process is commonly followed by the wholesale collapse of public facilities and services, which further heightens the ongoing crisis and reduces the likelihood of future recovery.

A rather different story has emerged in Spain's less remote, medium-sized rural settlements. With better accessibility and services, these have tended to draw in people from the smaller, and often more remote, communities. Those rural households avoiding the temptation to gravitate towards the centre (Madrid) or the affluent periphery (Catalonia, Basque and the Balearic Islands) tend to remain in these middle tier settlements, which become 'semi-rural/urban' holding points, better served in terms of housing quality and other infrastructure. They also display a lower dependency on agriculture and might be described as rural service-centres, typically with between 2,000 and 5,000 inhabitants.

But perhaps the key point to note on the issue of depopulation is that it has been demographically selective and biased towards younger people, particularly women. This means that declining areas have a greater abundance of men and an ageing population – resulting in a number of side effects. For instance, there are fewer marriages and births, a higher mortality rate, less 'innovative capacity' and a rejection of new technology. And this final side effect has been particularly unhelpful at a time when farming has needed to become more competitive in order to survive: areas such as Galicia and Andalucía, heavily dependent on traditional methods, have been badly hit by the combination of population and agricultural change.

Demographic changes have not all been negative, however. Some rural areas – especially those close to the larger urban centres – are experiencing notable population reinforcement as a result of the expansion of second homes, the in-migration of new residents and increasing development of tourism industry. Tourism, in particular, can generate new employment opportunities, broaden the local economic base, and lead to spin-offs in the form of new craft industries, and the restoration of historical heritage (Valenzuela, 1997). These developments can all be viewed in a positive light, leading to material improvements in quality of life. However, the introduction of new activities into rural areas can be accompanied by conflicts. Some conflicts are the result of poor integration between new economic opportunities and the old agrarian activities. Others may relate to competition for housing, but only where the supply of such housing is limited. Despite the patterns of depopulation described above, in some parts of the Spanish countryside, such housing conflicts do arise and often as a result of the desire amongst the urban population to seek homes in the country.

Housing pressure and housing conflicts

Housing pressure commonly arises when there are no, few or restricted opportunities for households to gain access to a desired place to live. This situation might be a result of supply restrictions, or changes in the demand for housing that do not coincide with current levels or patterns of supply. In the Spanish countryside, pressure points often emerge where there is a coincidence of agricultural revival or economic diversification (and consequent prosperity) and a simultaneous increase in urban or tourism-based housing demand. Pressure will also stem from the inadequacy of existing housing stock to meet the needs of an ageing population and an increase in the number of single person households in some areas.

A key pressure – and source of conflict – in some locations has resulted from the purchase, by either domestic or foreign buyers, of retirement or second homes. Extraneous demand – in the form of commuters seeking the perceived benefits of a rural lifestyle – may also contribute to the pressure experienced within the rural housing market. Although some areas are facing a deepening rural crisis, others are experiencing both expansion and prosperity. In the latter, the balance between housing supply and demand may become unsettled: those workers locked into the agrarian sector may not be able to compete against higher earning workers in the newer more prosperous sectors. In other words, the benefits of collective economic opportunity may not flow to all individuals.

It was noted above that house prices in rural areas are generally lower than in the cities. However, the resale prices of rural homes are not uniform across the country. In some regions (for example, across northern Spain) prices achieved for rehabilitated traditional houses can be exceptionally high as a result of strong external demand pressure. At a lesser scale, different social preferences as well as issues of landscape value, image, architectural attributes, etc., impact on house prices causing local variations. One consequence of depopulation, economic restructuring and local price variations has been the creation of clear divisions between the types of households competing for property in Spain's housing market. These divisions run along the following lines:

- Residents with incomes derived from the rural economy (not necessarily agrarian) and consequently with *low* purchase capacity. This purchase capacity becomes weaker in areas of greater housing demand. Access chances are dependent on subsidies and on their capacity to build up savings over a period of time. Such households may seek to improve existing homes rather than compete for newer (and perhaps better) property with other higher earning households.

- Former out-migrants who have returned to their place of origin (in the countryside) and now have the means (having engaged in urban employment activities) to purchase property for future retirement or investment. This is a very common practice in Spain's northern regions (especially Galicia) where housing for ex-rural dwellers is considered a long-term investment (Abellán, 1993).
- Urban buyers originating from the nearby cities (mostly the larger centres) and looking for a second residence or a permanent home in the country. These are usually middle-aged professionals, with high saving and purchase capacity.
- Foreign investors in rural properties who seek second or retirement homes. They frequently gravitate towards rural areas close to the main tourist hot-spots (e.g. the Mediterranean coast or Mallorca).
- Owners of large rural estates (more than 1,000 hectares) comprising luxury houses. These do not occupy a common housing group in rural Spain but it is the case that wealthy businessmen will sometimes purchase 'status-symbol' estates. This practice has been particularly commonplace in the agrarian regions of central Spain (Castilla La Mancha, Extremadura, etc.). Buyers often seek the aristocratic lifestyle associated with hunting, fishing, socialising and, above all, wealth.
- Immigrants who endure substandard housing conditions. These sometimes originate from the developing countries of north and sub-Saharan Africa. They are drawn to the employment opportunities found in the intensive agricultural areas of Andalucía, Comunidad Valenciana, Catalonia, but are then unable to afford decent or appropriate housing.

These different groups obviously have markedly different needs: few conflicts arise between very rich and very poor households, who remain socially and physically separate. However, at the fringes of wealth and poverty, some ex-urban and rural households seek homes in the same sections of the market and in these instances, it is local households who may find themselves priced out of the market. In the following series of sections, some of the different ways and vehicles for managing such pressures and conflicts are briefly examined.

Managing the pressure – the agencies

Across Europe, a hierarchy of agencies is commonly involved in rural development concerns. Table 8.1 lists the *public sector* agencies working in rural Spain.

Spanish central government provides support for rural housing initiatives through its general economic policy: it has also sponsored direct measures to assist sectors of the rural economy. Between the 1960s and 1980s, for example, the 'Agrarian Amelioration Agencies' played a significant role in taking forward 'Agrarian Development Plans'; plans that aimed to increase the quality of basic amenities (water, electricity, sewerage etc.) delivered to farming communities. Political reorganisation in the 1980s shifted responsibility for housing issues to the Regional Governments who would henceforth deal with such matters, though central government retains overall control of fiscal policy.

More recently – since the 1990s – the Ministry of Agriculture, Fishing and Food has started to exercise new powers, which have brought indirect benefits to the rural housing stock. Mechanisms, for example, were established to support the agrarian labour force and these included grants for young farmers and farm workers for the purchase and improvement of housing. Other tools appeared to tackle housing problems more generally, with some benefits for the countryside. The National Housing Plans for instance (the most recent running between 1998 and 2001) appear at first glance to ignore rural areas: though additional grants are targeted at municipalities with an abundance of small settlements. The stated rationale is that decline in smaller communities, affects the well-being of the entire municipality. Hence the complementarity of rural and adjacent urban areas is recognised in these Plans. It is the Regional administrations (see Table 8.1) however that wield the real power to design specific programmes and strategies for dealing with rural housing concerns. While this allows for flexibility, it also accounts for the lack of homogeneity in Spanish housing policy. This issue is discussed further in the next section.

At the widest scale, Structural Funds provided by the European Union offer an important source of money for dealing with housing problems. A number of different funds have been tapped into. For instance, the European Regional Development Fund (ERDF) has been used to support programmes focusing on difficulties relating to poor infrastructure provision; the funds assist with economic development strategies that will hopefully bring about a better quality of life (measured in terms of improved infrastructure) for many rural areas. Other money comes in the form of *Fonds Européen d'Orientation et de Garantie Agricole* (FEOGA). This is intended to support farms as individual production units, assisting in farm modernisation, rationalisation and – indirectly – investment in housing. And finally the LEADER (*Liaisons Entre Actions de*

Table 8.1 Agencies involved in rural housing in Spain

Agency	Description
The European Union	Offices dedicated to co-ordinating European initiatives and then monitoring the results of these initiatives
Spanish Central Government	Various ministries (e.g. General Directorate of Housing, Architecture and Planning and the Ministry of Agriculture, Fishing and Food)
The Regional Governments (Autonomous Communities)	Housing Departments and Institutes of Land, Housing, and Architecture
The Provincial Governments	Provincial infrastructure plans through the 'Housing Patronages'
The Counties ('*Comarca*')	Loosely defined except in the case of Cataluña, where they have political status and their own budgets
The Union of Municipalities ('*Mancomunidad*')	Municipalities coming together to co-operate on key strategic issues – though they rarely co-operate on housing issues
The Municipality	Rarely possessing sufficient administrative (or resource) capacity with which to address local housing problems, or design and implement effective housing policy. They are reliant on the integrity and co-operation of town councillors ('*Concejal*') who are charged with construction licensing and the supervision of projects

Source: Author

Dévelopment de l'Economie Rurale, or 'Links Between Actions for the Development of the Rural Economy') programme – conceived as an integrated programme for rural development – assists smaller communities through a range of initiatives and strategies. Recently in Spain, there has been an emphasis on the provision of subsidies for the refurbishment of traditional housing that can then serve as tourist accommodation. The LEADER (and more recent LEADER II) programme has been directed at economic diversification rather than the support of agrarian activities and therefore has the potential to help those communities suffering the consequences of agricultural decline (Beltrán, 1994; Blanco and Benayas, 1994).

Finally, and besides the various programmes developed by these governmental agencies, there have also been a number of private and self-help initiatives aimed at improving rural housing conditions. Some private companies, for instance, have been pro-active in the rehabilitation of rural dwellings, which are then turned into second homes. At the present time, however, there is a lack of enterprises specifically devoted to housing rehabilitation and the private sector tends to concentrate on new-build housing in rural areas.

Managing the pressure – land use planning

There is no overarching land use or housing plan for rural areas in Spain. The Autonomous Communities (Regional Governments – see Table 8.1) have a responsibility for planning and related activities within their own areas of juris-diction. During the 1980s and 1990s many Autonomous Communities enacted laws and approved special plans to be deployed in their rural areas and other instruments (included in the Spanish Land Laws) were used to regulate devel-opment pressures at the local, provincial and regional scales. These instruments were designed to stem the tide of urbanisation and bring land use change under stricter planning control. But the success of these measures has been limited.

While it is often assumed that the effectiveness of planning control has increased – particularly where regions have paid special attention to rural concerns (e.g. in the Balearic Islands and Comunidad Valenciana) – any regula-tory gains have been offset by continued problems with planning enforcement. These problems are often rooted in a distinctively Spanish tradition – that of erecting buildings in the countryside without any real concern for official rules or restrictions. This tradition has worked contrary to the interests of local plan-ning and meant that planning itself – resigned to failure – has rarely ventured beyond basic construction rules: and even these are regularly flouted. One cause of this difficulty has been poor resourcing for the planning function: a key outcome has been a lack of leadership in rural housebuilding and general devel-opment-anarchy in the rural landscape. And yet, despite these local difficulties, regional government has been more active and successful in intervening in the rural housing market. It has, for instance offered special grants to allow young people, couples or new residents to enter the housing market and subsequently remain in their homes. The programmes set by regional government have also supported dwelling improvement and repairs, ensuring that the condition of rural property reaches an acceptable standard. Though another critical issue affecting housing quality has been the lack of support infrastructure (water and electricity, or services and roads etc.) in some rural areas. The extent of disadvantage is, again, frequently dependent on geography. The remoter and less accessible rural areas suffer disproportionately in terms of poor service provision, while those closer to large urban centres tend to be better served. Programmes to improve rural living conditions are being implemented, though remoteness – and the additional difficulties this brings – is a significant problem affecting many of Spain's rural communities.

Managing the pressure – general housing policy

Of the three principal tiers of Spanish Administration – national, regional and local – it is the regional tier that has greatest influence in relation to housing policy, and the policy that has been developed has taken two broad directions. First, it has been concerned with permanently occupied dwellings and the industries that sustain the local population. Second, it has also been concerned – in equal measure – with that rural housing which supports an 'urban use'; i.e. dwellings used as second homes or those seen as supporting the local tourist industry in some other way. Though these directions may seem to address different sets of needs and issues, they are perceived as complementary, both addressing the problems of depopulation and decline through the following strategies:

1   the modernisation of rural enterprises (including the promotion of new economic forms);
2   direct housing amelioration, including dealing with issues of supply (of permanent and second homes); and
3   infrastructure and services available to rural communities.

Of course, local and regional implementation may differ in a number of important ways: objectives, detail and timescale will all be locally specific. Some examples of such specifics are given in Table 8.2.

It is reported (for the purpose of European Union Structural Fund monitoring) that different Regions have tended to concentrate resources on different areas of action. Aragón, for instance, has used its funding to support the tourist industry, building additional youth hostels. In the Balearic Islands, emphasis has been placed on the rehabilitation of traditional architecture; a similar emphasis can be observed in Galicia (see Table 8.2) (Barreiro and Novoa, undated) In Navarra, however, funding has been used to facilitate much-needed repairs or diverted into new construction. Pais Vasco has been promoting a programme of infrastructural improvement, concentrating on water supply and electricity. Spanish rural housing policy is very much a patchwork of varying concerns and objectives.

Finally, the LEADER programme mentioned earlier has, since its inception in 1991, been a key driver in the modernisation and reactivation of economic activity in rural areas. Although the programme's influence on rural housing concerns is indirect, its promotion of economic diversification (and support for

Table 8.2 Regional housing policy in Spain: examples

Andalucia: At a regional scale, Andalucia can be held up as an example of a region proactive in the promotion of a consistent rural housing strategy. The *Andalucian Housing Plan* has a range of specific policies for dealing with the needs of isolated dwellings, self-rehabilitation and general housing improvement (including energy efficiency gains and the use of solar power). Since the 1980s, the plan has contained policies for dealing with special categories of housing – such as 'cave-housing' or the traditional isolated farms comprising multi-functional buildings (*'Cortijos'*). The programmes developed by this particular Regional Government have covered almost every aspect of the regional housing stock.

Galicia: The case of Galicia illustrates another way rural housing concerns have been addressed in Spain. The Galician administration has developed two complementary lines of housing action. The first focuses on poor condition housing located in settlements with fewer than 1,500 inhabitants, and concentrates on families with particularly low incomes. The second focuses on the issue of preserving traditional architecture, with the aim of attracting new residents and supporting the tourism sector.

Castilla and Leon: A third example of better (or at least unique) practice can be found in Castilla and Leon, the largest region in the European Union. The Region's 'Regional Land and Housing Plan' is interesting in its attention to detail, cataloguing an intricate list of grants available for rural housing projects and schemes. Needs are carefully assessed by the Regional Administration which then budgets for dealing with these needs over the subsequent twelve months.

Source: Author

tourism) has brought huge improvements to the rural housing stock. Indeed, general economic strategies are likely to have as profound an impact on rural housing as any specific housing policy.

Managing the pressure – local initiatives

Local initiatives – and local solutions – remain important and many municipalities have come up with small-scale schemes to address the types of very specific, localised issues described in the last section. Some examples of such schemes are provided below.

A number of rural councils are supporting programmes for the rehabilitation, transformation and general improvement of rural housing stock as a means of curbing the process of depopulation. The UN Habitat Programme has heralded initiatives developed in Navapalos (Soria) and Valdicio (Cantabria) as examples of 'best practice'. In Navapalos, traditional construction materials and energy-saving techniques have been combined as a means of improving housing quality. Inexpensive materials such as sun-dried bricks and alternative energy sources (solar or wind power) increase the affordability of schemes. In Valdicio, traditional housing (which combines living space with accommodation for live-stock) has been the focus of a rehabilitation programme aiming to separate people from their animals while improving water supply and other amenities.

Elsewhere, housing co-operatives have been directly involved in house-building as a means of reducing housing costs, and therefore increasing unit affordability. Examples of this kind of activity can be found in El Burgo (Málaga) and to the south of Madrid. The schemes involve the future occupants in the construction of homes, providing them with new skills that add to the wider strategy of economic diversification.

Other local initiatives have sought to address the problem of low housing quality. Spain's *White Book of Housing* (Fundación de Estuidos Inmobiliarios, 1999) has recently revealed that 20 per cent of all rural homes are considered to be 'substandard'. Problems appear specific to particular regions (such as Castilla and Leon and Andalucía) where there are a larger number of multi-functional homes or '*Cortijo*'. Special grants for dealing with this issue have been assigned to these affected regions. Some of the traditional housing is viewed as necessarily poor. For instance, in Andalucía and other Mediterranean regions (Jessen, 1955) 'cave-housing' was traditionally reserved for lower income families, even if they could provide comfortable, temperature-balanced living space when all the modern equipment is present. There are presently 35,000 units of this type all over the south-eastern regions (including Almería and Granada) and the regional administrations are actively supporting their enlargement and improvement. Other buildings (military barracks, schools and cereal warehouses) are also being converted for housing use. At the same time, modern construction techniques are being employed in the provision of new 'bio-climatic houses' (in Almería, Sevilla and Cádiz) that combine passive energy saving devices (materials, design etc.) with active technology (solar panelling) to produce lower-impact develop-ment.

Finally, some abandoned rural housing has been recovered for alternative use. Entire villages have been completely renovated (by either public or private agencies) and now form summer camps, educational tourist centres, second homes and so forth. This type of use-change has been led by the public sector (at Granadilla in Caceres province), trade unions (at Morilla de Tous in Huesca province), the regional saving banks (at Bubal in Huesca province) and some private investors (at Villalbilla in Soria province).

The point to be made here is that local initiatives have played a critical role in shaping Spain's rural housing agenda. Structural support has been provided by Europe and by the Spanish government and this has defined the larger playing field. But these local initiatives have helped channel wider resources into the most deprived areas and ensure that money is used to tackle the most pressing and important issues facing particular communities.

Gauging success

Much of the discussion provided above has pointed to a clear dualism in the Spanish rural housing market. On the one hand, traditional housing occupied by agricultural workers, farmers and other settled rural inhabitants may fail to meet modern quality standards, while on the other, purpose-built dwellings intended to serve the tourist industry or an urban market offer a good level of comfort and amenity. The current thrust of Spanish housing policy is to ensure greater parity in housing quality across these two distinct markets irrespective of location.

This strategy is already bearing fruit. Private amenity standards (electricity, drinking water, sewerage and telephone connection) have increased considerably over the last fifteen years, with the entire country now better served in this respect (though it is acknowledged that more attention must still be paid to the needs of Spain's interior regions). Isolation is also less of a problem today than in the past, and most areas are accessible via an extensive and much-improved road system. The problem of regional disadvantage is being addressed through a corrective strategy that has sought to channel additional resources into laggard areas: this strategy has been focused on general economic advancement rather than the specifics of housing difficulties.

More general rural diversification – naturally occurring and bolstered by the LEADER programme – is making a strong contribution to the social and economic reactivation of Spain's peripheral areas, bring huge improvements to physical infrastructure (housing, services, utilities and transportation) and wide-spread job creation. However, land values have been driven up by these processes in many areas and there have been concerns that controls over the future development of tourist infrastructure may not be effectively enforced. This concern has been heightened by the past failures of the planning system.

Conclusions

While rural housing matters might indeed be obscured by a broader – and urban-dominated – national agenda, it is apparent from the above discussion that such matters are viewed as extremely important at the regional level. In Galicia, Andalucía, Castilla and Leon and many other areas with an abundance of small, farming communities, the issues of rural housing supply and quality have been subject to considerable attention and remedial effort. It is clear that these and similar areas in the Spanish countryside are subject to rapid and complex change. Housing no longer simply services the needs of a population engaged in agrarian activities; rather, there are multiple markets. The reduced importance of farming within the rural economy – along with associated demographic changes – indicates that there is an increasing external demand for rural housing, among both new permanent residents and those seeking second homes. Some of the rural stock, especially traditional housing types, form part of a new tourism base within Spain's countryside.

The economic decline and depopulation of rural areas are key issues for policy-makers. These processes are of particular concern in remoter rural areas, but tend to have a lesser impact in those areas closer to larger urban centres. Housing pressure is seen to stem from the economic impacts of a reanimation of agrarian activity alongside successful economic diversification (in the agro-business sector and tourism). In other words, success generates pressure, drawing in new forms of economic activity and new residents. But housing access in the countryside appears to be both easier and cheaper than in nearby towns and cities, as a result of lower construction and land costs. Access is less of a problem than housing quality. A clear quality division between housing locked into the traditional agrarian sector and that serving the new tourism industry is a key feature of the rural housing market. The main theme of rural policy has been to bring about greater parity in the quality of housing in these two sectors and has focused on the provision of running water and electricity. The same divisions exist between urban and rural municipalities and policy has focused on the equalisation of services and housing standards. Much of this policy is devised and implemented at the regional level or via local initiatives.

Future problems for the rural housing stock are also anticipated, and these will stem from two main processes. First, the ageing of the rural population will mean that many homes will become unsuited to the future needs of their current occupants. Second, an increasing number of immigrants continue to pour into the intensive agricultural regions (e.g. Andalucía, Comunidad Valenciana and Cataluña) piling further pressure onto Spain's already stretched housing resources. While existing policies have met with some success, it remains to be seen whether or not they are equal to the task of dealing with future housing pressure.

Chapter 9
Ireland

Joe Finnerty, Donal Guerin and Cathal O Connell

Introduction

Ireland's current high levels of economic growth are putting considerable pressure – via their many-faceted impacts on the existing system of housing
production and consumption – on housing affordability and access for recently
formed and aspiring households. The first part of this chapter examines the
nature of these nation-wide affordability and access problems. The ways that
these problems are exacerbated in two kinds of rural areas will be explored in the
second part. Policies to counteract both national and specifically rural housing
pressures are discussed in part three. And finally, the fourth part presents some
conclusions concerning key rural housing issues, challenges and policies.

Economic growth, demand for housing and the Irish housing system

It should be noted at the outset that there is no tradition of substantial research,
statistics or policy-focus on rural housing in Ireland. Moreover, rural housing is
more likely to be approached in terms of urban containment and preservation of
the countryside than in terms of the affordability and accessibility issues covered
in this chapter. Additionally, the term 'rural' is defined differently for different
purposes. However, in a recent research paper for the pending National Spatial
Strategy[1] 'rural areas' comprise District Electoral Divisions with a population of
fewer than 150 people per square kilometre or which do not contain a town with
a population of 1,500 or more (Centre for Local and Regional Studies *et al.*,
2000). On this basis, approximately 1.4 million people, or 39 per cent of the
population, live in rural Ireland (1996 figures).

Rural areas, which have been characterised for many years by population
decline, are unprepared for the general housing pressures sparked off by recent
Irish economic growth. An understanding of these pressures requires an overview
of the complex impacts of economic expansion within the context of existing
housing production and allocation patterns.

In recent years, the economy of the Republic of Ireland has been the fastest growing in the European Union, with a 9 per cent annual average increase in real GDP in the years 1994–2000. This growth has been accompanied by a rapid surge in population, particularly in the household forming age group (the national population has increased from 3.52 million in 1991 to an estimated 3.84 million in 2001, the highest population level since the end of the nineteenth century: Central Statistics Office, 2001), falling average household size, rising employment levels (the numbers at work have increased from 1.1 million to 1.7 million), rising real incomes and falling unemployment (down from 14 per cent in 1994 to 3.7 per cent in 2000 (DoELG, 2001: 4–5)). Another feature of Irish economic growth has been the maintenance of Ireland as one of the more unequal societies in the EU in terms of income distribution (Nolan and Maitre, 2000), with the emergence of a class of people with access to substantial sums of cheap capital to invest in residential property.

One consequence of this economic growth has been unprecedented demand for, and levels of, residential new-build, with 52,600 new housing units built in 2001.[2] However, this economic and demographic expansion has also contributed to a housing crisis whereby historically dominant patterns of housing production and allocation are coming under increasing pressure to cope with new levels of demand (Drudy, 2001; National Economic and Social Forum, 2000).

The most striking feature of the Irish housing system is its lopsided tenure profile, with an overwhelming dominance of home ownership over other tenures. Home ownership accounts for almost 80 per cent of dwellings in the Irish system, private renting accounts for approximately 11 per cent, while the remainder comprises social housing offered by local authorities and the voluntary sector.

While the reasons for the dominance of owner-occupation are beyond the scope of this review, recent hyperinflation in the housing market is giving rise to unease among commentators who are concerned that the current emphasis on owning one's home is leading to over-mortgaged or excluded households.

Since the start of the current economic upturn in Ireland, the average price of private new-build nationally has more than doubled, rising from approximately £61,000 in 1995 to £133,000 in 2000. While increases have been much more pronounced in the main urban centres of Dublin, Cork, Limerick, Waterford and Galway (for example the average price of a new house in Dublin soared from approximately £68,000 to £174,000 over this period) house prices have also increased substantially in rural areas. These increases have far outstripped the rise in real incomes, with the ratio of house prices to average earnings rising from 4.3 to 1 in 1994 to 6.4 to 1 in 1998 (Drudy, 1999: 6).

The private rented sector has undergone a minor revival over this same period, in part because of the prohibitive costs of entry into housebuilding. A second major factor in the revival of private renting is its use as a privatised alternative to social housing (the third factor, which is investor demand for rental units, is dealt with below). This new role is evident in the labour force status of these households: approximately one-third of private tenants are dependent on rent supplement (a form of housing benefit effectively available only to unemployed tenants) (Guerin, 1999). Unfortunately, problems of affordability, access and quality are rampant in this tenure. Many private tenants are vulnerable to minimal notice to quit (four weeks) and arbitrary rent increases, while a lax inspection and regulatory regime in the context of high demand means that exploitative rents can be obtained for poor-quality accommodation (Downey and Devilly, 1998). To add insult to injury, rental payments are eligible for far lower levels of tax relief than mortgage payments.

The small social housing sector comprises local authority and voluntary/co-operative providers. A narrow range of providers is involved in social housing, with little or no input from pension funds, banks, building societies, credit unions or trade unions (Drudy, 2001: 53). The tenure is currently overwhelmed by lengthening waiting lists with little hope of significant inroads likely in the absence of a massive increase in capital investment (see below for discussion on the social housing programme in the National Development Plan). The local authority tenure, which has catered for the poorest households in recent decades, is now the subject of new pressures from aspirant homeowners and persons who occupy sub-standard accommodation in the private rental sector. Though the overall stock of social renting dwellings has increased from approximately 97,000 in 1995 to 99,000 in 1999, the waiting list of qualified applicants in 1999 stood at a record 44,000.

As noted above, the problems of affordability and accessibility have as their proximate cause an exceptional and largely unforeseen surge in demand for housing by newly forming households, investors and those seeking second homes. Despite record levels of total new residential build, however, this increased demand has not produced a matching increase in the volume of new units nor improved affordability and accessibility of sufficient of this new-build.

The main reasons advanced for this failure to meet the full spectrum of housing need, manifested most clearly in increases in mortgage affordability problems, waiting lists for social housing, and escalating private sector rents, are:

- delays in the re-zoning and servicing of land for housebuilding;
- the slow pace of processing of planning proposals by an over stretched planning system;

- evidence of land hoarding by developers to maximise capital gains;
- the extensive activity of speculative landlords;
- super-profits being made by some developers and builders;[3] and
- a lack of sufficient investment in social housing by existing providers.

(Bacon, 1999; Drudy, 2001)

The affordability and access difficulties resulting from an insufficient volume of public and private new-build have been exacerbated by new patterns of ownership. Fuelled by a variety of tax incentive schemes in conjunction with unprecedented rates of house price inflation, a class of newly affluent private households and investors have been active in the purchase of housing units in both urban and rural locations. It is estimated that in 1999 alone, 12,000 out of a total of 42,200 private new-build units were purchased by investors[4] (see the sections following for details of the tax incentive schemes in rural areas). Available data on the income of those securing house loan approval show increasing activity by those at the upper end of the income distribution. Households with a combined income exceeding £50,000 increased their share from 9.4 per cent in 1996 to 31.1 per cent in 2000, while those whose combined income was less than £30,000 saw their share decline from 53.1 per cent to 18.9 per cent over the same period (DoELG, *Housing Statistics Bulletin*, 2000: 31). In 1999, the average industrial wage was just over £15,000.

Other key structural characteristics of the Irish housing system are also worth noting:

- Private new-build is based on either 'self-build' of single units or on speculative promotion where the development process is initiated and managed by private firms (Barlow and Duncan, 1994; Finnerty, 2000). Development gains arising from re-zoning and planning permission decisions accrue to private interests, which obstructs the development of effective policies promoting housing as a social good and a fundamental right for all (Drudy, 2001: 56–58).
- The legal and fiscal treatment of private tenants is compounded by the underdevelopment of Landlordism as a business sector. Rather than investment being committed at the development and construction stages by letting companies with a view to long-term investment, the typical private residential investor is an individual who becomes involved in housing provision at the allocation stage only, thus effectively competing for the same supply of housing as aspiring homeowners. Households may thus be faced with the scenario of having to rent a dwelling from a landlord who effectively outbid them for the purchase of that dwelling.

These are some of the general and structural problems facing the Irish housing system. More specific rural concerns are now examined.

The countryside

Many rural areas – even those in peripheral, non-scenic locations – are affected by the general problems of accessibility and affordability, which have characterised the Irish housing market over the last six or seven years. (These peripheral non-scenic areas rarely experience the kind of large-scale, entry level provision from builders and developers experienced in more pressured rural areas). Moreover, rental tenure options are more limited in the countryside: private and public rented accommodation is concentrated in urban areas, so that the proportion of owner-occupied units in rural areas is higher than suggested by the national average. The concerns mentioned above about the results of hyper-inflation have particular resonance for rural housing markets where a deeply rooted proprietorial ethic has meant that owning one's home is revered in cultural and economic terms.

While the sustainability of owner-occupation for new households is in question in both the urban and rural contexts, the almost exclusive attachment to ownership in rural areas has virtually eliminated rental options to the point that they are hardly considered to be realistic accommodation strategies even by households who cannot afford to buy. In many rural areas, the historic neglect of both private renting and social housing (in the context of the economic marginalisation of peripheral regions) has meant that as property prices rise there are no viable alternatives for newly forming households unable to buy their own home. In rural areas many local authorities are adding to their stock only in single digit figures, thus offering no realistic alternatives to owner-occupation for newly forming households on low incomes.

Irish rural housing faces a number of unprecedented pressures, which raise question marks over affordability and access for low-income households. However, the problems being faced in the countryside are not uniform and a distinction can be made between those areas adjacent to larger urban areas and those in scenic – often coastal or lakeshore – settings in peripheral areas.[5] A range of specific factors, comprising changing rural population patterns in response to recent economic growth, the absence of strategic spatial planning and the impact of second and holiday homes, has contributed to these additional pressures.

Changing population patterns

As noted above, approximately 39 per cent of the national population live in rural Ireland. The north-west, north-east, west, midlands and south-west regions of the country are predominately rural (NESF, 1997: 13). Due to the current sustained levels of economic expansion, eleven rural areas are now experiencing population growth. However, an analysis of population trends shows that certain rural areas are becoming more quickly affected by urbanisation in comparison with others. One of the most striking features of Irish settlement patterns is the rapid urbanisation of counties around Dublin. A similar effect may be seen in other smaller urban centres such as Limerick and Galway. It is also notable that the areas with the lowest degree of urbanisation in 1996 – the west and north-west – are also those that suffered the greatest population losses during the 1951–1996 period (NESC, 1997: 14–21).

The 1997 National Economic and Social Council (NESC) analysis of changing population patterns highlights the following issues:

- the dominance of a relatively small number of large centres within the overall population distribution;
- the very large number of small settlements that exist;
- the continuing importance, despite recent decades of urbanisation, of living on farms, in open country or in very small settlements;
- the emergence of satellite and dormitory towns around the main cities; and
- a widespread decline of towns and villages outside the zone of influence of larger settlements.

(NESC, 1997: 61)

The picture is more complex than a simple shift of households from rural to urban areas. According to the NESC:

> those counties with strong urban centres are in a position to retain and increase their populations whereas counties lacking such strong urban centres are suffering from population decline because of declining agricultural employment.
>
> (NESC, 1997: 20)

However, even those counties with a strong urban centre can experience population decline in their most peripheral parts.

Urban spill-over

The second distinct pressure/process facing rural areas could be described as 'urban spill-over'. The rapid house price inflation referred to above, coupled with the lack of an effective land use and transportation policy in the main urban centres, has resulted in many newly forming urban households finding accommodation in rural areas which are within commuting distance of their employment. While this phenomenon is most pronounced in the Dublin region where commuting distances can reach up to sixty miles, it is also a feature in the hinterlands of other urban centres.

The Economic and Social Research Institute has pointed to the role of underdeveloped strategic planning in creating a situation where the lack of affordable housing in the large urban areas generates a growing tendency for people to reside in and commute from 'outer' regions. This pressure has generated a growth in commuter towns in the counties surrounding the large cities e.g. Cork, Dublin, Limerick and Galway (ESRI, 1999: 122). A recent report for the National Spatial Strategy states that:

> One of the most striking aspects of the Irish Urban System is the primacy of Dublin [the Irish capital] . . . The growth of Dublin has been exerting increasing influence over urban centres in the Greater Dublin Area and beyond, so that much of the east of the country may be regarded as a single urban system of a scale comparable to other European cities.
>
> (Goodbody Economic Consultants *et al.*, 2000: 85)

This type of growth is radically changing the character of rural areas surrounding these urban centres. These changes are creating a number of distinct pressures. These are:

- High cost of housing: the cost of new and second hand houses in rural areas has risen dramatically because of the number of urban dwellers seeking to purchase cheaper homes.
- Encroachment on countryside: the number of new houses being built is radically reshaping rural villages and the open countryside.
- Affordability for local people: the cost of home ownership is now creating affordability issues for local people who wish to remain in these areas. The lack of affordable homes for sale, combined with the absence of a developed private rented sector and the small number of social housing units, is creating a situation where there is enforced population change in these areas.

The effect on rural towns and villages of accelerated urbanisation processes is similar to that of holiday and second homes on peripheral rural areas. The superior purchasing power of incoming households, many of whom are dual income, inflates the price of housing and sites, thus marginalising poorer local households who are trying to gain a foothold on the housing ladder. This process, at the same time, reduces the ability of local authorities to supply public rented housing as an alternative.

Impact of second and holiday homes

In many peripheral rural areas of high amenity value, house prices are boosted by the changing structure of the local housing market in another way: the impact of second and holiday homes substituting for the effects of urban over-spill. Reflecting the overall buoyancy of the economy and sustained house price inflation, there is a clear pattern of activity by investors and by those buying second homes. Encouraging the emergence of a pool of residential investors in peripheral rural areas have been certain tax breaks catering to this market, principally the Seaside Resort Renewal Scheme (SRRS). The Seaside Resort Scheme ran from July 1995 to December 1999 and cost an estimated £200 million in tax expenditures. It provided tax relief for the construction of, *inter alia*, holiday homes in twelve designated seaside resorts (Interdepartmental Review Group, 2001).

The greater purchasing power of residential investors or urban households seeking a second dwelling often puts prices of even modest dwellings out of the reach of locals. Given that there are no statutory restrictions on the purchase of second homes (or sites for second homes) per se, the problem is particularly acute in scenic and coastal areas (e.g. the western seaboard). The result is that an increasing number of homeowners do not reside in these areas for most of the year. In one remote area of County Donegal, for example, it is estimated that approximately 65 per cent of all out-of-town houses are owned by holiday home investors from outside the area (*Irish Times*, 28 May 1999). The weight of this external demand also bids up the cost of building services and of sites, and thus makes it more difficult for local authorities to meet unsatisfied housing need. This has implications in terms of depopulation, inability to sustain services on a year-round basis and over-stretching of infrastructure at the peak season, and the development of dual communities and social disparities (Heanue, 1998).

Holiday and second home construction in seaside and other high amenity areas can blur the true effect of housebuilding activity in such areas and have impacts that go beyond the immediacy of the housing market. In these areas housebuilding levels can match, and in many cases exceed, the output of much larger and more populous areas. There are however implications of an environmental, economic and community developmental nature raised by developments on this scale in small resorts and rural areas.

The exceptional level of new-build in Wexford, for example, is almost entirely due to holiday and second homes arising from the county's longstanding appeal as a holiday destination for households from Dublin and the eastern seaboard. In the village of Rosslare Strand in County Wexford, despite the massive increase in housebuilding, new estates and holiday home developments, staff numbers at the local national school are under threat due to falling pupil numbers. In other resorts in the county, the extent of new building has resulted in huge pressures on infrastructure such as water supply, sewerage and roads, etc., to the extent that during peak season, water shortages and overload of treatment plants often happen.

This displacement, in turn, has implications for the sustainability of existing communities and how their needs are met in light of virtually uncontrolled development. Many resort towns and villages become boomtowns during the summer months, but virtually shut down during the low season. Coupled with depopulation of the existing community they can become deserted, alienating, ghost towns surrounded but untouched by the trappings of affluence and incapable of supporting basic community facilities such as schools, public transport and so on.

The benefits of seaside renewal schemes and the phenomenon of second and holiday homes in general could at best be described as cosmetic, resulting in short term buoyancy in local building activity, speculative gains for investors and developers and related service providers. At worse they run the risk of inflating local housing markets out of reach of existing communities, overloading infrastructure, and bifurcating such areas into self-contained communities of affluent peak season visitors and increasingly marginalised permanent residents.

Dealing with rural housing pressure

The financial and exclusionary impacts of Ireland's housing crisis are infrequently discussed in a rural context, with attention more often being devoted to environmental considerations such as suburbanisation of the countryside or to sustainability considerations such as demands on transport and other infrastructure. The lack of public awareness of the issues of affordability and accessibility partly reflect the 'invisibility' of poverty and disadvantage in Irish rural society. Depending on the choice of relative poverty line, some 20 to 30 per cent of the

Irish population are living in income poverty, two-thirds of whom live in rural rather than urban areas. Indeed the proportion of households living in income poverty is largest in small towns and villages and smallest in Dublin (Jackson and Hasse, 1996: 61–62).

Jackson and Hasse identify six factors to explain this invisibility, which are also manifest through housing disadvantage. These are:

- The residential pattern: the physical separation and isolation, reflected in the lowest population density in Europe, can hide the presence of poverty, including poor quality housing.
- Landscape as consumption: the ideology of the urban or tourist gaze excludes the evidence of poverty. In such a view, a certain romanticism is attached to the countryside which may obscure issues such as the quality of dwellings and housing affordability for local people.
- Confusion between income and property: the emphasis on the value of property in Irish culture may conceal the evident economic desperation that is faced by many farmers. Research carried out in 1992 found that only one-third of farms were economically and demographically viable. The pressure on smallholdings and the need to generate off-farm incomes were key considerations in the *Government White Paper on Rural Development in Ireland* (Department of Agriculture 1999: 3). For some farmers, the selling of sites for new houses can prove a useful source of extra income. However, the consolidation of smaller farms into larger units provides greater opportunities for larger cash- and asset-rich farmers. This, in turn, is reinforcing inequalities between large and small farmers.
- Landless living in rural areas: the housing estates established by county councils have been ghettoised by virtue of their location outside the central areas of small towns. Their location means they have become marginal and effectively invisible. Research has also found that those living in local authority housing estates face the most extreme form of deprivation, including difficulties in finding employment (Nolan *et al.*, 1998).
- Strong ideological and institutional constraints: within Irish rural communities there are strong ideological and institutional constraints, which may prevent the recognition of objective differences in wealth and income opportunities, including those relating to housing.
- A property owning democracy: the culture of home ownership places considerable pressure on rural households to own property in order to belong and to have a place in the community.

(Adapted from Jackson and Hasse, 1996: 62–65)

National housing policy has of course impacted on rural areas and the government is planning or has implemented a number of measures designed to ameliorate the problems facing lower-income, often non-homeowning households. These have included the proposed reform of rents and the subsidies system within the social and private rented sector, and the setting up of a land-lord–tenant dispute resolution board and modest moves towards improving security of tenure. In order to ease access into home ownership and offset the pressure of house price inflation, policies have been introduced to increase the supply of zoned and serviced land.[6] It is also proposed – in the National Plan – that 4,000 extra homes should be provided annually by the voluntary housing sector.

But more specific measures have been taken (or are planned) in the countryside and have come on the back of general rural renewal, which has been a key emphasis in institutional reform in recent years. The primary focus has been on reversing population decline through generating higher agricultural incomes and the provision of off-farm incomes. Community development initiatives, however, have rarely taken the housing issue as a *primary* objective. Different responses, with relevance to housing, are now examined in turn.

Response of development agencies

At present there are a large number of agencies involved in performing many diverse roles in support of rural renewal. The varied work of these agencies does reflect to some extent a move away from equating rural renewal to agricultural development; however the principal minister with responsibility for rural renewal remains the Minister for Agriculture. An economic focus also forms the core elements of the thirty-four LEADER II programmes, which have been the mainstay of rural community development since the early 1990s. A review of the operational programme for the LEADER II Community Initiative suggests that housing has not featured as a concern with the companies. A greater concern with housing is evident in the work of some of the rural Community Development Projects which focus on poverty and social exclusion. However, evidence suggests that access to housing and issues of affordability are rarely seen as stand-alone priorities in their operational programmes.

Priorities of the National Plan

An emphasis on economic regeneration also forms the basis of the main priorities identified by the recently published National Development Plan, 2000–2006 (NDP) and by the *Government White Paper on Rural Development in Ireland*

(1999). The National Plan identifies agriculture as remaining critical to the well-being of the rural economy. Measures to promote agriculture feature prominently in the NDP. Extensive reference is also made to the implementation of a regional policy in which investment in roads and telecommunications can contribute to economic prosperity. Although it acknowledges the impact of urbanisation on rural hinterlands and the problems faced by more remote rural areas – including emigration and increased cost of service – the NDP makes no specific reference to *rural* housing, apart from reference to an allocation of £103 million, which is being provided for urban and village renewal (there will be an overlap in certain areas with the Town Renewal Scheme, described below). Economic regeneration in the form of measures to support agriculture, forestry and fisheries is the dominant focus of attention in planning for rural areas.

The planning system and local government responses

It remains the case that the main institutional response to problems in rural housing will continue to lie with the local authorities (city and county councils) within the legislative framework laid down by the DoELG and the pending National Spatial Strategy.[7] As part of the implementation of the NDP, each local authority is in the process of producing an integrated 10-year strategy across the areas of health, education, housing and social welfare. The development of this strategy provides an opportunity for rural local authorities to address the issues of urban encroachment and housing affordability.

A potentially important element in the housing strategies of local authorities is Section V of the Planning and Development Act 2000, which gives local authorities the power to acquire, at agricultural prices, up to 20 per cent of land for social or affordable housing in new housing developments. Related to this, the NDP also provides for a multi-annual local authority housing programme to deliver an additional 41,500 units over the lifetime of the Plan.

Additionally, a Town Renewal Scheme running from 2000 to 2002, aims to counter the trend for people to move out of towns into the surrounding rural areas. This tax-relief scheme, which applies to both commercial and residential developments is, in its first phase, confined to approximately one hundred towns with populations of between 500 and 6,000.

More immediately, many county councils in areas experiencing housing pressure have introduced various kinds of zoning and residency conditions for the granting of planning permission for residential developments as part of their rural settlement policy. The main grounds on which these requirements have been introduced are issues of housing affordability and access for local residents. The County Development Plan for Donegal (located in the north-west of the country), for example, states that priority for new permanent housing in rural areas should be given to members of the 'indigenous rural community' with higher density, multiple housing developments being permitted only on serviced areas within defined control points. Members of the indigenous rural community are defined as:

- family members from established farming, land owning and non-land owning rural households;
- returned emigrants originally from the area; and
- new rural dwellers working in the rural area.

(Donegal County Council, 2000)

Similarly, Kerry County Council (located in the south-west of the country) makes provision for people to reside in rural areas particularly where there are strong established links to the locality. In this context, the stated planning aims and policies of Kerry County Council are to:

- provide accommodation for local people with genuine housing needs, thereby enhancing and maintaining a vibrant local community; and
- recognise that one-off housing, functionally related to the rural area in which it is situated, is a vital component in sustaining rural communities, but should be limited to enable rural amenities, environmental qualities and the character of these areas to be maintained.

Much controversy has accompanied attempts to tackle 'uncontrolled' rural new-build, whether for holiday or permanent use. In County Clare on the western seaboard a draft proposal allowing anyone to build homes in the open countryside was modified with the addition: 'that the purpose of this policy is to facilitate local rural people who have a genuine requirement for housing'. Councillors also agreed that 'non-locals' would not now be allowed to build homes in areas under high development pressure on the county's west coast and vulnerable landscapes, including much of the Burren.

Regional planning guidelines

In terms of combating urban spill-over, Strategic Planning Guidelines (SPGs) were issued by the DoELG for the Greater Dublin Area in 1999. The SPGs seek to confine significant new housing developments within designated growth areas, so that new-build in other parts of the Greater Dublin Area would be for local population needs only. Local authorities in the Dublin and mid-east Regions must have regard to the guidelines when making and adopting development plans. However, these guidelines have been subject to much opposition from affected local authorities, who have attempted to rezone large tracts of land for residential use (O'Brien, 2001).

Conclusions

Key rural housing issues

The issues of affordability (of owner-occupied or private rented housing) and of access (to public rented housing, supplied by either the local authority or a voluntary housing organisation) are central to the housing pressures faced by all newly forming or newly formed households of modest incomes in Ireland today. The broad factors generating these pressures – rapid and unbalanced economic growth leading to increased population and to house price inflation – have generated rural housing pressures in two separate ways. First, the actions of affluent households and residential investors seeking second or holiday homes in peripheral rural areas have bid up the price of sites and units and made the provision of public renting opportunities more difficult. A similar outcome has emerged in urban hinterlands, through the actions of newly forming households seeking housing alternatives outside the main urban areas where house price inflation is most acute.

Present and future challenges

Challenges to the development of a rational spatial strategy include both the historic absence of developed political steering capacities, and the considerable influence of a clientelist political culture, at local and national levels. At the local level, and as noted above, the planning efforts of rural local authorities have clashed with a variety of interests, especially those who, while wishing to build on family lands, work in off-farm employment. Anecdotal evidence suggests that elements of the 'rural settlements' policies in County Development Plans are proving ineffective.[8]

Concern that Section V of the Planning and Development Act 2000, allowing local authorities to acquire building land for social or affordable housing at agricultural prices, would prove repugnant to the protection to private property afforded in the Irish Constitution, have proved unfounded. Nonetheless, the power that the prevailing model of housing provision gives to developers to resist public planning has led to forecasts of a slowdown in future new-build. At the same time, development gains from rezonings, planning permissions and the provision of infrastructure continue to accrue to private landowners (Drudy, 2001: 57).

In terms of voluntary rural housing, while a number of innovative schemes have been established by organisations such as Rural Resettlement – which have involved supporting families who wish to move to rural Ireland from Dublin – the capacity of such organisations to supply the number of units envisaged is in doubt. Most organisations are almost completely volunteer-based and are better prepared for dealing with the needs of small numbers of local elderly people than general provision on any larger scale.

In terms of social housing, even if projected targets are met, many areas forecast continued high and unsatisfied demand for social housing. For example, in the Joint Housing Strategy of Cork City and County, it is conceded that existing waiting lists of 7,500 households will have been reduced to 6,400 households by 2006 through traditional social housing provision. A reduction to 3,400 households is *possible*, but only under the unlikely scenario of the new mechanisms for procuring social housing, set out in the Planning and Development Act 2000, being implemented in full (Cork Planning Authorities, 2001).

The future

Despite a slowdown in rates of Irish economic growth, population growth in the absence of significant net migration seems likely to continue, prolonging existing demand for significant new-build. On current estimates, and in the absence of the long-awaited national spatial policy, 80 per cent of this growth will occur in Dublin and adjacent areas. The scale and depth of 'other' problems in many rural areas – including agricultural decline, high population dependency ratios and depopulation – has meant that the problems of rural housing have been largely overshadowed. The historic problems of poor quality and over-crowded accommodation have been joined by the new problems of access and affordability. However, the overview of current initiatives and responses provided above indicates that the problems of rural housing continue to be afforded low priority.

Today, planning is playing an increasingly important role in shaping responses to housing need. Rural housing pressures are multifaceted and often mutually self-reinforcing. These pressures suggest a need for additional planning policies, developer incentives, community and infrastructure development, and a broad strategy for dealing with structural weaknesses in the rural economy. Any future policy agenda must deal with all these issues in an integrated way: without this holistic approach, housing pressure is likely to remain a feature of these areas.

Notes

1   The National Spatial Strategy aims to provide a 'broad planning framework' for the location of development in Ireland over the next twenty years. It will 'identify potential development patterns for different areas and set out overall policies for creating the conditions necessary to influence the location of different types of development in the future'. In particular, it will select about four major growth 'gateways' outside Dublin for future development. See the website at www. irishspatialstrategy.ie

2   New residential build is at the highest rate in the EU in proportion to population, with 13.1 houses per 1,000 population in 2000, more than double the average EU rate (DoELG, 2001).

3   It is clear that the price of housing bears little relationship to the cost of production. According to official statistics the national housebuilding cost index rose by 15 per cent between 1995 and 1999 while the average sale price of a new house in this period rose by a massive 90 per cent from £61,000 to £117,000 (DoELG, *Housing Statistics Bulletin*, various years).

4   No comprehensive data are available on levels of second and holiday housebuilding.

5   In the absence of detailed and comprehensive research, the present analysis must content itself with pointing out the existence of these two distinct kinds of housing pressure without claiming that these pressures pertain to all rural areas. There do exist rural areas that are depressed economically, leading to out-migration and declining population, but not subject to the two external pressures of urban spillover or holiday and second homes. Nonetheless, these areas are still influenced by the general inflationary tendencies in the housing market. In this regard, the significance of (a) the relatively small land area of the Irish Republic, and (b) the improved accessibility of even the most peripheral rural areas via an upgraded road network, should be borne in mind.

6   See the DoELG website for more details on these various initiatives.

7   The physical planning system in Ireland is run by 88 local planning authorities: 29 County Councils, 5 County Borough Corporations, 5 Borough Corporations and 49 Urban District Councils. The DoELG is responsible for planning legislation (see the DoELG website, www.environ.ie/devindex/), and has recently acquired powers to impose regional guidelines on planning authorities, as in the case of the Strategic Planning Guidelines for the Greater Dublin Area.

8   A non-attributed background paper for the National Spatial Strategy notes that 'the desirability of a rural site has increased its value to the point where there is now a very real incentive to abuse the planning system by persuading a planning

authority to grant permission on the basis . . . of local need and then to sell. Occupancy conditions offer little resistance to this and perhaps consideration should be given to . . . binding legal agreements governing occupancy' (www. irishspatialstrategy.ie/docs/13).

Part Three:
Divisive Cultures, Unstable Regimes

The final group of chapters draws together contributions from England (Chapter 10), Scotland (Chapter 11) and Wales (Chapter 12). Obviously, these three countries share a political and cultural link which is far stronger that that joining our other two groupings. They occupy the same island, cut off (physically) from the rest of Europe. A thousand years of Anglicisation means that they share a common language and political system, though Scotland and Wales are home to both different languages and their own political traditions. The three final case study chapters differ from the previous seven in the sense that the authors were all conscious of the immediate link that would be drawn with the other British contributions. Hence, while Hoggart goes for a general overview, Shucksmith and Conway are quick to point out Scottish political nuances and Edwards argues that plain urban–rural divisions found in England are frequently dressed in cultural and language terms in Wales.

However, the joining of England, Scotland and Wales here is a reflection of the fact that they share an underlying culture of urban–rural division. Margaret Thatcher famously described the countryside as a 'repository of cultural values' as if there were something more explicitly English about living in a small village as opposed to a large city. This cultural distance between town and country-side, which is common to all three countries (though its form may differ), is expressed in UK party politics. The recent parliamentary debate on the future of hunting with hounds (March, 2002) revealed wholly expected divisions between the Labour-dominated cities and the more Conservative countryside. We suggest later in Chapter 13 that this greater division – termed a 'divisive culture' – is also expressed by a more transient and disputed form of power. It is often suggested that the state favours the urban population: planning, for example, is commonly viewed as an urban tool reflecting urban values (despite its original goal being to contain cities and protect the countryside). It either allows too much development (for incomers) and upsets conservative sensi-bilities, or allows too little and contravenes the rights of local people to gain access to housing. In response, planning policy is liable to constant challenge and there exists a rift between those who would like to see more planning and a more regulatory policy approach and those who would prefer less, favouring a laissez-faire regime in which those deemed local would be free from the constraints of an urban planning system.

In Chapter 10, Keith Hoggart's account of housing in England begins with a general overview, examining public versus private housing in Britain as a whole. Particular attention is paid to the low standing of public housing and the demand and supply pressures, which display such strong regional variations. Hoggart notes that rural housing pressure is at its most acute closer to cities, and especially within greenbelt land. Planning restraint is held up as a critical issue, driving up house prices with the most acute repercussions being felt by younger non-home-owning households. Affordability is a key rural pressure, brought on by the excess of demand over supply and the weakness of alternatives to home ownership in the English countryside. It is argued that a key definitional issue confuses any understanding of housing pressure in rural England: should rural mean settlements of fewer than 10,000 or 1,000 households? If the higher limit is used then the key pressure facing communities is general under-supply. But if the lower limit is used, the in-migration of more affluent households becomes critical. On the policy front, Hoggart points out that government has chosen to prioritise larger settlements, leaving smaller villages to fend for themselves, often attempting to employ ad hoc and largely ineffectual polices such as the exceptions approach (a strategy whereby low-cost housing is allowed on sites that would otherwise not be earmarked for housing use). But this comes as no surprise given that strategies to meet a range of needs are possible in larger centres, whereas villages are unable to cope with changing needs over time; they simply do not have sufficient stock variety. The entire situation is summed up as follows: 'market forces dominate rural housing access, with price discriminations in smaller settlements intensified by the operation of the land use planning system'. The English case study comes first because it neatly summarises many of the broad processes affecting rural areas in Britain. It also points out the key divisions: centred on social equity, the rights of incomers versus locals and the legitimate role of planning in the countryside. The policy instability caused by these divisions is clear.

In the next chapter looking at Scotland, Shucksmith and Conway begin by making a direct comparison with England. Rural areas in both countries have been affected by the process of globalisation, marked by the penetration of global capital into local markets and the colonisation of rural areas by consumption interests. There are, however, also important differences between the two countries. In Scotland for example, public rented housing has traditionally occupied a more dominant position, and is still seen in a less negative light, than in England. It is also the case that private interests north of the border have been weakened by a history of distrust of landlordism, largely because of its association with English intrusion.

The authors then turn their attention to rural markets with the assertion that 'housing markets in rural areas are not free markets'. On the demand side, the market has been augmented by the arrival of elderly people or those seeking second homes. On the supply side, it is heavily regulated through planning policy and the objective of containment. The weight of planning power is amplified – as in England – through well-educated and articulate anti-development interests, creating a situation in which 'planning has become a political arena through which the interests of the most powerful are imposed on the weak'. Hence, a picture of division ending in social exclusion emerges. And the key pressures affecting the Scottish countryside are summarised as:

- supply-side constraints resulting from planning and land monopoly;
- increasing demand from external sources and single-person households;
- declining stock of affordable housing;
- a small and expensive private rented sector, which is also declining.

In the late 1980s and early 1990s, such problems became the focus of intense discussion if not immediate action. This culminated in a paper from Scottish Homes identifying what it considered to be 'The Rural Housing Challenge'. This challenge was thought to have four strands: increasing supply, improving conditions, ensuring affordability, and tackling tenant participation and involvement as part of community development.

In response, moves were made to use existing grant structures in more flexible and innovative ways: funding was, for example, directed towards self-build and towards care and repair. The Scottish Office also looked to innovations developing elsewhere in the UK, and particularly the use of planning mechanisms to secure an additional supply of affordable housing. The basic philosophy, reflected in the Shucksmith and Conway chapter, was one of innovation. There was also a strong desire to experiment with different ideas and thereby create a distinctly Scottish response to pressures being experienced across the United Kingdom.

It emerges from Chapter 11 that, for the most part, Scotland possesses the same urban–rural conflicts as those found in England. This is expressed in the way policy struggles to balance competing interests. That said however, the struggle in Scotland may have been eased by greater faith in public sector housing provision and a 'weakening of private interests'. This contrast in underlying values has resulted in a political debate, which although fundamentally similar to that of England, is perhaps more willing to embrace a policy regime characterised by stronger intervention.

The final case study chapter, looking at Wales, reflects the same balance of fundamental similarity and local difference. Chapter 12 focuses on local action in managing or resisting housing pressure. Edwards identifies three phases of engagement with planning and housing issues in Wales. Prior to 1980 the patterns of population and social change apparent today were slowly taking hold and there was a period of emergent concern over migration and how this might be managed. In the second phase – throughout the 1980s and into the first half of the 1990s – Wales had to come to terms with the withdrawal of state subsidy from social housebuilding and the need to promote local voluntary action. The third phase began with the arrival of the National Assembly for Wales and was – and continues to be – characterised by hopes that a distinctive Welsh policy agenda will emerge, better able to cope with cultural needs and the pressures inherent in the current housing market.

Edwards asserts that in rural Wales 'the recognition of an entrenched rural housing problem is apparent in local media reporting and in local claims of disadvantage and in the concerns of the academic and policy community'. The problem itself is seen to stem from the strength of housing demand. And this demand is a result of steady in-migration, often affecting language and culture, and disadvantaging certain local groups more than others: especially the young who find it increasingly difficult to afford homes. In all, six key problems and challenges are identified:

- competition for existing stock;
- the uneven geographical distribution of tenures;
- the lack of affordable property to rent or purchase in low-income rural economies;
- the need to maintain local communities and cultures;
- the problems faced by younger families and single parents;
- the growing problem of a rural underclass and those who become homeless and marginalised.

With some optimism, Edwards suggests that economic change may bring modest gains for rural communities, and these will drive demographic shifts in the form of both endogenous growth and sustained in-migration. The housing challenges therefore, will remain much the same as they are today. But pressure to deal with environmental consequences and cultural impacts is likely to grow, both on the ground and politically. There is a belief in Wales that past policy designed by a government at Westminster did not adequately express Welsh conditions: rather it was out-of-step, particularly in the way that it consistently failed to respond to issues of language, cultural sensitivity and the different planning needs of dispersed settlements in many parts of Wales. So while Wales may share aspects of England's divisive urban–rural culture, there is perhaps a hope that current instability in the policy regime can be eased in the future by bringing policy design closer to the people of Wales.

Chapter 10
England

Keith Hoggart

National housing concerns

According to the media, 8 June 2001 was historic in British politics. The day heralded a second consecutive term in office for a Labour Government with an absolute Parliamentary majority. Had this occurred earlier, commentators might have expected housing to be a major policy priority. For most of the twentieth century, Labour was associated with state involvement in housing, especially over the provision of homes for the poor. But this is the twenty-first century. When Labour came into office in 1997, its government took unto itself a new mistress. This companion's influence was often unacknowledged but it did mean that Labour's former affections now came to be portrayed rather patronisingly as beyond their sell-by-date. This shadow-like mistress, whose power became obvious in the Chancellor of the Exchequer's loving references to his Prudence, induced minor changes in housing policy. In a first term in which the health of the economy was given priority over social equity, Labour did little to mitigate the accumulating disfunctionalities of national housing trends for low-income people. In the previous two-to-three decades, these disfunctionalities had both intensified and mutated into new forms. This generated paradoxical tensions. Housing shortages came to be accompanied by over-supply. Unwanted homes now came alongside housing shortages. Rising house prices sat beside demands for a larger housing stock. Yet these tensions were not spatially even, with rural areas facing peculiar kinds of housing problems.

Set within an estimated need for an increase in housing supply of almost one-quarter by 2016 (Barclay, 1997), the key pressures on the housing system are high prices, the low standing of non-ownership options and supply short-ages. As Table 10.1 indicates, in terms of their impact on the disposable incomes of families, housing in the UK is substantially more expensive than in the rest of the European Union. This generates real affordability problems, especially given strong inflationary pressures within the owner-occupied sector. This aspect of home ownership needs to be emphasised, for other housing tenures have lost favour. For private rental tenures, which dominated the housing scene at the start

Table 10.1 Cost of living comparisons for the EU 1999

Member state	Total	Total without rents	Total for housing, water, electricity, gas and other fuels
Austria	110	104	134
Denmark	132	129	149
Finland	118	115	124
France	119	107	160
Germany	108	104	124
Greece	87	87	76
Ireland	110	98	148
Italy	101	98	114
Netherlands	114	101	172
Portugal	85	83	95
Spain	92	96	100
Sweden	120	116	139
UK	157	116	307

Note: These figures are computed with Belgium equal to 100.

Source: Adapted from Eurostat (2001: 248)

of the twentieth century, the cumulative impact of rent restrictions and long-term growth in the value of dwellings has encouraged landlords to sell their properties. Add to this an antagonism from some quarters toward state involvement in housing provision. This arises even though failings in the private sector prompted large-scale state intervention in housing provision (Swenarton, 1981). But, as Orbach (1977: 46) noted, such interventions were never expected to endure: 'The story of housing legislation is the story of the permanent adoption of solutions to what was conceived as a temporary problem' (e.g. Bowley, 1945). Even decades later, by which time shortcomings in private sector provision were writ large, the political Right viewed state housing as necessary for political rather than supply or equity reasons (Bridgen and Lowe, 1998). Under Conservative governments, cutbacks in state provision became regular, leading to rising rates of homelessness (Greve *et al.*, 1971; Greve, 1991). This reduced state role was intensified in the 1980s when the Thatcher governments made it attractive for public sector tenants to buy their homes (Forrest and Murie, 1988), at the same time as public sector rents were force-fed above the inflation rate and investment in social housing was cut. In 1988 new state provision effectively ended. Following a variety of inducements to encourage local government to shift their housing into the non-profit sector (Rao, 1990), the 1988 Housing Act effectively removed their capacity to provide housing; handing this task to non-profit housing associations. At the same time, private owners continued to receive tax and other privileges (albeit in declining abundance as the century neared its close), which further confirmed that the nation's housing market was dualistic, unlike many of its European counterparts (Harloe, 1995). But even if government policy had been more even-handed, the wealth that could accrue (and be passed on) from property price rises made ownership highly desirable (e.g. Hamnett, 1995).

The consequences of all this for state (and private rental) housing has been a lower standing in the general public's eyes. This is not surprising. Although some high-quality public sector dwellings have been built, ongoing disputes over the 'right' of the state to construct and manage homes has resulted in deliberate steps to lower quality at various points in time. Add to this, in the 1980s and 1990s, an unwillingness to invest to maintain the dwelling stock. This led to deteriorating standards (Deacon, 1991). But the low standing of the public sector was not just a matter of investment. Other negative images flooded into people's minds. For one, a perceived linkage with high-rise dwellings came about during the mass housing programmes of the 1960s, with negative lifestyle images associated with apartment living (Dunleavy, 1981). Then there were images of hard-edged, unsympathetic treatment for traditional communities, which were blighted as 'slums' (Dennis, 1972), in need of eradication in a modern society (Davies, 1972). With families uprooted from traditional homes, often dispersing longstanding neighbours (Kirby, 1979), the public sector came to be seen in negative terms (Cooper, 1985). This is one reason why there was considerable support for the 1979 Conservative policy of selling council homes to tenants (Forrest and Murie, 1988). Not only have council tenancy and council estates come to be viewed negatively, but this imagery has extended to whole neighbourhoods, decreeing them as poor places to live (e.g. Maclean, 1974). Early signs of this came in the identification of 'difficult-to-let' public housing estates, where local councils found it hard to attract tenants to vacant properties (Byrne, 1976). Another layer to these problems were racially discriminatory systems of housing allocation, in part the result of white reactions to ethnic minorities having homes on certain estates (Phillips, 1987). The ascription of uneven assessments of residential desirability is harsher than the so-called mental maps of residential preferences that geographers once studied so assiduously (e.g. Gould and White, 1986), for an outcome of these evaluations is vacant housing. More recently this process has extended beyond the public sector, with dwellings of all tenures abandoned in some neighbourhoods. As Power and Mumford (1999) report, getting toward two-thirds of homes in some streets in Manchester and

Newcastle-upon-Tyne have been abandoned; including high-quality housing association dwellings that were built less than ten years ago. Even cash incentives to get households to move into such areas have proved unsuccessful, although housing is of high quality and would likely be gentrified if these neighbourhoods were in other regions.

It follows that there is a regional dimension to inequity in housing conditions (Shucksmith and Henderson, 1995). Partly explaining this, Power and Mumford (1999: 35) note that as it was cheaper to develop in the north of England and jobs were in short supply in the region, the area was for some time favoured in social housing allocations. This raised the number of units constructed, so giving the appearance that 1980s' Conservative governments were responding to housing need. In reality, the impact of the Thatcher governments on social housing was primarily seen in reorienting construction away from areas of highest need (Boyne and Powell, 1993). The reorientation of social housing provision toward the non-profit sector in the 1988 Housing Act reversed this trend in some measure (Hoggart, 1999), but the number of low-income dwellings built is still too low (e.g. London saw an 84 per cent reduction in its 1979–1989 housing investment allocation (Brownill and Sharp, 1992)). Severe shortfalls in some areas result in estates with heavy concentrations of deprivation, accompanied by high levels of social and health problems (Page, 1993). In other regions there is a notable over-supply of low-income housing, with Power and Mumford (1999) reporting public sector vacancy rates (by ward) of 13–20 per cent in Manchester and Newcastle-upon-Tyne. Here, local councils report no waiting lists for social housing.[1]

What this means is that the nature of housing pressure is geographically uneven across the country, with housing markets characteristically segmented by place and tenure. Housing costs are generally high, which generates real problems for household finances, with slumps in the housing market generating major burdens for homeowners who need to move (Dorling, 1994). But price rises and slumps both have marked spatial manifestations (Hamnett, 1992, 1993). Most extreme in terms of housing costs is the south-east, where prices are so severe compared with other regions that net migration into the region is higher when the regional economy is depressed (Fielding, 1993: 139). When it is buoyant, house prices run so far ahead of other regions that potential in-migrants are dissuaded from moving to the region. Meanwhile, retirees find the monetary bounties of leaving for other regions appealing. In areas of high private housing costs, social housing provision has been timid, just as it has been 'over-generous' in other regions, even if provision has too often been linked to a downward spiral of neighbourhood social standing and negative attitudes toward non-private accommodation options. But it is not just across regions that disparities are identified but also between housing types (e.g. Tinker *et al.*, 1995), and geographically within regions.

The extent and nature of rural housing concerns

One dimension of intra-regional distinctions is that between rural and urban areas. But views on the distinctions between these two are affected by what is understood by rural and urban. The definition of 'urban' used by the UK Office of National Statistics is of areas with land uses that are irreversibly urban. The National Land Use Classification system identifies such spaces, taking them to be land that is covered by permanent built structures, transport corridors and nodes, buildings for mine working and areas surrounded by built-up sites. Once these are identified, urban areas are viewed as urban land use zones that cover at least 20 hectares, in which separate units of urban land are not more than 50 metres apart (UK Office of National Statistics, 1997). The minimum population threshold for such 'urban' areas is 1,000 persons. Rural in this scheme is non-urban, so the term covers places of less than 1,000 inhabitants. This definition might be acceptable to some, but it is not universally acknowledged. For one, the national government agency, the Housing Corporation, uses a cut-off of 3,000 inhabitants (Housing Corporation, 2001), while, according to the national government's quasi-independent 'watchdog' over rural affairs, the Countryside Agency (1999: 39): 'Rural areas are those wards or postcode sectors which are outside settlements of 10,000 or more people'. Many use this definition, even if this means that 'rural' comprises small market towns. One of its advantages is that it gets away from the conceptual complications that used to exist. Thus, Francis (1982: 33) lists the definition used by the Association of District Councils as places outside a 5 mile (8 km) radius of an urban area with a population of at least 20,000 as well as being at least 10 miles (16 km) from an urban centre with a population of at least 100,000, whereas the then UK Office of Population Censuses and Surveys (now the UK Office of National Statistics) was taking rural districts to be those in which the majority of the population lived in parishes with less than 5,000 inhabitants,[2] where no town of 25,000 persons existed and the district population density was less than two per hectare.[3] Faced with such confusion, Newby's (1986: 209) words are noteworthy: 'There is now, surely, a general awareness that what constitutes "rural" is wholly a matter of convenience and that arid and abstract definitional exercises are of little utility'. At one level this statement is easy to agree with. However, the definition of rurality that is adopted has bearing on how far government policies are seen to respond to rural housing problems. This is an issue to be returned to below. For the present, note that rural housing pressures are significant whether we assume rural is under

10,000 inhabitants or less than 1,000 (albeit the intensity of pressures is greater for the lower figure).

One reason for this is growing demand for new homes, given high rates of new household formation (Barclay, 1997). This demand has fuelled recognition that expansion of the housing stock will heighten pressure on greenfield (open country) sites. Although the Labour Government has made clear that at least 60 per cent of new dwellings should be on brownfield (already non-farm) sites by 2006 (UK Department of the Environment, Transport and the Regions, 2000),[4] this still leaves a substantial demand to be met by rural zones. Yet rural housing demand in England tends to be higher closer to cities. It is in precisely these areas that green belt zones provide the land use planning system with its most stringent restraints on new housing. Indeed, even when the national government has encouraged a more lenient view on new housing applications, local councils have often been reluctant to comply (Elson et al., 1996). One feature of local government contexts that makes this understandable is the adverse reaction to growth amongst the general public. Even when the Conservative Government was seeking to water-down planning restrictions, to give builders greater freedom, internal conflicts within the Conservative Party indicated deep opposition to intrusions into the countryside (Barlow and Savage, 1986), which consequently led to a restatement of the sanctity of rural restraint (Thornley, 1993). But restraint is regularly ascribed as a key cause of higher housing prices, especially in areas of high restraint (Monk and Whitehead, 1996). In this context it might be no surprise that 17 of the 20 districts that record the highest levels of mortgage arrears are defined as 'rural' by the Countryside Agency (1999). Such districts are especially noteworthy in the south-east and eastern regions, as well as in proximity to cities (Cloke et al., 2001a). Apart from land values, one reason for higher dwelling prices close to cities appears to be that builders respond to restrictions in land availability by raising the quality (and price) of new homes (especially if local councils apply planning regulations tightly). As Monk and Whitehead (1996) found for the Cambridge region, this results in lower cost homes being built in areas of relatively low demand or where councils adopt a more laissez-faire attitude toward new-build. While it might be that homes in rural areas as a whole are cheaper than comparable units in urban zones, for lower cost homes the differential is meagre, and with generally inferior incomes for rural workers (Chapman et al., 1998), a real rural affordability problem exists. Added to which, rural house prices are estimated to be higher than their urban counterparts in one-fifth of all districts (Bramley and Smart, 1995). As 75 per cent of rural homes are owner-occupied, compared with about 65 per cent nationally (Chaney and Sherwood, 2000), the end-product is that access to rural homes is more difficult for the young (Rugg and Jones, 1999) and those who are not already homeowners. This feature is made more evident with high demand for rural homes amongst those of higher income. Not surprisingly in this context, change in rural home occupancy tends to see those of lower social status being more inclined to find dwellings in larger centres, while professional and managerial workers are increasingly making up village populations (albeit, one has to be careful not to exaggerate the inevitability or generality of such trends; e.g. Hoggart, 1997).

Despite obvious problems of housing affordability, local government districts have devoted little attention to the peculiarities of their rural housing problems. Thus, a survey by Tetlow and associates (1996) found that rural housing needs were generally neither identified nor articulated in local housing policies. That few councils conduct surveys of need is confirmed by Cloke *et al.* (2001b) who report that just 3 of the 77 authorities they investigated had undertaken surveys of rural homelessness. Indeed the Tetlow and associates survey reports that only one-fifth of districts break down information on housing needs, so they can identify rural problems. One consequence, as Cloke *et al.* (2001b: 109) put it, is that: 'It is as if the magnitude of the urban problem throws a shadow over the plight of homeless people in other (particularly rural) locations'. This provides a distorted image of the nature of rural housing, as rural problems are intimately bound up with other forms of service provision. Tinker *et al.* (1995) offer one indication of this, when noting that housing in villages can become inappropriate for elderly persons, not because of housing deficiencies but because local retail outlets and public services decline or cease. In similar vein, lone parents in rural areas face similar problems to those in urban centres, although issues like access to childcare are compounded by low provision and poor public transport (Hooper, 1996).

As valid as this point might be, the broader issue is the availability of homes for those on lower incomes. Of course, this is only a problem if you believe in the benefits of socially mixed rural communities or in the appropriateness of enabling those whose families have lived in a village for generations, if not centuries, to be able to continue to live there. This is not how many in-migrants see the situation, with the self-interested assertion of letting 'the market' talk being manifest in the comments of one of Bell's (1994: 111) informants:

> What did those local people used to do? They didn't all stay in the village. Not everybody used to stay in their own village, did they? A certain percentage used to go out. They always left. So why should we turn around and say, right, they all ought to be allowed to have a house to stay in the village? It's stupid, because it would just get bigger and bigger and bigger. It would be a town.

Integral to this vision is the growth of second housebuilding. Although the level of second home owning in England is much lower than in many parts of Europe (Gallent and Tewdwr-Jones, 2000), in a context of limited low-cost housing supply its existence further restricts local options for the less well-paid. Again, note regional differences, with the rural pressure group the Countryside Alliance recently identifying the Lake District (16 per cent) and North Cornwall (10 per cent) as rural zones with high shares of their housing stock as second homes (see http://www.countryside-alliance.org/edu/housing.htm/ read on 31.5.01). Indicating where it feels government sentiments lie, a Rural Housing Trust (2000) press release of 5 October 2000, pointed out that while the national government made £21 million available for affordable rural housing in 1999–2000 it gave £150 million in council tax relief to second home owners.

This is simply icing on the cake. The real story of rural housing in England is essentially twofold. On the private, home-owner side, the issue is one of a general excess of demand over supply, with professional and managerial workers, whether in employment or in retirement, being particularly notable for their capacity to outbid others for scarce housing. Add to this a willingness, almost an internal drive, for those who already own rural homes to resist an increase in local housing numbers, even if the incomers would be from the professional and managerial classes (Cloke and Thrift, 1987; Murdoch and Marsden, 1994). Fuelling this fire is the land use planning system. This significantly reduces the prospect of new homes being added in small villages, restricting most growth to larger centres. The trend is toward a social exclusive countryside.

This tendency is reinforced by the second key issue in rural housing. This is the weakness of alternatives to owner-occupation. There is a private rental sector, but this is largely a hangover from the large landed estates of the past. As the fortunes of estates waned, and their employment of local workers fell, the usefulness of such properties declined (Mandler, 1997). Sales to owner-occupiers resulted (Bird, 1982; Bowler and Lewis, 1987). But whereas shortfalls in low-income housing were addressed through public sector provision in many cities, in most rural areas this tenure is less evident. Illustrative of this, just over 10 per cent of the rural housing stock is said to be in the public sector in England, compared with almost 21 per cent in urban centres (Chaney and Sherwood, 2000). The precise reasons for this would take a longer chapter than this to address. At one level some local political leaders were ideologically disinclined to support state provision, as well as seeing benefits accruing to 'their class' from not offering alternatives to private rental (Rose et al., 1976). At another level, biases in government allocation policies favoured cities in their applications for state housing (Hoggart, 1998).[5] Added to which, despite a legal requirement that local authorities respond to a recognised housing need, rural councils have not been aware of needs within their jurisdictions (Cloke *et al.*, 2001b). Whether the issue is unawareness or unwillingness to find out is another matter. What can be concluded is that residents in rural districts tend to expect a weak housing response from their local council (Cloke *et al.*, 2001a). Rural councils have, however, recognised inadequacies of provision. This is indicated by 130 rural districts applying for exemption from the provision of the 1980 Housing Act that tenants have an automatic right to purchase their state-owned home (Flynn, 1986). That the role of the national government figures large in eventual housing outcomes is made clear by only eighteen (partial) exemptions being granted. The result is that public sector dwellings, many constructed with special grants so they would be affordable for low-paid agricultural labourers, are now increasingly occupied by professional and managerial homeowners (Chaney and Sherwood, 2000). In short, the public sector and the private rental sector offer scant respite from aggressive aggrandisement by the profit-driven private housing market. Hardly surprisingly, rates of homelessness in rural areas have been held to be rising more rapidly than their urban counterparts since 1980 (Greve, 1991; Bramley, 1994).

Policy and strategy to address rural housing pressure

What are government responses to this? Here the rationale for policy has changed over time, but the long-term thrust of policy has reinforced the tendencies identified above. Take for instance the 1997 Labour Government's acceptance of spending targets set by the previous Conservative administration. According to the Rural Housing Trust (2000), this means that Labour's housing proposals do not foresee a return to 1996 construction levels for affordable rural housing until around 2006. Offering some insight on the under-provision this signifies, the Trust notes that even if 3,000 social housing units are built by 2004 this falls well short of the estimated need for 50,000 dwellings. Further biases in provision arise in expectations for smaller villages. Hence, the Labour Government's Planning Policy Guidance Note on housing explicitly directs that homes should be provided in areas where previously developed land is available (UK Department of the Environment, Transport and the Regions, 2000). This should be done while maintaining the green belt, with only limited new housing expected in villages. Even if villages get unexpected favour, these are to be the larger ones, as: 'The Government's policies for meeting new housing needs are based on the principles of focusing new development on existing towns and villages' (UK Department of the Environment, Transport and the Regions, 2001, para. 3.18). This rationale favours sustainability ideals and focuses development on settlements that offer a range of services. At this point the significance of your definition of rural becomes transparent. If rural is taken to be less than 1,000 inhabitants then many rural areas are excluded from the provision of new dwellings. This applies generally, but it is especially noteworthy for low-income housing, given the premium that accrues to small village homes on account of their 'protected' land use planning status. That the Labour Government is intent on ensuring that its objectives are implemented is apparent in new stipulations for housing development, such as the requirement that all proposals for more than 150 dwellings have to obtain ministerial approval (UK Department of the Environment, Transport and the Regions, 2000).

Welcome as some might see the environmental sustainability dimensions of this emphasis, the implications for villages are marked. Previously, local councils were instructed to predict demand for new housing and propose land-release to cater for this demand. This stipulation has been changed in significant ways, including the requirement that estimates build in an expectation that 'windfall' land sites become available (such as unexpected factory closures, whose land could be slated for new homes). For villages themselves new pressures are placed on local councils. As one example, if housing expansion is to take place in villages the council has to demonstrate that any extra housing will support services (i.e. enable them to stay in operation), as well as ensuring houses are sympathetic to local architectural styles. Moreover, for the principal mechanism for building low-cost homes in small villages – the so-called exceptions policy – councils must now show that there is a demonstrable lack of affordable housing (UK Department of the Environment, Transport and the Regions, 2000).

Appreciate this point. First, note that councils exert little effort to identify the magnitude and character of rural housing needs (Cloke *et al.*, 2001b). As the Tetlow and associates' survey (1996) found, only one-quarter of councils consulted rural interests on housing policy, although this is a national government requirement. Second, record that the exceptions policy, whereby local planning authorities can 'ignore' approved plans so low-income housing is built in small settlements, is not easy to implement. Reports from non-profit housing associations confirm this (Tetlow *et al.*, 1996), with the Herington and associates' (1995) investigation of exceptions policy recording that 81 per cent of local authorities faced difficulties securing new homes under this scheme. Illustrative of this, financial institutions often place a lower value on such dwellings, fearing restrictions on future occupants, which makes securing construction loans more troublesome, with some schemes even having to be abandoned (with the suggestion that this can cause housing associations to restrict social access to their rural homes (Bevan, 2000)). This problem is of heightened significance given that small schemes incur higher per-unit construction costs, with the primary national funding agency for social housing (the Housing Corporation) only making allowances for this in 1996–1997 (Elson *et al.*, 1996). Third, note that there are substantial differences in how local councils interpret national directives. This is seen for one measure that has been introduced to alleviate tense rural supply–demand relationships, which is to allow existing buildings to change usage, such as from productive activities into housing. As Elson and associates (1995) found, one-third of councils were imposing various 'presumption against' criteria on such usage transfers that limited the potential to address housing need.[6] Similarly, there are noteworthy differences in the ways local councils respond to settlements in 'green belts' around cities. In the south-east, where development pressure is highest, places with as many as 500 dwellings are often 'washed over' by green belt designations. This leads to new construction being resisted in such villages, with councils often interpreting this stipulation strictly (Elson *et al.*, 1996). However, in northern regions, where employment supply falls below job demand, in-filling in such settlements is widespread (Elson *et al.*, 1993). For how long will the national government allow such variation? With environmental objectives increasingly pressing on decisions about the location of new dwellings, the Government has intervened to ensure that it overviews 'large' construction decisions. This is not seen in direct interventions alone but also applies to directing the parameters governing housing construction. These parameters guide social housing providers toward little new construction, except in large settlements, with little impetus behind efforts to ensure there is a supply of affordable dwellings for low-income residents. At the same time, restrictions on new-build mean that house prices are rising rapidly, in many regions creating affordability problems even for those in full-time, white-collar employment.

Conclusions

To return to a point made earlier, the definition of 'rural' does bear on images of the intensity of rural housing pressures. If we adopt the lower figure offered by the UK Office of National Statistics (1997), so places of less than 1,000 inhabitants are 'rural', a somewhat different vision of rural housing problems emerges than that associated with the Countryside Agency's idea that rural means places of less than 10,000 people. Most obviously this is seen in the greater likelihood that settlements in this latter class will receive a share of social housing, much as Milbourne (1998) reports for central Wales, where larger local centres are the (almost exclusive) focus of new social housing. If rural is defined as places of up to 10,000 people, the net flow of low-income residents (or households with manual workers) from smaller toward larger villages constitutes an intra-rural movement, for many flows in this settlement size-range are local (e.g. Herington and Evans, 1979). In this framework, the magnitude of discriminations in rural housing markets are much less severe for the low-paid than if we define 'rural' as under 1,000 inhabitants. A bigger 'rural' problem is apparent if we use the 10,000 figure, with a greater under-supply of low-cost housing. With a 1,000 cut-off a professional and managerial takeover of the countryside comes across more strongly. Given that national agencies use these different delimitations of rurality, we need caution in comparing research results from their studies, as we do in interpreting what commentators define as 'the rural housing problem'. That said, given the high cost of housing in England, alongside the declining role of social housing (plus the status problems of this sector), no matter what definition is used, a key pressure on rural housing in England is the supply of quality, affordable housing. This problem is not restricted to the low-paid but also impacts on the aspirations of those in middle income brackets.

Built into this is a key geographical dimension. It is futile to assume that low-income housing can be provided easily in rural England in locations where social housing demand exists. As various studies have shown (Phillips and Williams, 1982; Richmond, 1985), many rural residents want a new home in the village they currently live in. But the nature of this demand is variable, which creates a real dilemma if authorities seek to over-provide for the mix of housing needs that arise (Mullins, 1993). The difficulty is that it is expensive to change housing provision to meet different needs (for large families, then single parents, then the elderly with special physical disability needs, for instance), but, with a small social housing stock, such changes will be required if people are to take up new tenancies where they already live. Such variability can be better catered for in larger centres, where more houses might exist, since variety can be built into dwelling supply. This is not feasible for schemes of (commonly) six-to-ten dwellings in small settlements. Moreover, while national governments put ideology or cost cutting a long way before responding to housing need (Flynn, 1986), the chances of such units surviving in the social housing realm are much reduced. More likely they will be snapped up by wealthier in-migrants who desire a rural home (Chaney and Sherwood, 2000). In effect, the response of government agencies toward the magnitude of low-income housing scarcity in rural areas has been limp. The Housing Corporation's Rural Programme illustrates this. Following criticism that the Corporation's allocation policy discriminates against small-scale housing developments (e.g. Warrington, 1994), a special Rural Programme was introduced in 1989 so smaller settlements could secure social housing units. However, in 1999–2000 the Programme only funded 955 rural units in the whole country, having never achieved a higher annual rate than 2,355 and only completing 16,670 dwellings in its eleven years in existence (Housing Corporation, 2001). Such a minimal response has barely slowed pressure on rural housing access for low-income residents. Market forces dominate

10.1 Detached homes being built in Lower Quinton, 2001 (Stratford-on-Avon District): S.J. Gallent.

10.2 A new development of mixed size units on the edge of Stratford-on-Avon: S.J. Gallent.

10.3 Recently built red-brick houses on the edge of Moreton Morrell, 2001 (Stratford-on-Avon District): S.J. Gallent.

rural housing access, with price discrimination intensified by the land use planning system. Although this intensity is regionally specific, in each region it is the relatively wealthy, whether through earnings or inheritance, that have privileged access to a rural home. This results both from the operation of private sector housing markets and from state policies.

Notes

1   This was not just an issue of regional inequity but of differentiation by house type. The politics of the short-term Conservative agenda embodied visions of restricting social housing to the 'deserved' needy. This led to an over-supply in sheltered housing (e.g. for the elderly). Despite the fact many councils changed entry criteria to fill these homes, Tinker *et al.* (1995) found 91 per cent of non-metropolitan districts, 96 per cent of London boroughs and all metropolitan boroughs in England had difficult-to-let sheltered housing schemes.

2   Parishes come in a variety of sizes, with their boundaries defined initially (and in many cases still) by ecclesiastical decisions. Some can be smaller than enumeration districts (which are used to collect the population census, comprising something like 200 households, although less in low density areas), others can be large, being NUTS5 areas in their own right, or even larger in towns and cities. The

Countryside Agency (1999: 39) defines a rural parish as that with a resident population of 10,000 or under, of which there are 9,677 in England.

3   Districts are NUTS4 zones. There were 296 non-metropolitan districts for the whole of England (and 67 boroughs/districts for metropolitan areas) at the time this definition was used. Acknowledging the messy situation that still exists, the Countryside Agency (1999: 39) rather unhelpfully indicates that: 'Rural districts can be classified in a variety of ways'.

4   Langton (2000) cites the House Builders' Federation as indicating that 58 per cent of new homes are already being built on such sites, with 70 per cent achieved by the largest builders. These figures contrast with the views of lobbying organisations and some academic evaluations, which hold that government targets for brownfield sites are unattainable (e.g. see Barclay, 1997).

5   Linked to this, even within rural districts the emphasis has clearly been on centralising provision, unlike the situation in the inter-war years. Thus, Tetlow and associates (1996) found that only 10 per cent of rural districts had policies to disperse social housing to villages in which there was housing need. For the vast majority, spatial dissonance between need and supply was barely commented upon (for case studies see Phillips and Williams, 1982; Richmond, 1985).

6   With an approval rate for re-using older buildings of about 90 per cent even in national parks, these stipulations are powerful in thwarting applications, and so the potential for building re-use.

Chapter 11
Scotland

Mark Shucksmith and Ed Conway

Introduction

Many of the issues identified by Hoggart in Chapter 10 in the context of England apply for Scotland too. Rural areas in Scotland, as in England, are affected by the globalisation of production and the move towards post-Fordist systems of production associated with flexible specialisation (Lipietz, 1987). A core of workers is highly paid, while others (perhaps elsewhere) are made 'flexible' through low wages, insecure contracts and casualisation. This has allowed the colonisation of many rural areas, whether by global capital penetrating local markets or by consumption interests. Much has been written about the rise of a rural professional and managerial 'service class' such that certain regions, notably the south-east of England, may be colonised by knowledge-workers at a distance from production activities. This phenomenon also exists around the major cities of Scotland. In attractive remoter areas too, retirement migration and distance-working may produce similar effects, though in less attractive (or ex-industrial) rural areas, with low wages and low rents, low-grade jobs may be all that can be attracted. Overall, the population of rural Scotland is growing while the cities are losing people, but this conceals wide variations and different processes operating at different scales. This migration also tends to be age-specific, with young people often leaving rural areas, and older families moving in. Swain (1999) sees this trend in rural areas of Western Europe as the 'supplanting of a traditional production-oriented dominant class of farmer by a new consumption and leisure-oriented dominant class of ex-urbanites', so breaking the identity of the rural with agriculture.

In the 1980s and 1990s Scotland also experienced similar changes in the role of the state. These changes are summarised by Cloke *et al.* (2001) as: reduced levels of spending; reductions in the power and responsibilities of local government; an increased role for the central state in controlling welfare spending; and marketisation of the delivery of welfare services: 'An important outcome of these forms of restructuring has been the complication of welfare provision and its delivery at the local level, which now involve a range of agencies drawn from public, private and voluntary sectors.' Although this may be seen as a peculiarly British experience, associated with Thatcherism from 1979, Jessop (1991, 1994) sees these changes in a broader political economic context, linked to the processes of globalisation, post-Fordism and flexible specialisation discussed above. He sees the provision of welfare as a key form of social regulation that meets sets of shifting economic needs: thus, emerging post-Fordist modes of production, and their associated flexible labour force, required new forms of welfare provision such that the Keynesian welfare state had to be replaced by what he calls a Schumpetarian workfare state. This tendency may therefore extend beyond England, Scotland and Wales to have a broader European resonance.

Similar processes therefore set the context for rural housing pressures in Scotland as in England, but there are significant differences. One cultural difference derives from public rented housing being the majority tenure only 30 years ago, with more than half the population of Scotland renting from local authorities. For this reason, public sector housing is still seen much less negatively north of the border. Another difference lies in the institutional structures and, until devolution, in the role of the Scottish Office as a bastion against the implementation of English initiatives against Scottish interests (Midwinter *et al.*, 1991). The potent memory of landlordism, in both rural and urban Scotland, is associated with a wariness of the private sector, more socialist values, and weaker anti-development interests. It would be unthinkable for rural England to have embraced land reform, let alone with the enthusiasm current in Scotland.

In rural Scotland, as in rural England, there is a predominance of owner-occupation and often (but not everywhere) the same 'expensive scarcity'. This was the clear conclusion of the series of rural housing market studies commissioned by Scottish Homes in 1990 (see Kirk and Shucksmith, 1990) and of a review of more recent evidence by Shucksmith *et al.* (1996a). Overall, 61 per cent of housing in rural[1] Scotland is owner-occupied, compared with 56 per cent in urban areas; and rural Scotland has a much smaller social rented sector (26 per cent compared with 38 per cent in urban areas). Since 1990 there has been an overall decline in both the private rented sector (from 15 to 13 per cent) and the social rented sector (from 29 to 26 per cent), the latter primarily due to the mandatory sale of council houses (Scottish Executive, 2000). The relative importance of the private market in allocating houses is one legacy of difference between rural and non-rural areas, and its concomitant, the lack of social housing, has been widely identified as the most important issue facing rural communities (see Shucksmith *et al.*, 1994a, 1996b).

Housing markets in rural areas are not 'free-markets', of course. On the demand side, the growing number of single-person households and the increase in the number of elderly people have heightened the demand for housing in most areas. In the more pressured rural areas these sources are augmented by the increased purchase of retirement and holiday homes, and/or by commuters seeking the perceived benefits of a rural lifestyle. It is on the supply-side, though, that regulation has the greatest impact, through the constraints on supply imposed by the planning system and by policies of urban containment (Hall *et al.*, 1973; Newby, 1985; Shucksmith, 1990a). Policy guidance presuming against permitting new housing in the countryside has been reinforced by the desire of some rural residents (often the most articulate and powerful) to preserve the countryside in its existing state, so that planning has become a political arena through which the interests of the most powerful are imposed on the weak. As Newby noted in 1985, before the term social exclusion had been coined:

> As prices inexorably rise, so the population which actually achieves its goal of a house in the country becomes more socially selective. Planning controls have therefore become – in effect if not in intent – instruments of social exclusivity.

The importance of land ownership constraints on housing provision in some rural areas of Scotland have also been noted, as an instance of market failure in land markets and thus in housing markets. Local monopolies in land markets are a particular source of social exclusion, and have been the subject of policy development by the Land Reform Policy Group.

The Scottish Executive is aware of these issues and makes the following comments in its recent policy statement (Scottish Executive, 2000: 64):

> The low levels of social housing in rural areas means that provision is generally limited to those regarded as in 'priority need' and research suggests that demand considerably exceeds supply. Pressures on the owner-occupied sector are associated with demands from those moving to live in rural areas, the improvement in the road network leading to the potential for more commuting and, to a lesser extent, from the demand for second and holiday homes. The effect of the steady levels of migration to rural Scotland has been to increase house prices, which coupled with the low wage levels of much rural employment, has served to exclude low income groups from the housing market.

Because of the overemphasis on owner-occupation and the concomitant lack of housing to rent, especially public housing, there is thus a lack of choice within rural housing markets, particularly for those who do not have the financial means to compete effectively within the private sector. For these households and individuals, the allocation of houses through the state and voluntary sectors is crucial to their chances of finding an affordable home. Analysis of council allocations and waiting lists in rural Scotland (Shucksmith, 1990a) has identified those most favoured by the application of needs-based allocation criteria (families with children) and those most likely to be excluded (young, single people, young couples and to a lesser extent older people because of the shortage of small houses owned by rural councils.)

Of course, these must be considered in conjunction with the allocation processes of the voluntary sector (i.e. housing associations). Increasingly, state responsibilities for social housing provision in rural areas are being transferred to the third sector, namely housing associations, which have been asked to replace the local state as the primary provider of social housing in rural areas. In many cases, voluntary organisations who assume such responsibilities become increasingly dependent upon the state for funding, and may become more closely regulated by the central state agencies as a condition of funding. One result of this is that they become more and more like state agencies themselves, adopting the discourse of business plans, efficiency gains and the like. This has certainly happened to housing associations (Shucksmith and Watkins, 1990) whose central aim of meeting housing needs (especially special needs) has sat uneasily at times beside the priorities of their funding agency (Scottish Homes), particularly over the level of rents to be charged (leverage of private finance) and the balance between the affordable rented programme and building for low-cost home ownership. Allocation policies have also been subject to regulation, and the tendency now is towards waiting lists operated jointly with the council. In Scotland, as in England, there is considerable pressure from central government on councils to transfer their stock to housing associations.

It was widely perceived by respondents in Shucksmith *et al.*'s study (1994a, 1996b) that the state allocation system together with the operation of the private market limited the options for local people wishing to stay in a rural area and especially affected newly formed households. Young families and single-person households were frequently seen as being groups with the most restricted housing choice in rural areas. As a consequence of high uptake of the right to buy in many rural areas, there has been a considerable reduction in the number of social housing units available. This compounds problems for those who do not have the financial means to enter the private housing market.[2]

Taken together with supply-side constraints due to planning and land ownership, the demands for rural housing from commuters, retirement buyers and holidaymakers, lead to problems of affordability for many in private markets for rural housing. Meanwhile the social housing stock has diminished for a variety of reasons already described by Hoggart in Chapter 10, leaving few options for many potential households in rural Scotland, so contributing towards social exclusion, and indeed towards spatial exclusion.

Apart from these issues of housing pressure, there is also a problem of the quality of housing in rural Scotland (unlike rural England). A high proportion of housing of 'Below Tolerable Standard' (BTS) can be found, many of them damp and insufficiently maintained, largely in the private sector. In 1990 there were an estimated 24,700 BTS properties in rural Scotland, with rural households being three times more likely to live in a BTS home than the Scottish average (Scottish Homes, 1990a). The total estimated cost of repairs was £412 million. In rural Scotland, '1 in 8 dwellings experience dampness; 1 in 4 experience condensation; and 1 in 4 have poor energy ratings. A higher proportion of rural housing was built before 1919' (Scottish Executive, 2000). Previous efforts to tackle rural disrepair had been less effective than in urban areas largely because no appropriate strategy had been developed or pursued. Elderly and poor households were most likely to be living in damp or otherwise unsuitable dwellings (Church of Scotland, 1988) and many were unable to afford the cost of the improvements needed. Private landlords were often reluctant to carry out improvements due to the large capital outlay required and the poor returns.

Key issues emerging in pressured rural areas of Scotland are therefore:

- supply-side constraints, notably planning regulation and monopoly land ownership;
- increasing demand, both from external sources and from smaller household size;
- the declining stock of affordable social housing, both because of the right to buy and because of severe cutbacks in public investment; and
- the small and expensive private rented sector, which is also declining.

Development of a rural policy

Increasing recognition of the issues identified above led to calls for the development of distinct policies and instruments to tackle the problems that were facing rural areas. Interestingly, the 1987 White Paper on Housing in Scotland (which preceded the 1988 Housing Act, creating Scottish Homes[3]) offered little in the way of change for rural housing. It did acknowledge that the problems of rural areas were different to those in urban areas, and stated that policies 'will be developed, with due regard to the circumstances of rural areas' (Scottish Development Department (SDD), 1987). The paper also noted that the contribution of Scottish Homes in rural areas was likely to focus upon the extension of housing associations into those areas, and on co-operating with local authorities in the development of improved strategic planning (SDD, 1987). It is argued in this chapter that the formation of Scottish Homes allowed Ministers to deflect pressure for the Government to address rural housing problems on to that agency.

In 1988, in addition to continued lobbying from Rural Forum and Shelter (see Alexander *et al.*, 1988), the Church of Scotland Independent Inquiry into Scottish Housing called for the recognition by Government of the special problems of housing in rural areas, through: 'the adoption of a pluralistic strategy to increase provision of low-cost housing, including adequate subsidies for the provision of social housing by both housing associations and local authorities' (Church of Scotland, 1988). In its response the Government noted that it found common ground on several issues. Of particular relevance to rural housing was the statement that 'It is the Government's intention to give Scottish Homes, as one of its early priorities, the task of formulating a rural housing strategy within which agencies can contribute to meeting housing need in its widest sense, in the rural areas' (The Scottish Office, 1988). It was this statement which required Scottish Homes to address rural housing issues, albeit with reluctance on the part of their Board.

In January 1990, Scottish Homes issued a consultative paper entitled 'The Rural Housing Challenge' (Scottish Homes, 1990a). The paper identified a series of principles which would guide the development of its rural policy. These included: working in partnership with other agencies and housing authorities; the development of a new approach rather than merely revamping an inappropriate urban response; that the approach should reflect varying local circumstances; that the policy should contribute to broad rural development objectives as well as more specific housing goals; a policy of support for rural development through working with rural communities; to consider affordability as well as development costs; and that investment and resources should be directed to where they are most needed and to those who most need them (thus requiring a better information base). The paper also identified what Scottish Homes saw as four key challenges in rural housing. These were: increasing supply; improving conditions; ensuring affordability; and tackling tenant participation and involvement as part of community development. This analysis was generally supported by those responding to the consultation.

The Rural Policy

Following this consultation period, Scottish Homes' Rural Policy was published in September 1990. It was the very first policy to be announced by the agency, and in fact preceded the development of their own strategic aims and objectives. The document reiterated the principles underlying the delivery of the Rural Policy, and the four key challenges identified in the consultation document.

In terms of the first key challenge, that of increasing the supply of housing in rural areas, the policy stated that Scottish Homes could only contribute to housing provision through private sector bodies and identified housing associations and landowners as appropriate vehicles through which to do so. The policy also specified the range of grant mechanisms that Scottish Homes had at its disposal. Housing Association Grant (HAG) was available to registered housing associations for the provision of both rented and owner-occupied (or shared ownership) accommodation. HAG was also available in urban areas, but Scottish Homes had clearly taken note of calls for higher levels of grant in rural areas (see Shucksmith and Watkins, 1990), stating that:

> We will use the existing flexibility within the Scottish Housing Association Grant (HAG) procedures to consider higher levels of grant, for example where it can be demonstrated that there are additional justifiable costs of site acquisition, servicing and procurement in rural areas.
>
> (Scottish Homes, 1990)

Grants for Rent or Ownership (GRO-Grants) were available to private sector bodies and developers to help reduce the costs of development, and so the price of housing for the consumer. The Rural Policy document proposed an additional set of GRO grants consisting of awards to individuals to build their own home and assistance with infrastructure costs, which later became known as Rural Home Ownership Grants, or RHOGs. In order to tackle the problem of poor conditions, the policy noted that Scottish Homes had further powers to award Improvement Grants for private properties in need of repair. These powers paralleled those of local authorities, however, and so support was instead to be given to agencies employing project workers in Care and Repair initiatives. These involved the provision of advice, assistance with grant applications and personal finance, and was particularly aimed at elderly households. Scottish Homes undertook to encourage additional organisations to participate in Care and Repair projects, subject to the findings of an evaluation. (Scottish Homes, 1990b) The policy also noted the possibility of assisting landlords to improve houses for rent, or let them on repairing leases.

The key issue of ensuring affordability identified in the Rural Housing Challenge was broadened in the Rural Policy document to become 'improving access' to housing. The document made a number of suggestions in this area, focusing on extending the range and variety of housing options. These included promoting the expansion of new suppliers, both small local and major national developers. Houses were also to be made more affordable by reducing the costs of development. Measures included: consideration of higher HAG rates for rural housing associations (as noted above); consideration by government and local authorities of the disposal of publicly owned land for less than full market price if suitable for the development of social housing; and finally measures under planning regulations. The policy recommended the Scottish Office consider issuing guidance to planning authorities in areas with particular supply constraints, that local plans might indicate that 'exception sites' could be released for low-cost housing for local needs in addition to the provision made in the plan for housing demand. The use of Section 106 agreements,[4] as operated in England and Wales, to reduce housing costs was also suggested (see Gallent, 1997 for a discussion of Section 106 measures in England and Wales).

The document made few references to tenant and community involvement, the fourth key issue identified by the Rural Housing Challenge. It was noted that tenants and local communities had not really chosen to become involved in the consultation process, and that this was an area requiring further development. Supporting economic development and partnership were considered as underlying principles. Again, few references were made in the policy to the links with economic development, aside from the consideration of the experimental provision of workshops related to housing developments. The policy stated that Scottish Homes would 'work in partnership with others', that they would 'work closely with local authorities', that they would 'strive to work with communities in community-based projects' and that they would contribute to more general rural development objectives by 'working with the agencies responsible for social, economic and environmental development' (Scottish Homes, 1990b). The document did not, however, state how this was to be achieved. One notable exception to this was the considerable prominence given in the policy to the concept of a local housing agency, an organisation which it suggested could provide a range of housing services within local communities in co-operation with housing authorities. The idea was that almost any private sector organisation might establish such an agency, as long as it could provide a broad enough range of services and that it had a genuine basis in the community (Shucksmith, Conway and Henderson, unpublished) Such agencies would be able to work together with economic development agencies, and it was envisaged that a network of local housing agencies might be established. The potential for local housing agencies to contribute to involvement of tenants and communities in the broader rural development process was also discussed.

As the document itself noted, the Rural Policy was very much a first step. The policy can also be seen as an attempt by an agency to make itself sensitive to the rural context, something to be applauded given the urban nature of many of its challenges and pressures, and the lack of rural policy emanating from other bodies such as Scottish Enterprise. The paper announced that a series of demonstration projects were to be established and ten Rural Demonstration Areas (RDAs) were announced to act as test beds in which the new instruments could be piloted in a variety of rural housing situations. A further aim of the RDAs was to demonstrate the commitment of Scottish Homes to the implementation of the Rural Policy. As part of the experiment, a monitoring and evaluation exercise was undertaken to assess the effectiveness of the new instruments and their applicability to other parts of rural Scotland. This was undertaken by the University of Aberdeen and CR Planning and provided the first opportunity to review the mechanisms within the Rural Policy. The results of the exercise were published in 1994 (Shucksmith *et al.*, 1994b), and suggested that overall the RDA test-beds had demonstrated that these instruments were effective at increasing supply and ensuring affordability. However, the instruments were less successful in improving house conditions or encouraging residents' participation, and the underlying principle of economic development had not been effectively addressed. The general conclusion of the RDA evaluation was that the broad objectives of the Rural Policy were not always fully translated into operational objectives, although the approach was effective in encouraging innovation and piloting new initiatives, and also for providing lessons to steer the way forward. The study made a number of recommendations in relation to specific mechanisms, and in particular with regard to more effective partnership working. One of the key recommendations was that home ownership policies should be complemented with investment targeted at those who were unable or unwilling to aspire to owner-occupation.

The review of the Rural Policy

In 1996 Scottish Homes commissioned the Arkleton Centre for Rural Development Research, University of Aberdeen, to undertake a review of its Rural Policy, in the light not only of experience but also of two other events: the publication of a White Paper, 'Rural Scotland: People, Prosperity and Partnership'; and the reorganisation of the structure of local government in Scotland. The first stage of the policy review was to examine relevant prior and current research and evaluation work. Together with an examination of quantitative outputs, this provided a focus for the main part of the research required by Scottish Homes, which was a consultation process with stakeholder organisations and individuals, including end client groups who were invited to contribute to the process from four case study areas. This methodology placed some limits on the type of information collected in that, apart from the statistical analysis, much of it was restricted to stakeholders' and consumers' perceptions of Scottish Homes and the Rural Policy. These perceptions were not always supported by other evidence.

The review focused on the four objectives and the underlying principles of the 1990 Rural Policy, but incorporated a new principle of sustainable regeneration. Views were sought as to whether Scottish Homes had achieved these objectives, and whether the underlying principles had in fact guided the delivery of the policy. The review was also able to examine whether lessons and recommendations highlighted in the monitoring and evaluation of the RDAs experiment in 1994 had been taken on board.

The first stage of the review suggested that the 1990 analysis of the Rural Housing Challenge was accurate and still relevant. The intensity of the problem had worsened, however, with a further diminution of the social rented stock, increases in waiting lists and homelessness (Corbett, 1996). The evidence suggested diminishing housing choice for those unable to afford home ownership. Nevertheless there was a perception that Scottish Homes' policy had made a significant and positive impact, with the main constraints on rural housing being outwith the control of Scottish Homes (for example Government investment constraints, the imposition of VAT on the rehabilitation of property, planning restrictions and contemporary pressures on rural housing markets). The policy review noted that some respondents felt Scottish Homes should be trying to lobby Government to implement changes in these areas. Further, a number of respondents suggested that national policies and Government priorities (for example increasing owner-occupation) were the driving force in rural practice, and over-rode the Rural Policy.

Increasing supply

In terms of increasing supply, the review highlighted that Scottish Homes had invested over £300 million in rural areas since the start of the Rural Policy, resulting in over 10,000 unit starts of new or improved homes. They had also progressively increased the level of investment in rural areas each year (until the 1996–1997 programme which proposed a 20 per cent cut in rural spending, compared to an overall budget reduction of 14.7 per cent). At the time of the policy review, 28.8 per cent of Scotland's households were living in rural areas and this proportion was increasing. Only 20.2 per cent of Scottish Homes' total expenditure, however, was going to rural areas. This differential raised one of the most important questions in the review, which was how is the balance of investment in rural areas determined? Despite enquiries, the review was unable to identify any transparent rationale articulated by Scottish Homes.

There was also an issue about the composition of the programme as between rented housing and low-cost home ownership (LCHO). In 1993–1994 and 1994–1995, just over half of Scottish Homes' investment in rural areas was

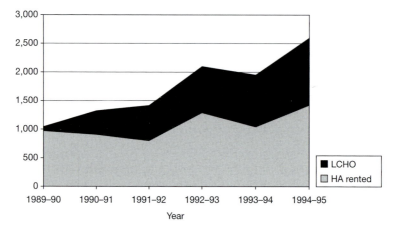

11.1 Housing Associations and Low Cost Home Ownership in rural Scotland.
Source: Scottish Homes

through HAG for rent. Around a third supported various forms of LCHO, and the remainder assisted market rented properties. The proportion spent on LCHO had increased substantially over the review period, as shown in Figure 11.1, partly because of the Conservative Government's emphasis on promoting home owner-ship and partly to lever more private funds into rural housebuilding. Stakeholders were unanimous in thinking that the tenure balance in investment was inappro-priate, and that greater emphasis should be placed on housing for rent, and less on LCHO.

A major impact of the rural policy was felt to be the increased involvement of developers in the provision of rural housing for LCHO or market rents, through GRO grant assistance. There was general support for the GRO mech-anism, although some developers and landowners were keen to see the development of a similar mechanism which would facilitate private sector devel-opment of affordable rented housing. As was found during the RDA evaluation, the RHOG programme remained very small and its uptake was uneven and concentrated in few localities. Concerns highlighted at the time of the RDA eval-uation continued to be relevant, for example space restrictions and a lack of flexibility with regard to economic development criteria. Two other important issues raised by informants to the review included the crucial role of a local contact in promoting the grant; and the inappropriateness of the mechanism for low-income households. Land availability was also a problem, and the use of Section 106 (s.50) agreements to try and reduce land costs had not been pursued, despite earlier recommendations in the RDA evaluation report.

Improving house conditions

The RDA evaluation had found that little progress had been made in the RDAs towards the objective of improving house conditions. This finding was echoed in the Rural Policy Review, except through Scottish Homes' support for Care and Repair projects. Activity in this area expanded markedly during the three years prior to the Policy Review amounting to a total repair programme of almost £8 million. The success of the programmes depended on Scottish Homes working together with local authorities, who contributed about 65 per cent of capital costs from their non-housing revenue account improvement and repair grants (non-HRA), while Scottish Homes supported the associated staff costs. However, council non-HRA funding was seriously under threat at the time of the Policy Review, so posing a significant threat to the future of Care and Repair projects. Care and Repair was felt by repondents to the Policy Review to have made a major contribution to improving the quality of housing in rural Scotland, with the benefits of schemes extending beyond housing to Care in the Community policies and economic development. The potential loss of this scheme was a matter of the utmost concern.

Other Scottish Homes activity in improving conditions centred around the Rural Empty Properties Grant (REPG), which assisted private landowners to bring empty properties back into use as affordable housing. The Policy Review found that the impact of the REPG was limited, although the grant was only extended nationally at the end of 1995. Suggestions as to how Scottish Homes might further approach the matter of housing conditions included enabling housing associations to purchase private property and renovate it for rent. HAG targets were said to militate against this at present.

Accessibility

Gaps in terms of customers targeted by the available mechanisms were identified by informants across household types, particularly low-income households who fell outside the housing benefit qualification criteria. These were mainly young single households on low-wage incomes. Homelessness was acknowledged to be a serious and worsening problem, but the lack of factual information indicated a need for further research to investigate the nature and scale of the problem. Geographical targeting was also highlighted as an issue by respondents, who sought a clearer articulation of how Scottish Homes' investment was distributed across areas.

A further issue was the lack of advice and information about housing options available to people in rural areas. The difficulty of providing a local information and/or advice service in rural areas was highlighted by the review, some respondents suggesting that elderly households were particularly disadvantaged. (See also Shucksmith *et al.*, 1996a). A local contact was seen as crucial, although this has obvious resource implications, and emphasised the need for joint working and sharing of resources by housing providers.

Community involvement

Increasing resident participation and involvement was seen by respondents to the Policy Review as being the hardest objective to achieve, and the one which has been least successfully met since the introduction of the Rural Policy. This was partly because it was not clearly defined, as was noted in the RDA evaluation. The review suggested that this objective should be renamed 'community involvement' as this was a better representation of what Scottish Homes were trying to achieve, and that this should be pursued in partnership with other agencies. One way in which this had been addressed in practice was through the establishment and support of local housing associations and local housing agencies. These two types of body had enabled a greater level of community involvement, although some respondents felt there was still considerable scope for more local housing associations. It was felt that local housing associations were not only more rooted in their communities but also participated in joint working at the local level and to engage in local partnership activity. Large housing associations were seen as less able to achieve local involvement, but it was suggested that these associations could act as umbrella bodies for smaller associations, supporting them through a 'constellation model' (Shucksmith and Watkins, 1990).

Partnership

The Policy Review noted that a partnership approach had underpinned much of the work undertaken by Scottish Homes in rural areas. The extent to which this had been the case had varied considerably across Scotland but had included, for example, the drawing up of strategic agreements between Scottish Homes and local authorities as well as with national economic development agencies. A wider implementation of the partnership approach was seen by many as being essential to the future operation of Scottish Homes' activities in rural areas. This was particularly so given the emphasis placed on partnership activity in the Conservative Government's Rural White Paper for Scotland and in subsequent labour policy statements. A number of areas for future joint working with organisations such as local authorities, local enterprise companies (LECs) and others were highlighted by respondents, including the provision of information and advice, common waiting lists, and the adoption of a multi-sectoral approach to rural regeneration. Respondents felt that there had been little activity in relation to economic development since the introduction of the Rural Policy, with a few notable exceptions, although the principle had been accepted by Scottish Homes. Given that strategic agreements had been reached with national agencies it was suggested that more effort had to take place in networking at the local level so that LECs and Scottish Homes, and indeed other agencies, could grasp opportunities for synergy.

Sustainable regeneration

The lack of clarity as to what Scottish Homes meant by the third underlying principle of sustainable regeneration was raised as an issue by most respondents to the Policy Review. As such it was difficult to establish whether this principle had underpinned the work of Scottish Homes in practice. Most respondents interpreted it as meaning sustaining rural communities, 'keeping people in rural areas', and taking a more holistic approach to housing development. This view is consistent with the current Government's policy objectives for rural Scotland which have sustainable development as a central theme, and which incorporate economic, social and environmental aspects of sustainability (The Scottish Office, 1997). In these terms, some respondents felt there was little evidence of Scottish Homes' commitment to this principle on the ground, and that its proper pursuit would require a shift away from HAG target-determined decisions and the development of broader targets which valued the safeguarding of a local school or post-office, for example. There is a general issue here about the difficulties of reconciling such performance targets with 'joined-up' government. Interestingly, the review noted that Scottish Homes staff themselves had no shared or common understanding of the term 'sustainable regeneration'. A point articulated clearly during the consultation was that if Scottish Homes were to pursue the objectives of supporting community development and sustainable regeneration seriously then they might reasonably be expected to commit funds and staff to assist communities to develop their own housing solutions.

The conclusion to the Policy Review stated that overall the Rural Policy was seen to have had an important and valuable impact in rural Scotland, notwithstanding the worsening housing problems in rural areas. Apart from relabelling the 'resident participation' objective and clarification of the 'sustainable regeneration' principle, the objectives and underlying principles of the Rural Policy were considered to be appropriate for the immediate future. It was felt that the most important of the issues emerging concerned the distribution of investment and the practical implementation of the Rural Policy.

Rural Policy Statement 1998

Scottish Homes issued a revised policy statement in 1998 (Scottish Homes, 1998), in the light of Labour's election victory, a new national Scottish Homes Strategy for 1997–2000 and the Arkleton Centre's Policy Review. The statement recast the agency's rural objectives to fit within its new national strategy, and responded to many of the findings from the Policy Review. Notably Scottish Homes moved to redress the over-emphasis placed on investment in LCHO. While the agency will continue to invest in LCHO projects, 'Within available resources, we will now place greater emphasis on the provision of affordable rented housing in rural Scotland'. Further, the document noted that in terms of the issue of land availability, Scottish Homes are considering how it may play a more pro-active role in relation to land use planning at both national and regional levels, including the use of its, as yet unused, compulsory purchase powers.

In terms of addressing housing conditions in rural areas the policy statement renewed Scottish Homes' commitment to the Care and Repair programme. The statement also noted that the agency would acknowledge the crucial role of local authorities in funding improvement and repair work, and work closely with them in a number of key areas such as the identification of ways to assist lower income owner-occupiers to fund repairs to their properties (together with the private sector); and the development of strategies to improve housing conditions in the private rented sector. This latter approach included a re-evaluation of the REPG and other mechanisms.

The policy statement renewed the agency's commitment to partnership at the national, regional and local levels. Of particular interest is that housing associations and voluntary organisations operating in rural areas will be invited 'where appropriate, to represent our interests on partnerships' as suggested in the Policy Review. Further, the strategy states that 'we will seek to achieve real community participation in these partnerships'. This is to be achieved through a number of initiatives including: the publication of a good practice guide for housing practitioners which draws upon the experiences of tenant and community participation experiences throughout rural Scotland in the 1990s; giving consideration to awarding grants to support services for community regeneration initiatives; and supporting community involvement in achieving both housing solutions and the broader objectives of creating and developing sustainable communities. Even at this stage, the new Government wished community participation to be given greater prominence in Scottish Homes' activities. Further, in line with the Government's broader rural policy (Scottish Office, 1997), the concept of sustainable regeneration was now to be interpreted as developing sustainable rural communities, rather than focusing on housing provision exclusively. This is not to say that sustainable 'development' has been ignored – energy efficiency and appropriate building design are also given prominence in the policy statement. The point is that these concepts have been clarified and given much greater emphasis in as far as they relate to the rural policy.

While a good policy statement can never be a substitute for policy implementation, Scottish Homes had attempted to address at least some of the concerns raised by the Rural Policy Review, as well as the imperatives and objectives of the new Labour Government.

The most important question raised by the Policy Review, that of exactly how the allocation of investment for rural areas is calculated, still remained unanswered. The policy statement was defensive on this matter, stating that:

> Scottish Homes current resource allocation process is based upon a coherent and comprehensive planning framework, which reflects the National Strategy and direction . . . Scottish Homes' investment programme is a balance between 'top-down' and 'bottom-up' influences. It is informed by Government policy and objectives; the Board's strategy and stated investment priorities; ministerial direction on priorities and the resources available taking into account committed expenditure. In addition, the programme allocation is informed by existing partnership agreements, the capacity of the market to assimilate housing investment and increasingly the willingness of partners to subscribe to a holistic approach to housing investment. At a local level, priorities and projects are informed by a rigorous analysis of local housing markets to identify needs and demands. Judgement will always be a part of any resource allocation process.

The impression that there remains no clear rationale is encouraged by the announcement that 'we are currently developing a resource allocation system' based on indicators of social exclusion and performance criteria, for introduction in 1999–2000. Despite the urban bias of many such indicators (Shucksmith, 1990b), the document asserts that 'we will ensure that rural areas are not disadvantaged by the nature of the resource allocation method adopted'.

This impression is further confirmed when one examines the process by which the planned level of Scottish Homes' investment in rural housing was determined that year. Internal documents reveal that Scottish Homes' Board intended to make disproportionate cuts to their rural programme in 1998–1999, but that, as a result of heavy lobbying by Shelter, Rural Forum and the Rural and Islands Forum of Housing Associations, the Housing Minister (Calum MacDonald, MP for the Western Isles) directed them to maintain the rural share of their programme.

Devolution: towards Communities Scotland

Following the establishment of a Scottish Parliament, the Labour/Liberal Democrat coalition issued a further White Paper, *Rural Scotland: A New Approach*, in 2000. This acknowledged the importance of affordable housing in rural areas and announced:

- an increase in Scottish Homes' development spending in rural areas by over 10 per cent to provide 1,550 new and improved homes, of which 1,250 were to be for social renting;
- new research into the availability of land for housing in rural areas; and
- a new 'Rural Partnership for Change Initiative' anticipating a suspension of social housing tenants' right to buy in pressured rural housing markets in the forthcoming Housing Bill.

The Rural Partnership for Change consisted of two strands. A rural pilot project, taken forward by a local partnership led by Highland Council, examined new and innovative ways of tackling the problems of pressured rural housing markets. To achieve this it had access to £10 million of additional funding over three years. Alongside this, a National Steering Group, chaired by Scottish Homes, monitored the pilot and, drawing also on the experience of other countries, considered how the lessons might be applied across Scotland. The report of this group is unpublished, but clearly offered the desired support for the Housing (Scotland) Act, 2001 to include powers to suspend the right to buy in pressured rural areas for five years, as well as reducing the levels of discount substantially in all areas and exempting registered social landlords that are charities, co-operative housing associations and special needs housing.

Apart from this welcome measure, the Housing Act contained two other principal provisions. The first was the replacement of secure and assured tenancies with a new Scottish Secure Tenancy which applies to council, Scottish Homes and housing association tenants alike. This is intended not only to simplify legislation but also to facilitate stock transfers from councils and Scottish Homes to associations.

The second principal measure was the replacement of Scottish Homes by a new executive agency, Communities Scotland, under direct Ministerial control and with a much broader remit for regeneration and community empowerment, in addition to improving the effectiveness of housing investment. Over time its resources, amounting to £400 million in 2002–2003, will be shifted from housing investment towards area-based regeneration, including social inclusion partnerships and neighbourhood renewal. The new agency has only recently published its draft corporate plan, and it is unclear how this transformation will affect rural areas and rural housing. But most of Communities Scotland's early statements betray a prime concern with neighbourhoods, an essentially urban concept, encouraging the belief that people in rural areas will once again be the poor relations.

Conclusions

This chapter has presented a brief outline of how a policy for rural housing in Scotland has evolved over the last ten to fifteen years in response to a variety of factors, including lobbying from concerned groups and individuals, research and evaluation work and changing government policies. A number of conclusions may be drawn from this experience.

One notable aspect is the extent to which policy has been informed by research. The original 1990 policy was developed in response to a Church of Scotland report (itself research-based) but was formulated with the aid of nine rural housing market studies and a part-time academic adviser. The continuing development of the policy was then informed both by the testing of instruments and ideas in the RDAs, and the evaluation of these, and then by the Policy Review itself. Unsurprisingly, Scottish Homes has taken selective notice of research findings, quoting conclusions it wished to hear and ignoring some others, but it cannot be said to have been uninformed. As such, this offers an interesting case study of the interaction between research and policy, and a model for policy development in the future.

A central issue, and a perennial one, concerns the influence of research on policy, even in such a case as this where the two have articulated closely. Even from the inside, however, the strength of this influence is very hard to judge. There is evidently a dialectical process through which researchers frame their recommendations and even their research questions in the light of the politically possible, while at the same time what is politically possible may be altered partly by research findings. In this case, there were certain policy options which were imperative to the Conservative Government, whatever the research evidence (e.g. promoting home ownership as against rented housing), and others which were unacceptable to Scottish Homes Board (e.g. resourcing growing rural areas to the same extent per capita as declining urban areas). Outside these taboo areas, however, there appeared to be scope for research to inform policy, both in problem definition and in helping to formulate appropriate forms of intervention. Nevertheless, the influence of political changes and pressure groups may well have been stronger.

Another issue is whether an agency like Scottish Homes should have a distinct rural policy: Scottish Enterprise, for example, argues that all its policies are both rural and urban, but it is widely perceived as being insensitive and inactive towards rural Scotland. The experience of Scottish Homes' development of a rural policy is that this made the agency more aware and more sensitive towards the specific problems of rural areas, and that this was recognised by its partners and clients. This offers a lesson to other agencies working in Scotland, especially in the context of the Labour Government's commitment to 'joined-up policies' initiated by local communities in pursuit of sustainable rural development. Communities Scotland is well placed to engage in this community-based, territorial approach to rural policy, but whether it looks beyond problem neighbourhoods in urban areas may depend upon Ministerial direction.

Whatever the virtues of Scottish Homes' policy development, however, it is apparent that housing problems in rural Scotland have worsened over the last 10–15 years. Scottish Homes has not been able to offset the loss of council houses through its expanding programme, with the result that opportunities and choices for lower-income households in rural areas have diminished. It would be churlish to blame Scottish Homes for this, since the right to buy dates from 1980, the policy of curtailing council housebuilding was announced by the Conservative Government in its 1987 White Paper before the establishment of Scottish Homes, and the resources available to Scottish Homes have been inadequate to the task. What can be argued is that the development of Scottish Homes' Rural Policy deflected political pressure from the Government, who might otherwise have found it harder to damage housing opportunities in rural Scotland quite so systematically.

Acknowledgements: In addition to the two present authors, Mairi Henderson and staff of CRPlanning worked on the Evaluation of Scottish Homes' Rural Demonstration Areas, and Polly Chapman worked on the Review of Scottish Homes' Rural Policy. The authors acknowledge their input and are grateful for their contributions. We also acknowledge the help of the project advisory groups, and of Scottish Homes' staff. As usual, however, the present authors alone are responsible for any errors or omissions in this chapter.

Notes

1   Hoggart's arguments about the importance of the definition of 'rural' to the nature of the processes at work apply just as much to Scotland too, as discussed later. This 'official' definition of rural Scotland is based on local authority areas.

2   Considerable concern was expressed within rural Scotland about the future loss of social housing in rural areas as a result of the Housing (Scotland) Act, 2000 which

establishes a Single Social Tenancy. Concerns that this would open up housing association stocks in rural areas to the right to buy led to amendments to the bill in the Scottish Parliament.

3   Scottish Homes, the national housing agency for Scotland, was created by the 1988 Housing (Scotland) Act, taking in both the Housing Corporation in Scotland and the Scottish Special Housing Association. In November 2001 this became Communities Scotland, with a broader remit, particularly in relation to regeneration (see later).

4   Section 50 agreements in Scotland.

Chapter 12
Wales

W.J. Edwards

Introduction

The last thirty years have seen three phases of engagement with planning and housing issues in rural Wales. Each of these phases indicates *how* the rural housing problem has been defined, *what* housing pressures are evident and *how* these might be addressed. Central to such engagement has been a rising concern to prioritise *local* needs and the hope that, with the new National Assembly for Wales, *local* policies will be developed to address regional circumstances.

National housing concerns

Prior to 1980 the consolidation of the role of planning and housing departments through local state intervention played a key role in directing concern over rural housing issues. Their concerns were with the inadequacy and improvement of the existing ageing stock, the containment of new-build and the development of local authority housing. During this period, depopulation of younger and more active residents and the *in situ* ageing of local residents provided the opportunity for a steady flow of new residents from outside Wales (Champion and Watkins, 1991). Some arrived for retirement in coastal and more remote locations, other younger in-migrants chose smallholdings (as part of the 1960s and 1970s counterculture), while isolated or village properties were favoured for second home purchase (Bollom, 1978; Davies and O'Farrell, 1981). As this process gathered pace during the 1970s it generated a growing debate, culturally founded, over the consequences and how they should be managed or resisted (Welsh Language Society, 1971).

The second period from 1980 to the mid-1990s was marked by central government's emasculation of local housing through the encouragement of 'right to buy' opening doors for many into subsidised ownership (Milbourne, 1998). Such changes precipitated a vociferous demand to relax centralised planning control on private development in the remoter countryside (Cloke, 1995). There was, as a consequence, increased funding of housing association provision as registered social landlords, and an emerging, enabling 'partnership' role between local authorities and the 'third sector' (Gallent, 1997, 1998). Increasing concern became apparent over the unequal competition for rural housing that was emerging, the changing mix of tenures that were available and the low levels of stock provided by these new agencies (Cloke and Edwards, 1985). This led to an intense debate over the priority that should be given to local needs, affordability and to the cultural and community expectations implicit in policy (Dyfed County Council, 1989; DoE, 1996; Tewdwr-Jones *et al.*, 1998).

The third and current phase runs from the mid 1990s to the present. Although past trends continue, this period has seen a greater focus on regeneration, while the referendum vote and the emergence from 1998–1999 of the National Assembly, raised hopes that a new policy agenda addressing rural needs might emerge (Welsh Office, 1997a; Devolution Unit, 1999; National Assembly, 1999c). However, notwithstanding the intention to introduce new Welsh Planning Policy Guidance (PPG) and Technical Advice Notes (TANs) addressing planning and housing issues, at the time of writing, few have emerged. It is also interesting, given the current partnership rhetoric so dominant in Wales, particularly given the success in obtaining EC Objective 1 funding, that there is a noticeable 'silence' over the impact on housing of that regeneration process. This current phase has seen a continuing pressure to prioritise the local, which highlights the long difficulties of meeting local affordability requirements and cultural needs in a market-driven housing system.

Recently, the Welsh Assembly Government has defined a national housing strategy for Wales and many issues addressed in this strategy cover expected ground. Emphasis is placed on the age of stock (36 per cent built before 1919), the high level of investment necessary in the renovation of both local authority and private properties and the need to maintain housing provision across all sectors. Particular attention is given in this policy document to developing energy efficient forms of housing and producing a sustainable strategy for housing provision. Recognition is also apparent of the intractable question of affordability and of the need to reach out to the socially excluded, minority communities and those in need of supported housing provision. These goals are to be addressed through partnership working between established housing agencies, the voluntary sector and communities within Wales.[1]

Central to achieving such an agenda is a process of continued refurbishment of stock[2] and the effective monitoring of need and demand about which still too little is known. To encourage local authorities to undertake surveys to identify need and demand, grant-aid is now forthcoming to allow these issues to be more precisely specified by local authorities throughout Wales. In so doing, particular attention will be given to demands arising from those with special needs, the homeless and rough sleepers and to the broader issue of affordability of stock, so that the needs of the most vulnerable may be addressed. A scheme of licensing Houses in Multiple Occupation (HMOs) is also proposed, as well as an intention to support Area Renewal Schemes and maintain steady investment in renovation.

While many of these elements are simply a continuation of past strategies, the priority given to *needs assessment* indicates that, in Wales, still too little is known of actual local needs and demand for housing.[3] Interestingly, there is only passing reference to any differences or similarities that might exist between rural areas and urban districts and a common agenda is set for both, though clear differences exist between such areas in both the priority and intensity of particular problems. Most notable is the pressure placed on the maintenance of language and culture in the rural heartlands of Wales by current levels of inmigration and its impact on the housing market (Cymuned, 2001).

Defining rural areas

It is not surprising given the absence of territorial differentiation in the National Housing Strategy that there has been no attempt to produce a sophisticated categorisation of rural areas. Prior to 1996, seventeen districts formed the basic units for any rural analysis[4] (Tai Cymru, 1992); since then, the reorganisation of Wales into twenty-two unitary authorities has modified this spatial framework and now only nine of these authorities are considered to be predominantly rural[5] (Gallent and Tewdwr-Jones, 2000b). The use of such administrative definitions has the major disadvantage that certain urban and suburban areas within predominantly rural districts are included, and that some suburban and rural districts in both South Wales and the Valleys and in North-East Wales get overlooked. These districts are much more extensive than those specified as 'rural' in the Housing Act of 1980 where, with the exception of the Brecon Beacons National Park, the designated districts had a distinctly west coast bias, a pattern replicated in the specification of West Wales under the recent EC Objective 1 designation. When statistical rather than administrative definitions have been used they follow the multiple attribute census classifications used by Cloke (1977, 1978 and in Cloke and Edwards, 1986, recently revisited by Harrington and O'Donoghue (1998)).

Alongside these broad definitions of rural Wales, a piecemeal collection of housing studies has been undertaken in rural locations. The national park authorities undertook rural needs surveys during the early 1990s (Beresford, 1989). Subsequently, under the Jigso Community Development Initiative between 1988 and 1994, Tai Cymru, as a joint sponsor, introduced an element of housing need assessment into local village appraisals[6] (Edwards, 1992b). Such surveys were continued in those areas benefiting from LEADER 1 and LEADER 2 funding.[7] However, these studies were often very fragmented, lacked contiguous territorial coverage and were mainly undertaken in rural communities of less than 1,000 population.

To encourage more comprehensive survey work during the 1990s local authorities were also encouraged to explore housing provision and needs. Such studies did distinguish between the housing circumstances of key rural towns, suburban pressure points and remoter rural areas, but at that time no standard methodology or standard designation of rural settings was employed (Edwards, 1995, 1996).[8]

Although the absence of formal definition may be considered a weakness, there are advantages in a broad specification of authorities that are stereotyped as rural. Inevitably the isolation of supply, demand and access criteria on more localised spatial frames denies the interconnectedness of housing markets and raises expectations of local delivery. Local Housing Markets are effectively maintained through travel-to-work engagements between town and countryside, particularly in the owner-occupied sector, and to fragment such functional units too much and raise expectations of local entitlement to provision creates for planners, housing officers and housing agencies an unrealistic task. However, within such functional regions obvious housing distinctions exist at a more local scale between different places and between local urban centres and the surrounding countryside in terms of stock availability, access and housing pressure.

The countryside: key concerns and housing issues

The last twenty years have seen considerable research effort devoted to the nature and consequences of change in rural Wales. Uneven demographic change and increasing social recomposition has led to three main lines of enquiry, each of which impinge on the debate surrounding rural housing. First attention has concentrated on the consequences of market forces and state restructuring on access to and service provision in rural areas (Higgs and White, 1997b; White et al., 1997; Ribchester and Edwards, 1999). Such work has highlighted the opportunity, service and accessibility deprivation that is present and the unevenness of 'quality of life' within the Welsh countryside (Higgs and White, 1997a). This has encouraged a wider level of community engagement with needs and delivery of alternative options (Edwards, 1992b; Tewdwr-Jones, 1998). Second, a suite of studies arising from research on rural lifestyles has exposed the diversity of residents in the Welsh countryside, the varied lifestyles and the poverty and disadvantage many experience (Cloke et al., 1994, Cloke et al., 1995a, Cloke *et al.*, 1995b, 1997a, 1997b). Third, the process of in-migration has challenged Welsh identity and led to contestation, which has often been seen to focus on the issue of access to housing (Cloke and Davies, 1992; Cloke and Milbourne, 1992; Fevre *et al.*, 1999; Gallent and Tewdwr-Jones, 2000b). Each of these lines of enquiry encouraged a direct engagement with housing policy and practice.

In rural Wales the recognition of an entrenched rural housing problem is apparent in local media reporting and in local claims of disadvantage and in the concerns of the academic and policy community. Central to representations of the problem are heavily publicised demand-side issues, which can only be met by either supply-side solutions or an overall improvement in wage levels in the rural economy.

First, the steady increase through *in-migration* has led to an increasingly competitive housing market across all of rural Wales, whether for permanent (Edwards 1996; Milbourne, 1999) or second home accommodation. (Gallent *et al.*, 1997; Gallent and Tewdwr-Jones, 2000a). Rates of in-migration vary across rural Wales as do the age and type of migrant. Nonetheless in all areas it is seen as the dominant contributory factor to the pressurised situation that exists for rural housing providers.

Second, the impact of in-migration on the language and culture of rural regions has produced, in the west and north, *a cultural dimension* to the concept of rural housing pressure. This has been accommodated in part by PPG 12 (Welsh Office, 1988, 1992c, 1999), but planning and housing authorities are increasingly facing assertive voices seeking to control access and maintain the cultural distinctiveness of the traditional language communities of rural Wales (Aitchison and Carter, 2000; Fevre *et al.*, 1999; Gallent and Tewdwr-Jones, 2000b; Welsh Language Society, 1989, 1992c, 1998).

Third, *age specific needs* from both the young and elderly compound the housing pressure experienced in many areas (Shucksmith, 1990; Milbourne 1997). Here, studies have explored the marked changes in the distribution and availability of social housing and recognised the pressure such changes have produced for those in need of affordable provision (Tai Cymru, 1990a; Milbourne, 1998). Such changes in supply make the retention of young people more problematic, a difficulty compounded by the low incomes that are available in the region, which marginalise them in a competitive housing market (Tai Cymru, 1990b). While some Housing Associations are seeking to address this issue through age-specific provision, it is widely asserted that young people are finding appropriate housing inaccessible.

It is widely recognised that retaining young people as residents within rural communities is essential for demographic balance, sustaining local culture and the maintenance of basic services. Sustaining schools and other services in such communities depends on a regular renewal of child-rearing families. The steady ageing of rural populations also contributes to a rising demand for more specialist and supported provision, invariably concentrated in small towns and regional centres. Finally, the requirement for care in the community from a range of disadvantaged and marginalised groups compounds the housing pressure on particular types of accommodation.

This demand-side problem can only be met through the balanced provision of housing opportunities and the regular movement of newly established, growing and ageing households through the stock. Creating social balance in the process requires a mix of tenures, thus opening opportunity for all groups irrespective of income. This can in part be achieved for some residents by Section 106 agreements and the use of exceptions policies, but even these face difficulties in their operation. Alongside these issues are those that arise as life expectancy increases and a rising proportion of the retired live independently for longer. Shaping the pattern of provision to meet such needs in rural districts, where in- and out-migration further confound the situation, makes the task of those planning for the future increasingly problematic and demanding.

Consequently, there has been an ongoing debate over the extent and nature of pressures operating in rural housing markets and attempts to mitigate the problems through supply-side solutions. Here, the restrictions on new-build in open countryside have generated much debate (Welsh Affairs Committee, 1993), as has the loss of social housing (Tai Cymru, 1990a; Milbourne, 1998) and the competitive demand for private sector provision to rent or purchase (Milbourne, 1997, 1999).

Throughout all these studies common problems are identified, namely:

- competition for existing stock;
- the uneven geographical distribution of tenures;
- the lack of 'affordable' property to rent or purchase in low-income rural economies;
- the need to maintain local communities and cultures;
- the problems faced by younger families and single parents; and
- the growing problem of a rural underclass and those who become homeless and marginalized.

Recognition of these issues was apparent in the consultative paper from the Wales Rural Forum (1994) and developed in the Rural White Paper (1996: 13–19). They have also been central to the initiatives that rural authorities have implemented, many of which seek to address local needs and establish procedures for prioritising them. This is now illustrated through a review of strategies recently employed in selected authorities in rural Wales.

Policy and strategy to address local housing needs

In the search for solutions to the housing problems that have been identified, planning and housing departments in local authorities throughout rural Wales have attempted to identify the key issues arising and to devise policies that seek to ameliorate these pressures.

Housing needs surveys

Most districts in rural Wales are seeking to devise criteria that define those in need, prioritise the local and work towards some definition of affordability.[9] Particular attention is also given to *Circular 53/88 The Welsh Language: Development Plans and Planning Control*, which establishes the principle that maintaining cultural balance is a material consideration in the planning process, though the degree to which this subsequently shapes policy is more explicit in some Local Plans than others. As Table 12.1 reveals, a mix of local authority and locally based need assessments is seen as essential in establishing village 'exceptions' policies and encouraging affordable low-cost housing to rent or purchase throughout much of rural Wales.[10]

Strategies of survey prior to investment do give an indication of *demand* for particular types of provision, but only in part answer the question of *the degree of need* for such investment. The *needs* element is most clearly evident for local young people seeking to set up their household, for local, low-paid or unemployed households, for those leaving tied-accommodation on low pay and for certain of the elderly who find it difficult to find appropriate lower cost housing for their retirement. While these circumstances are recognised in general terms and incorporated into the criteria for establishing *local* housing needs *no authorities explicitly define need in precise terms.*

Defining local housing priority

Most local plans choose to set out their priorities for housing *local* residents who may be identified as in need of affordable housing for rent or purchase. Districts, in specifying the local priority given to applicants in need of accommodation, use a variety of criteria (Table 12.2). Certain authorities begin with or include a series of general criteria that are important in defining *housing need.*

Table 12.1 Specification of housing need survey and local and affordability definitions in Wales

	Housing needs survey required	*Local defined*	*Affordability defined*
Dyfed			
Ceredigion	Yes (Local)	Yes (Born/5yrs)	No (Market)
Carmarthen	Yes (Local)	Yes (CCArea)	Yes (£30–35k)
Dinefwr	Yes (LA)	Yes (5 yrs)	No (Market)
Preseli	Yes (LA)	No	No (Market)
South Pembs.	Yes (LA/SPARC)	Yes (Need)	No (Market)
Pembs. Coast N. Park	Yes (LA/SPARC)	No	No (Market)
Eryri N. Park	Yes (Local)	Yes (Born/2–5yrs)	Yes (Local pay)
Gwynedd			
Aberconwy	Yes (Local)	Yes	No (Market)
Arfon	Yes (Local)	No information available	
Dwyfor	Yes (Local)	Yes (5yrs)	No (Market)
Meirionnydd	Yes (LA/Local)	Yes	Yes (£30–55 week)
Ynys Mon	Yes (Local)	Yes	Yes (£30–45k)
Powys			
Brecknock	Yes (LA/Local)	Yes	Yes (General)
Montgomeryshire	Not specified	Yes	Yes (40% of average income)
Radnorshire	Yes (LA)	Yes	No (Market)

Source: Author

The elements included here are typical of some of the criteria traditionally used by local authorities and housing associations in awarding points for priority on their waiting lists.[11] The length of residence criterion is fairly general in most districts, though it varies rather more when consideration is given to past residents who may have worked in the area and now wish to return. The link between employment and housing is also emphasised both for key workers and for those who, having obtained a job locally, cannot afford to buy or rent on the open market.

Most districts specify that those in need should fulfil at least one of these criteria, though some districts offer a wider range of specification than others,

Table 12.2 Criteria used to establish priority for local affordable housing to rent or purchase

---

General

> Must be in housing need (Brecknock)
>
> Elderly and disabled (Brecknock, Dwyfor, Meirionnydd)
>
> Unfit property (Dwyfor, Meirionnydd)
>
> Tied accommodation (Dwyfor, Meirionnydd)
>
> Needing separate accommodation (Ynys Mon, Meirionnydd)

One or more of the following

Lived in the Community Council Area for 5 years

> (Brecknock, Radnor, Dwyfor, Dinefwr, Aberconwy, Montgomery (3yrs), S. Pembs. (no length of residence), Ynys Mon, Meirionnydd, Ceredigion (within 25 miles of boundary))

Born, family links, brought up, worked in the area,
left but intend to return

> (Radnor (worked 5yrs), Montgomery (worked 3 yrs), Brecknock, Dwyfor (worked 5 yrs), Dinefwr, S. Pembs., Ynys Mon (worked 5 yrs), Aberconwy (worked 10yrs))

Return to look after relative

> (Montgomery, Aberconwy)

Currently employed as a key worker locally
within community

> (Radnor (12 months), Montgomery, Brecknock, S. Pembs., Ynys Mon, Aberconwy, Meirionnydd)

Obtained a job, can't afford housing in the
community

> (Montgomery, Brecknock, S. Pembs., Ynys Mon, Meirionnydd)

Caveats

Applies to those who do not own/ have not recently owned property

> (Radnor, Montgomery, Meirionnydd)

Source: Author

and all, as noted earlier are conscious of the impact of their decisions on the maintenance of the cultural characteristics of the communities within their district. Each of these criteria are employed to ensure that local residents in need of housing are first served, once housing needs surveys identify them and exceptions procedures and the construction of affordable housing to rent or purchase make property available.[12]

The affordability issue

The need for affordable housing to rent or purchase for those who cannot compete in the open market is central to the procedures for provision and the criteria for preferential access outlined in these Local Plans. Few plans however have anything to say in precise terms about how affordability is to be measured and assessed.

Most statements operate rightly on the presumption that certain households are on lower incomes and that even in a stable, let alone a rising housing market for rents and purchases, they are unable to compete. It is widely recognised that income levels are low in rural Wales, with significant numbers of households well below national and regional average income statistics. However, no adequate data are collected in a systematic manner that would provide detailed local evidence of available household income.[13] Most Local Plans refer to affordability in general terms related to levels of unemployment and wage rates in the local employment market (e.g. Eryri, Meirionnydd).[14] Affordability therefore is generally recognised to be a function of the existing housing and employment markets and much more detailed work needs to be undertaken on a regular basis to define it in precise terms.

This evidence highlights some of the uncertainties that current practices still contain. It points to the real requirement to identify precisely where housing need exists, through local survey and other strategies. It reveals that in assessing housing need, first, objective need has to be identified in terms comparable to those used by local authorities and housing associations, conceivably through some sort of refined 'pointing system', but which also includes some clear indication of 'affordability' through income assessment. Second, included in this procedure has to be a clear priority for local households and a sensitivity to maintaining cultural traditions in different parts of rural Wales.

The geography of rural housing provision

Sustainability

The location of rural property that is available to rent or purchase is a key factor in evaluating pressures within local housing markets. Current land availability forecasts and existing planning consents are considered by local authorities in specifying current and future expectations for land release for housing development through to 2005–2006 following structure plan requirements. Each district provides specific allocations of land to be released for housing development to meet the required Land Availability targets. All proposals reflect and emphasise *sustaining* the existing settlement pattern, in order to reflect the current pattern of community, employment and service provision.[15] The emphasis is on the hierarchical release of sites, with more in the urban centres and a graduated release of land in each of different grades of village centre.[16] Development in these centres is to be within the specified village envelopes or development boundaries except where other 'exceptions' policies are permissible.

As Table 12.3 reveals, local authorities seek through limited, controlled development in open countryside and through village exceptions policies to depart from these tight land use-zoning controls. In determining the balance of provision between market and affordable stock on land that has been released, opportunities are created for lower cost provision.

Table 12.3 Adoption of strategies for open countryside and village exceptions policies and local/affordable provision on larger sites

	Open countryside (agric/for/other)	*Village exceptions*	*Large estate local/affordable provision*
Dyfed			
Ceredigion	Yes 106	Yes Need/106	Yes 10 + 106
Carmarthen	Yes 106	Yes Need/106	Yes 20 + 106
Dinefwr	Yes 106	Yes Need/106	Spec by site
Preseli	Yes 106	Yes Need/106	No
South Pembs.	Yes 106	Yes Need/106	Yes 12 + 106
Pembs. Coast N. Park	Yes 106	Yes Need/106	Yes 20 + 106
Eryri N. Park	Yes 106	Reluctant/106	Yes 5-10/106
Gwynedd			
Aberconwy	Yes 106	Yes Need/106	Unspecified
Arfon	No plan available		
Dwyfor	Yes 106	Yes Need/106	Yes 6 + 106
Meirionnydd	Yes 106	Yes Need/106	Yes 5 + 106
Ynys Mon	Yes 106	Yes Need/106	Yes 10 + 106
Powys			
Brecknock	Yes 106	Yes Need/106	Yes 20 + 106
Montgomeryshire	Yes 106 (density)	Yes Need/106	Yes 10 + 106
Radnorshire	Yes 106 (density)	No	Yes 20 + 106

Source: Author

Provision in open countryside

The use of an exceptions policy under PPG7 to facilitate the local provision of accommodation for agricultural, forestry and other rural workers who have to live at, or near, their place of work has been, and still is, incorporated into all policy statements. In all districts the design and form of new development has to meet local requirements, there is emphasis on rehabilitation and improvement of existing properties and discussion of property conversion to residential and other uses. Most local plans emphasise that this strategy is to be tightly administered and against a presumption of no development in open countryside has to be earned, with the burden of proof lying with the applicant – it is not an entitlement.[17]

All authorities require the implementation of Section 106 agreements on the future resale or occupation of such properties, although the terms attached to these agreements vary between districts.[18] The Local Plans indicate that tighter guidelines are intended for this type of provision. These are determined in some districts by limiting the floorspace of such developments and by operating firm policies on the exceptional circumstances when occupancy agreements will be removed. It is clearly intended that these 'exceptions' to the policy of no development in open countryside are to be tightly controlled. Nonetheless, properly used, these policies do provide a sympathetic and appropriate option to provide affordable and suitably located property for key rural workers.

Village exceptions policies

In the release of land for new housing developments all authorities recognise the need for balance in the tenure and cost of provision on proposed sites within specified village boundaries. The presumption is that adequate land is released to meet these needs in most circumstances, but again most authorities recognise that there may be situations where exceptions have to be accommodated. Thus, the exceptional release of new land adjoining village boundaries is recognised as a possibility for local needs affordable housing to rent or purchase provided it is supported by:

- locally produced or local authority housing surveys;
- proof that existing local authority and housing association provision and the private market cannot meet such demand;
- proposals to provide low-cost, affordable housing to rent or purchase;

and the provision, once made, that the property will be bound in perpetuity for this purpose by Section 106 agreements. Local Housing Trusts or Housing

Associations will normally manage such developments.[19] The precise terms of Section 106 clauses vary from district to district. Thus they are very explicit in some and less so in others.[20]

   This type of policy is widely used, but is dependent for its success on proof of need, the availability of land and the willingness of housing associations or housing trusts to carry forward the development strategy. Much therefore rests with Community Councillors in the first instance or other interested parties to establish objectively the difficulties local residents have in obtaining appropriate property in the local market (through local needs surveys) and identifying house-holds objectively in need to justify such investment.

Large site/estate specification of local needs affordable housing

The final option utilised by Local Plans and widely employed in those examined here is the requirement for private developers of larger sites to set aside a nego-tiated or fixed proportion of the units constructed for local needs affordable housing. The size of site to which this policy applies varies between districts (Table 12.3) from sites of over 5 to those over 20 units. The type of provision should meet local and affordable criteria and may be of a number of forms. It may be housing for rent, shared-ownership, low-cost homes for sale or low-cost serviced plots for self-build. It may involve a local housing trust or housing association and occupiers should meet local needs criteria, and in all cases subse-quent purchase or re-let is bound by Section 106 agreements.[21] This means that there is considerable variation in both the location and number of units potentially likely to be provided by, or through, this policy in different districts in rural Wales.

Overview and future challenges

In rural Wales, the last decade has seen a growth in co-operation between plan-ning and housing departments and housing associations in devising policies that address needs and prioritise the local. However whatever policies have been, or are in future, adopted, it has to be recognised that any effective resolution of the long-term housing problems facing rural Wales is dependent on four inter-related issues.

- *The economic change.* Here, the fortunes of the land-based industries as they adjust to their current difficult financial plight and subsequently to Agenda 2000 will be critical in determining the extent to which deeper rural Wales diversifies, moves to organic production and local value-added products and sustains employment. Much also depends on how other sectors within the region maintain employment in an economy dominated by tourism, local professional and other services and state dependent employment. Incomes 75 per cent below the national average contributed to EC Objective 1 designation, and investment in the next six years will be critical in determining the extent to which the Welsh countryside remains a marginal, lagging region. Accessibility within local markets is in large part determined by regional income levels, if these can be boosted some, but not all, difficulties may be ameliorated.

- *Demographic changes.* One of the consequences of success under EC Objective 1 might be encouragement of endogenous growth and the retention or return of more local young people. This together with exogenous inputs to the regional economy through in-migration may well increase competition for existing stock and pressurise an already highly competitive market. In-migration for retirement, *in situ* ageing and other age-specific housing needs through increasing family fragmentation will also stretch a stock that is limited in terms of appropriately located specialist provision. This and the need to find solutions to rural homelessness and housing or conversion for other special needs groups will tax housing agencies.

- *Environmental responsibility.* Much of rural Wales is designated 'protected' landscape. This limits land availability and increases the price of new-build through design controls. This factor together with an established practice of concentrating land release for major housing investment in larger towns and key settlements will inevitably maintain an uneven geography of provision in both the private, social and specialised sector. While such territorial concentration may constitute a sustainable strategy in terms of access to transport and services and have less direct environmental impact on conserved areas, it may increase the demand for provision in open, more remote, countryside.

- *Local needs and regional cultures.* Prioritising local needs and meeting community requirements has become a dominant element in the rhetoric of housing provision: in Wales this is compounded by a desire for language maintenance. Action by Education Authorities throughout rural Wales has led to bilingual primary provision in most key villages and secondary facilities in market towns. While this does much to ensure cultural exposure to the use of Welsh by new residents, the sub-text of the call for local priority often appears to go beyond this. A major challenge facing housing agencies is to re-establish measures of 'normative' rather than simply 'expressed' local need to address part of this problem. This might be achieved through a revised 'pointing system', which really specifies those most in need, the

12.1 An old slate quarrying community, Corris (Meirionydd): W.J. Edwards.

12.2 A coastal tourist village with an abundance of second homes, Little Haven (Pembrokeshire): W.J. Edwards.

12.3 Housing Association new-build (Cymdeithas Tai Clwyd), Bala (Gwynedd): W.J. Edwards.

volume of such demand and then allows investment in the type of provision necessary to satisfy it. This will allow an appropriate balance of stock to be created. That noted, such provision, if small to be cheap, will be limited and the operation of an effective and sustainable housing market will depend on greater encouragement of household filtering through property that is available. The past provision of general needs social housing and ageing *in situ* has led, throughout much of rural Wales, to inertia and under-occupancy. In a managed market this needs to be addressed to ensure, conceivably through modified Section 106 agreements, a balance of households of different ages to maintain schools and community development in key centres.

Finally two other issues need the attention of policy makers. First the establishment of effective housing surveys of both private and public sectors, owned and rented property are required. Such surveys could reveal the true extent to which Welsh rural housing markets are pressurised, rather than relying on anecdotal evidence and stereotypical views of how pressure is generated. Here the current initiative from the National Assembly is welcomed. Second, the growing partnership engagement in housing provision and management needs to continue between public, private and third sector developers and participation in this process widened. Evidence throughout rural Wales indicates that while many residents are aware of the loss of local authority stock they are less informed of other routes to social housing. Far more publicity needs to be given to the alternative forms of housing that are available, so that the choices are better known.

A distinctive Welsh housing policy has yet to emerge from the Assembly. However the current trends and past policies emphasising, as they do, the priority that should be given to those locally experiencing housing needs, indicate that the future poses challenges in designing procedures that will provide for all in the Welsh countryside.

Notes

1   This information is based on reports listed on the National Assembly's web site (www.wales.gov.uk).
2   Though it should be noted that the recent House Condition Surveys reveal progress has been made on this count with only 8.5 per cent of property still 'unfit', a major improvement on the house conditions present in the early 1980s (Welsh Office, 1986; National Assembly, 1999b).

3   During the 1990s, local authorities have been encouraged to measure housing need following an official guide, *Taking Stock*, produced by the Housing Management Advisory Committee (1993). Many have done so, but practices have varied. Consequently the guidelines have been recently updated to develop a standardised process of monitoring by all agencies, which should allow a more comprehensive assessment of housing needs and pressures (Welsh Office, 1998).

4   Aberconwy, Arfon, Brecknock, Carmarthen, Ceredigion, Colwyn, Delyn, Dinefwr, Dwyfor, Glyndwr, Meirionnydd, Monmouth, Montgomeryshire, Preseli Pembrokeshire, Radnorshire, South Pembrokeshire and Ynys Mon.

5   Carmarthenshire, Ceredigion, Conwy, Denbighshire, Gwynedd, Monmouthshire, Powys, Pembrokeshire and Ynys Mon.

6   A set of standard questions were introduced specifying current need, need within five years and sought to identify other households who might be seeking to return.

7   These territories, particularly in Preseli, South Pembrokeshire and Antur Cwm Taf and Tywi (Carmarthenshire), were essentially rural in designation and with few major urban centres (Edwards, 1992b).

8   No attention was given to this issue in the Wales Rural Forum Consultative paper (1994) nor elaborated on the Rural White Paper (1996) nor addressed in Fisk (1996) or Fisk's and Hall's (1997) review of the housing challenge facing Wales, where only a brief reference is given to rural housing issues.

9   Central to the discussion of housing is an established procedure for undertaking Local Housing Needs Assessment. During the 1990s in order to encourage the development of consistent practice an early guide to local housing needs assessment was published. In the light of subsequent practice, the Welsh Office issued a Consultation Draft on Needs Assessment in 1998–1999 with the aim of encouraging proper strategic planning to allow the effective delivery of housing services. This outlined the appropriate strategy for undertaking Housing Needs Assessment, specifying what was involved, the key elements in needs assessment both for owner-occupied and for social housing and provided definitive guidance on how local housing needs surveys should be undertaken to arrive at comparable data between authorities and how such results might be utilised to develop new-build, conversions, renovation and repair policies etc. This document will shape subsequent practice in identifying housing needs in both the urban and rural Unitary Authorities in Wales.

10   Ceredigion, Dinefwr, Meirionnydd, Preseli and Radnor have undertaken comprehensive reviews of housing. South Pembrokeshire and the Coastal National Park have utilised comprehensive local surveys undertaken by South Pembrokeshire Action with Rural Communities (SPARC) alongside planning and housing department reviews of the current housing market. Other authorities including Arfon have adopted this strategy of a centralised overview using Waiting List and

other census evidence to establish housing circumstances. Alongside these, pilot local surveys have been undertaken in Montgomeryshire and Ceredigion to establish housing needs in particular localities.

11   It is also of interest that the *need element* is further specified in Radnor, Meirionnydd and Montgomery were they include a caveat against priority being given to those who do own or who have recently owned property. Presumably this is done to make it more likely that those most in need will actually be considered first. It may well be that other districts do consider these key general points in their considerations, but they do not choose to specify them as sharply in their documentation.

12   Interestingly, on re-let or resale of such property some of this local specificity is relaxed. Carmarthen indicates that subsequent occupiers should come from within the Community Council Area and this is presumably the intention in most districts. That said, in Aberconwy subsequent occupiers, if not forthcoming from the local area, may be drawn from throughout rural Aberconwy within a 10 mile radius; while in Meirionnydd subsequent occupation extends to households within 30 miles. In Dinefwr, second occupiers may come from anywhere in Dyfed and its adjacent Community Council Areas and in Montgomery, sale or re-let is extended to the whole of Montgomery. These policies indicate some flexibility in the subsequent criteria used for allocating affordable provision, but raise questions as to whether the expectation is that such provision is tied to local needs.

13   Arfon, Ynys Mon and South Pembrokeshire indicate that they monitor local prices of properties on the market, as a context for establishing availability and affordability, operating on the assumption that the mortgages required are determined by roughly 2.5 times the principal earner's salary. Reference is also made in other documents to the level of local authority and housing association rents and eligibility for housing benefit.

14   All districts recognise that affordability changes with wage rates and the market. Only a few plans give examples appropriate at the time of writing. For example, Carmarthen suggest that affordable property to purchase given local rates was in the £30–35,000 range in early 1990s; Ynys Mon suggest £30–45,000 for purchase and Meirionnydd a weekly rent of between £30–55. However, most documents do not specify the actual level, but do imply that often significant numbers and proportions of local households are existing on incomes well below the average.

15   This is in line with current thinking in the National Planning Strategy for Wales, 2000.

16   This strategy with an initial town focus, then moderate, modest and minor developments in smaller places produces in most districts a three- or four-tiered pattern of land release for future development.

17   All authorities require formal proof of functional need, evidence of the absence of property locally to meet need, and details of the circumstances of those applying. Certain authorities, Montgomeryshire and Radnorshire, specify the floor area size (100–140 sq. metres) of properties that will be constructed to meet these needs and all restrict applications to those who are currently employed or will be employed in the local enterprise.

18   The variation in terms occurs over the precise phrasing of those who are eligible and in the details of the 106 agreements. The latter is critical when attempts are made to revoke such controls should the houses be offered unsuccessfully on the local market. Thus Montgomeryshire initially proposed that the property had only to be on the open market for six months, but this was subsequently changed to a year and one or two years is far more normal as the time specified for advertisement to find a suitable *local* worker. Only then, if the price asked is not reached, can other options be considered.

19   None of the local plans examined specify where such exceptions might occur. South Pembrokeshire indicate that the normal practice will be only to release such sites adjacent to settlements where adequate community and other services are present. Montgomeryshire recognise that in order to meet local housing needs there may be a requirement for individual plot provision in smaller settlements in addition to such proven exceptions, while in Radnorshire there is no expectation that such exceptional development will be necessary.

20   In Montgomeryshire it is suggested that at least 50 per cent of such property should remain in local occupation on re-let or sale, elsewhere 100 per cent is expected.

21   In most authorities the proportion for such provision is not fixed. A fifth to a quarter of all units is suggested by Montgomeryshire, but most authorities set no precise requirements. Dinefwr actually specify in their plan the mix of cost and type of property on certain sites. Carmarthen suggests certain densities and size controls for such property, which should serve to make the property appropriate for specific clients. In Ynys Mon where the local authority controls nearly a third of the land allocated for future housing it opens considerable options for local provision. Elsewhere, fewer large sites are available and they are most likely to be located in the larger settlements.

Chapter 13
Housing pressure and policy in Europe
A power regime perspective

Nick Gallent and Chris Allen

Introduction

The aim of this penultimate chapter is to identify common themes and messages emerging from the previous ten chapters. The chapters were organised loosely around the idea that different policy regimes, and particularly 'planning policy' regimes, may create situations in which rural housing markets are more closely regulated (Part One), more reliant on informal regulation (Part Two) or generate an unstable relationship between town and country (Part Three). But added to this broad classification, the intention now is both to revisit the comparative structure set out by Allen (this volume), and to seek an explanation for observed differences in terms of underlying housing cultures and the way these influence political discourse and consequent housing strategy and policy. A key focus for the chapter is the form that *power* (to drive or regulate development and change) assumes in the case study countries, who wields it and to what end. The rationale of this focus is made apparent in later sections.

The intention is also to provide a reasonably detailed policy analysis, which identifies commonalities and broader 'headline messages' to be taken into the next and final chapter. First then, how can the detail and description in the case studies be unravelled?

A comparative structure

It was noted earlier in this book that while the practice of 'lesson learning' has become more popular in recent years, there has also been a growing recognition of the dangers inherent in assuming that simple comparisons are possible. It would be difficult to argue that the countries of western Europe – Spain, France, Italy, Sweden, Britain etc. – all sit on the same linear path and that at a policy level differences are merely a consequence of how far they have each travelled down the same road (see Allen, Chapter 2). This would assume that over the long term, these countries all want to reach the same point or achieve the same goals: such is the assumption in the 'convergence' thesis. Heins (in Chapter 5) does suggest that in strategic policy, the Netherlands is becoming 'more European' with a less 'comprehensively and intensively public sector led' approach to providing new homes. The implicit comparison being drawn is with those countries that have withdrawn from state housing provision: Britain being the immediately obvious example. But using the convergence thesis, this assumes a common European history; one in which the power of the state was once pervasive, but has now waned. At this particular policy level, there may be some merit in comparing the outward similarities of the Dutch and British housing systems. But at a pan-European level, the plausibility of identifying such a common history or path appears to diminish when the southern European or Scandinavian examples are drawn into the equation.

The alternative view introduced in Chapter 2 is that at a number of levels, different countries and societies are divergent. That is not to say that the general characteristics of modern societies are not similar, but that they may have taken very different routes to their present situations. And any similarity in the present situation does not mean that a common destination has been reached. Societies may remain on different paths (though seek to define common ground through pan-national institutions such as the EU), making it impossible to accurately predict their future trajectory. This is because – as divergence theorists have pointed out – these paths have been, and continue to be, determined by a complex interplay of unique economic, political and cultural forces. From our own perspective, the danger is to see everything that passes in Europe through British eyes and thereby offer a very Anglocentric analysis of the processes and events discussed in the previous ten chapters. But let us concede now that the risk of cultural contamination is very real and even if the 'Romeo error' mentioned in Chapter 2 is avoided, any diagnosis arrived at here will be far from perfect. Our strategy is to minimise the risk by offering an analysis structured at three levels: a cultural level, a broad political level and at a policy level (the second and third are fused in this analysis for the sake of brevity). At each of these, we begin by asking basic questions relating to the way in which different societies and systems seek to provide housing opportunities and access in the countryside. Therefore:

* At a cultural level: how have cultural factors shaped the 'power regime' (see below), influenced the political process, and thereby affected issues such as housing supply and land use constraint?
* At a political level: what is the political background, and what form has the 'power regime' taken and how has this affected issues such as housing supply or land use constraint?
* At a policy level: how have these political and cultural forces been manifest in policy?

Social and cultural factors in this analysis are seen as a *link to* politics (shaping the broad 'power regimes' that were alluded to in the organisation of case study chapters) and a *driver of* policy. This is a simplification of Figure 2.1 and at each level we ask broad 'nature of' questions that lead into 'type' or 'example' issues. The focus of the questions themselves draw on the broad division of countries into those that adopt a more protectionist and regulatory stance towards the countryside (regulatory regimes – Part One), those that are more ready to accommodate growth (and are more laissez-faire in their policy regime – Part Two) and those that sit between these two 'extremes' and are unstable in the sense that there are elements in these countries that desire a move towards one of the two other regulatory approaches (Part Three). If this were a political exercise in 'lesson learning', then our intention might be to seek and justify particular policy transfers. Back in Chapter 2, Allen ended his introduction to comparative methods with five basic questions, the last three of which were concerned with the political and cultural context of policy engagement and how this might be transported and recreated. Our goal in the remainder of this chapter is less ambitious. In asking key questions at different levels, the hope is that detailed themes, which provide relatively secure and useful comparative anchors, can be identified.

Cultural conditions and policy regimes in western Europe

This section takes two transects across the ten case study chapters. The first of these focuses on cultural conditions and the second on 'policy regimes', examined in terms of broad political discourse and consequent policy measures. We began with the general assumption that the ten examples fall in three regimes depending on outward attitudes towards rural land use and protection. This assumption was introduced in Chapter 1. The issue for the next two sections is how these general attitudes break down into key themes that are manifest at the cultural, political and policy levels. The first looks at underlying cultural conditions, the second at politics and policy expressed in terms of different types of 'power regimes': i.e. regulatory regimes in which power is wielded to (for instance) achieve 'universal' social objectives, laissez-faire regimes in which power is less formalised and unstable regimes subject to divisive debate over the extent of state regulation.

Level 1: culture

What are the cultural conditions and values that underpin rural housing politics and policies? For example:

- What is the nature of 'the countryside', what are its traditions, how is it used and who uses it?
- What is the relationship between town and country? How are town and country distinctions formulated in different places?
- To what extent is this relationship mediated by issues of consumption and production?

The arrangement of levels used in this analysis should not suggest a simple primacy of culture over politics. The development and direction of political debate is as much a determinate of culture and tradition as it is a reflection of it. In the discussion that follows, the ten case study chapters are divided into three main 'cultural types'. These cultural types correspond to the division of 'regime types' used in the organisation of the chapters. The aim is to describe the conditions under which particular regimes have evolved. We focus on different views and uses of the countryside, on how these views shape both perceptions of, and the relationship between, town and country, eventually expressing this relationship in terms of the changing balance between consumption and production interests in rural areas.

In Chapter 1, we forwarded the broad proposition that the regulatory regimes under which rural housing issues have evolved across western Europe sit between two extremes. At one extreme political debate has resulted in a system of tight regulation. At the other, far more laissez-faire approaches have either consciously been developed, or have been allowed to develop under the auspices of weak state direction. Between these two extremes, it was suggested that some countries have engaged in a political debate that has resulted in a factional split between groups who desire a gravitational shift towards a more fixed position where either the market or informality are assigned primacy. These were labelled 'unstable regimes'. The political and policy debate is returned to in the next section. Here, however, we use the same three-way division to explain the cultural circumstances underpinning the current use of particular policy tools.

As Table 13.1 illustrates, three distinctive rural cultures can be identified. These are cohesive cultures (underpinning regulatory policy regimes), atomistic, family oriented cultures (which are associated with laissez-faire regulatory

Table 13.1 Level 1: culture

Country	Cultural conditions	Cultural examples
Cohesive rural cultures (regulatory policy regimes)		
Norway	Society characterised by weak urbanisation with the retention of strong ties between the urban and rural populations. Declining reliance on agricultural production and increasing levels of recreational consumption. Dispersed settlement pattern.	Strong culture of owner-occupation in the countryside and a tradition of self-build and production of 'extra houses' (second homes).
Sweden	Countryside of dispersed settlements as opposed to nucleated villages. Agricultural rural society, but with a tradition of urbanites consuming the countryside for recreational use.	High levels of domestic residential tourism. Recent incursion of 'outsiders' into the housing market.
The Netherlands	Symbiotic link between town and country. Weak rural culture, but desire to create some form of rural heritage. A 'peri-urban culture'.	Desire to halt urban encroachment into peri-urban areas, which are seen as a repository of a manufactured brand of Dutch rural culture.
France	Tension between the countryside's agricultural past and a new social and cultural diversity in many areas. Past rural isolation has been replaced by new levels of access that have opened up the countryside to new forms of consumption, i.e. second homes, commuters, home workers.	Sometimes this is linked to new economic strengths, at other times it is a product of immigration from former colonies.
Atomistic family orientated cultures (laissez-faire policy regimes)		
Italy	Family rather than the state as the agent of welfare. Culture of resisting regulation. Thus emergence of a new culture of innovation, including new forms of economic activity and social praxis.	Flouting of planning regulation in some parts of the country. Reliance on family centred networks for housing and support.
Spain	An ageing population in some rural areas has meant, on the one hand, the retention of traditional values but, on the other, a rejection of the types of innovations required to ensure the viability of agricultural	Sporadic conflict between production and new forms of consumption. Consumption relatively unconstrained, e.g. new housebuilding, second homes.

Table 13.1 *(continued)*

Country	Cultural conditions	Cultural examples
	production. A changing mix of social groups.	
Republic of Ireland	Family rather than the state as the main agent of welfare. Thus, cultural resistance to regulation of private interests. Historical neglect of both private renting and social housing. Small and under-planned dispersed settlements; a continuing tradition of living on farms.	Planning efforts of rural local authorities have clashed with a variety of interests, especially those who, while wishing to build on family lands, work in off-farm employment. Similar clashes with incoming non-local households.

Divisive urban-rural cultures (unstable policy regimes)

Country	Cultural conditions	Cultural examples
England	Culture of conflict within the countryside, resulting from market distortions being heightened by planning constraint. Social reconfiguration as the countryside moves away from cohesive communities based on production to fragmented ones based on different forms of consumption.	The distorting effects of new demand pressures heightened by planning policy and creating housing scarcity. Second homes are a sporadic concern, but with their impact determined by the strength of planning constraint.
Scotland	Similar culture of conflict within the countryside, as in England. Greater emphasis on, and trust in, public provision linked to historical wariness of private interests (drawing from past experiences of landlordism). This results in a more forceful attempt (than in England) to manage local conflicts.	Culture of innovation in the way that grant funding is distributed and used. Greater concern for the way in which social housing is allocated.
Wales	Market conflicts centred upon cultural divisions expressed through language. Decline in agricultural communities. Diversity of residents in the countryside with varied lifestyles and backgrounds. A cause of conflict often mobilised through pressure groups. Traditional reliance on private housing provision.	Struggles over second home ownership, in-migration and retirement. These sometimes overshadow fundamental economic growth considerations.

Source: Authors

approaches) and divisive cultures (which belie the existence of unstable policy regimes).

Cohesive rural cultures

Sweden, Norway, the Netherlands and France can be characterised as having cohesive rural cultures. As the entries in Table 13.1 indicate, this is partly explained by the lack of an explicit division between town and country. In the case of the Netherlands, this is expressed by Heins in Chapter 5 as a 'symbiotic relationship' between town and country which is most visible in the 'peri-urban' fringe, but which also can be found in more marginal rural areas. Here, this relationship is to some extent a product of high population density within a limited land mass and therefore proximity between town and country. Norway and Sweden, however, have developed a similar condition for different reasons. Here, it is partly due to the lateness of industrialisation and consequent urbanisation across Scandinavia, which is commonly expressed through close family ties between members of the urban and rural populations. It is also linked to the historical perception of rural areas as a legitimate recreational landscape and not the exclusive preserve of agricultural values though, of course, these remain important.

This avoidance of a strict division between town and country has resulted in three trends. First, the lack of an identifiable 'rural culture' has meant that the countryside has been more willing to embrace the future, focusing on new forms of tourism, accepting new ways of living, experimenting with new types of development and, to some extent, more easily accepting social change. Second, this blurring of the urban–rural division has resulted in a more cohesive 'national culture'. In some cases, such as Sweden, this has meant that the struggle over the countryside has been between Swedish nationals and non-nationals who are to be kept out, rather than between the rural and urban populations. Third, it has resulted in a centralisation of political power within a 'strong state' that, as we will see below, pursues a heavily regulatory approach that prioritises neither town over country nor vice versa. This is most clearly demonstrated in Auclair and Vanoni's account (Chapter 6) of the apparent neutrality of French economic policy.

Atomistic family-oriented cultures

In our second category – which includes Italy, Spain and the Republic of Ireland – it is also the case that town and country divisions are relegated behind more fundamental concerns when it comes to defining the root of culture. For example, in Italy, Padovani and Vettoretto (Chapter 7) highlight the importance of family structures in delivering welfare support and, more specifically, helping meet the housing needs of those living in the countryside. Family and informal networks have a central role to play in Italy and this role crosses urban–rural boundaries. Often it becomes more important than state provision and, in many instances, rides roughshod over formal regulation. For example, in the south of the country, the enforcement of planning regulation has been limited where local people are choosing to illegally erect dwellings on family-owned land. While state intervention and enforcement of regulation might strengthen away from the southern part of the country, this remains an important feature in the history of the Italian rural landscape.

However, there is a paradox. In social theory, the family is associated with tradition, whereas the state is more readily associated with modernity. But, the resistance to the state that is created by the primacy of the family, paradoxically results in the modernisation of the countryside through largely unfettered development. The state, therefore, might be viewed as a hindrance to different forms of development; social, physical and even economic. The informality of regulation in this group of countries might be seen as socially progressive though it is more commonly judged to be environmentally malign. This is certainly the case in parts of Ireland and in Southern Italy. In Spain, however, tradition has proven to be a greater barrier to innovation in some areas, particularly in relation to farming method. But, there is evidence of the same informality in terms of development control in relation to private housebuilding. It is this more relaxed approach to land use planning that some commentators in other countries have sought to replicate. This issue is addressed in the next section.

Divisive urban–rural cultures

Our third category can be distinguished by the existence of a continuous tension, and sometimes overt conflict, between town and country. This tension is often used as a frame of reference in the analysis of rural problems by British-based researchers (given that it is a defining characteristic of rural culture across much of the United Kingdom). Application of this frame of reference to other countries, and the notion that politics and policy elsewhere have a similar cultural root, commonly results in what Kemeny (1992) has termed the 'Romeo error' (see Allen, Chapter 2). We would argue that despite particular key differences – amplified recently by devolution – England, Wales and Scotland all share this divisive urban–rural culture. Early industrialisation and urbanisation in the

United Kingdom resulted in a severing of links between urban and rural populations. These links remained severed for an extended period and this resulted in the development of distinct cultural types. In the countryside, Bell and Newby (1971) have argued that communities became organised around simple landless/landowner classes and were dominantly 'farming communities' with the majority of people engaged in agriculture or related activities. A process of counter-urbanisation, which gathered pace during the latter half of the twentieth century, brought an 'encapsulation' of rural communities along consumption lines, with a residual element of people still engaged in agriculture being joined by a new class of retired households and those seeking second homes. These are commonly thought to represent an urban class. The consequent 'clash' between a rural and an urban culture has become the defining feature of the countryside.

Conflicts are sometimes expressed in terms of housing market distortions, issues of housing access and questions over affordability. The rural culture may be viewed as being predominantly 'productionist', while the encroaching urban culture is largely one of consumption underpinned by greater market power. Resultant inequalities between 'newcomers' and local populations have driven a wide ranging debate over the role of the state and the nature of policy intervention. Some observers argue that less regulation is the logical response to stronger market pressure, and seek to adopt a more 'atomistic' approach. Others contend that only stronger regulation and market intervention will meet both local need and the need to protect the rural environment. Hence, they would see greater wisdom in a more regulatory approach, akin to that which has developed under the more coherent cultural conditions described earlier.

In England, conflict is expressed in terms of general market pressure and the power wielded by incoming urban elites. It commonly results in opposition to new housebuilding and it has been said that planning has become an instrument of social exclusion (Hoggart, Chapter 10). In Wales, a similar urban–rural conflict is frequently couched in cultural terms, though its root in the general market is the same. In Scotland, the clash of urban–rural cultures is again present, though the solutions being sought are more likely to be public-sector led. This is a key difference between Scotland and the rest of Britain.

This tension within the third category has, we suggest, resulted in an unstable regulatory regime characterised by a political debate swinging between strong and weak policy intervention.

Levels 2 and 3: politics and policy

What is the nature and focus of rural housing politics in different societies? And, in order to meet particular political objectives, given specific cultural conditions, what rural housing policies are employed? For example:

- Are there differing social objectives and views of the market (that find political expression)?
- What policies or strategies do different countries use in order to regulate their rural housing markets or development (and so forth)?

Different attitudes towards the countryside are perhaps most obvious at the political level, where social and cultural factors are mobilised behind a particular agenda. In England, Hoggart (Chapter 10) argues that this agenda is largely concerned with protecting a limited rural resource from an urban threat. Protectionist attitudes are given a political voice via a planning system that prioritises the need for public consultation on strategic policy and development matters. Hence in England, cultural and social values attached to the countryside have been increasingly politicised since the introduction of the 1947 Town and Country Planning Act. Today, these have culminated in an emphasis on planning constraint, giving rural housing a significant scarcity value and resulting in policy that tinkers with the market (perhaps by controlling the occupancy of some new homes) rather than dealing with the fundamental issue of supply. Both Edwards (this volume) and Shucksmith and Conway (this volume) confirm this link between attitudes towards the countryside in Britain, political discourse and the nature of policy tools.

This example demonstrates the link between our comparative levels, revealing that the end can be interpreted as a product of the context. Further discussion on links is provided nearer the end of this chapter. Here, we build on the three cultures identified in the last section. The notion of distinct cultures feeds into a broad suite of policy regimes, which can be distinguished from each other by the way in which power is held and exercised. Our cohesive cultures link to regulatory regimes, our atomistic family-oriented cultures emerge as laissez faire policy regimes; and our divisive urban–rural cultures become unstable policy regimes characterised by a polarised and unresolved policy debate. Particular characteristics of each of these regimes at a broad political and a policy level are noted in Table 13.2. Each is discussed more generally in the following

Table 13.2 Levels 2 and 3: politics and policy

Country	Political focus	Policy examples
Regulatory policy regimes		
Norway	Preservation and support of agricultural communities, and ensuring year-round occupancy of rural dwellings. Limiting the power of private interests within rural housing markets.	Primary legislation governing use of property and seeking to restrict the transformation of farms into normal residential units.
Sweden	Regulation of rural housing markets in order to achieve 'social sustainability', i.e. protection and preservation of 'traditional' rural communities.	Easing property tax burdens on local communities. Additional controls on the housing market governing foreign acquisitions.
The Netherlands	Management of population pressure on a limited countryside. Promotion of 'urban compaction' and environmental protection.	National spatial planning framework allowing only limited encroachments into the countryside.
France	Management of growth in particular regions, and sharing prosperity across regions. Emphasis on social equity across the countryside.	Primary legislation establishing universal 'housing rights'. Local action plans, in which local authorities set out how they are going to secure these rights.
Laissez-faire policy regimes		
Italy	Weak regulatory regime, with a traditional reliance on the family as an agent of social welfare.	Poor enforcement of planning regulation. 'Policy tolerance' of illegal housebuilding in parts of the country.
Spain	Limited concern for pressures on local housing markets. Greater political emphasis on the economic fortunes of rural area.	'Dual track' housing policy that accommodates new forms of consumption (tourism/second homes) *and* local housing needs.

Table 13.2 *(continued)*

Country	*Political focus*	*Policy examples*
Ireland	Management of economic growth. Lack of a distinction between rural and urban areas in political debate.	Economic strategies guided through *national* planning and development agencies. Limited policy responses to new housing pressures (sporadic house building in the countryside).

Unstable policy regimes

England	Promotion of market principles combined with weakened public sector housing provision. Planning restrictions amplifying market distortions.	Right to buy (sale of public housing). Emphasis on environmental protection to be achieved through planning restriction.
Scotland	Strong support for public sector housing provision, compared to England. Mistrust of private market interests. Political desire to engage in land reform.	Resistance towards the right to buy. Innovative use of grant funding for different forms of provision, e.g. self-build.
Wales	Shared context with England. Greater emphasis on community and local inputs into policy design. Welsh culture and language permeate political debate, particularly in relation to migration. Desire to embrace European agendas.	Resistance towards 'English' planning policy. Desire to establish distinctively Welsh agenda given the opportunities afforded by devolution. Establishing a cultural agenda within broader development policy.

Source: Author

three sections, and each section begins with a brief explanation of the form of power underpinning a particular policy regime.

Regulatory policy regimes

Regulatory policy regimes, linking to our cohesive rural cultures, represent a Hobbesian form of power (see Clegg, 1989), in which the omniscient state is deemed to act in the best interests of society and therefore individuals, irrespective of where or in what type of community they reside. The manner in which 'regulatory' policy regimes exercise power tends to be repressive[1] in the sense that they frequently aim to prevent or halt specific processes or changes. Hence they may emphasise the need to protect or preserve and might be viewed as inherently conservative.

In the case of Norway, a prevailing philosophy has been the need to minimise the exploitative capacity of private interests in the housing market. This is manifest in key policy that seeks to regulate the way in which property changes hands, the use of that property and the potential profits that might be realised from property transactions. Regulation is generally applied and concerned with broad issues of social equity, though there has also been a desire to retain a particular level of primary production in Norway's countryside. Broad social equity concerns are also apparent in Sweden where 'social sustainability' is interpreted as the need to balance production and consumption interests: the political debate is generally focused, but in the countryside is manifest as a desire to strike an accord between the needs of traditional communities and recreational pressures.

Similar approaches and policies emerge in France and the Netherlands. A cohesive culture in the Netherlands is articulated through a national spatial planning strategy in which the links between town and country are clearly set out. In France, a strong socialist tradition and an emphasis on levelling regional disparities results in policies that set and prioritise rights. Though policies might eventually operate differently in town and country, this is more by fortune than design, with government – central, regional and so forth – prioritising general interest.

Laissez-faire policy regimes

Laissez-faire regimes emerge as a product of more 'atomistic cultures: they are hollow' (cf. Rhodes, 1997) in the sense that they concede power to the market. In contrast to the repressive manner in which regulatory policy regimes exercise power, under laissez-faire conditions, power tends to be an enabling force. This is because it is exercised by market agents with a direct interest in property development and who, by virtue of this interest, drive change in the countryside.

Examples of this weaker regulatory regime are found in Italy (particularly towards the south of the country), Spain and the Republic of Ireland. In Italy, Padovani and Vettoretti (Chapter 7) describe the family as the central agent of social welfare. In a sense, power has been devolved to families that, in many respects are left to their own devices in the exchange of inter- and intra-generational support. In terms of the production of homes in the countryside, this can mean that the central state will turn a blind eye to the illegal erection of new dwellings by families to meet family needs. Stronger enforcement of planning regulation would, in this light, be seen as a direct challenge to the power of the family to deliver welfare support and would therefore run contrary to the prevailing cultural conditions. There have in recent years, however, been moves to strengthen planning enforcement. But the hope is that this can be achieved without completely closing the door on informal housing provision: in other words a compromise is being sought between the laissez-faire regime and a more controlled approach to development which fits a new paradigm – that of sustainable development.

On a less extensive scale, the same informalities in political and policy terms exist in Spain and the Republic of Ireland. Here they are expressed not only in terms of illegal housing development, but also a desire to relax regulation to create what are considered to be the right conditions for economic growth. Spain's 'dual track' housing policy is, in part, a recognition of the impracticalities and dangers of erecting barriers between local markets and new forms of housing consumption. These new forms of consumption – particularly centred on tourism – are thought to be essential to enhancing the economic vitality of many rural areas. Informality and handing power to local agents is seen as the best way of securing the future prosperity of communities. Whether or not the same philosophy exists in the Republic of Ireland is unclear, though there has been an obvious desire in recent years to ensure that development constraint does not become a barrier to incoming investment.

In all three countries, housing market distortions are rarely 'managed' in the same sense as they might be under regulatory policy regimes: rather, they tend to be 'ironed out' in more informal ways, whether through large-scale illegal housebuilding, as in Italy, or the sporadic development of cottages in open countryside (regulated, but only loosely), as in Ireland. Hence we see an antithesis to Hobbesian repression, in which informal power becomes a potent force for change.

Unstable policy regimes

Our third cultural condition centred upon the division between town and country; a product, in part, of historical process. This division underpins a political debate between rural and urban interests in which no group has been able to claim absolute hegemony. Unstable policy regimes are therefore best represented as a Machiavellian form of power (see Clegg, 1989). This is because power has not been 'won' (for example, by the state) but remains the subject of a continuous political struggle between competing interests.

Across the entire United Kingdom, unstable policy regimes prevail. The precise nature of these, however, differs between England, Scotland and Wales largely as a result of contrasting cultural priorities and divergent views on the role of state housing provision in the context of strong market housing demand. The south-east of England is a classic battleground for an unstable policy regime. It has been the focus of fierce political debate for several years, with government seeking (unsuccessfully) to balance competing pro- and anti-development interests. A culture of division between town and country centres upon significant market distortions, often attributed to the purchasing power wielded by urban interests in rural locations, and amplified by the restrictive nature of the planning system. The situation is worsened by the fairly recent withdrawal of the public sector from subsidised housing provision and the inadequacy of voluntary sector provision, partially as a result of declining grant levels, but also because of general land constraint policies. The environment, and the desire to protect it from encroachment, is another complicating factor. The underlying divisive culture discussed earlier, and the entrenched views of many of those engaged in the 'great housing debate', all drive an almost iterative debate surrounding the rural housing question. On the one hand, the situation might be lamented; but on the other it might be viewed as overtly democratic, with town keeping country in check and vice versa, avoiding the emergence of overly powerful hegemonies.

Again, the same debates are played out in both Scotland and Wales, each of which is subject to the same global changes and fluctuations in state welfare provision. Moreover, the same cleavages between economic production and residential consumption are also apparent. But in Wales, market conflict in many areas is couched in cultural terms with patterns of migration identified as a threat to a particular way of life (Edwards, Chapter 12). At the same time, Wales has displayed a greater traditional reliance on owner-occupation and an unwillingness to embrace public sector housing provision. These factors have heightened the political discord in some areas and fuel numerous campaigns to regulate the housing market in new ways, perhaps taking on board some of the 'lessons' that can be drawn from regulatory political regimes: particularly those found in

Scandinavia. In Scotland, the situation in relation to public provision is reversed, and council housing is viewed in a more positive light. But this has not prevented the large-scale loss of council housing in recent years or the market distortions that may stem from new forms of housing consumption.

Overall, the emphasis on market power within these unstable political regimes combines with a planning system that constrains market supply, to create social inequalities and exclusion. This drives the urban–rural cultural debate and sustains a dichotomous conflict. But does this mean that conflict is necessarily inflated under such regimes? A different perspective is that regulatory policy regimes, by virtue of their neutral focus, 'play down' conflict, whereas unstable policy regimes more readily advertise points of discord.

Linking themes: discussion

The emphasis up to this point has been on categorisation and the identification of key differences between countries resulting from particular cultural conditions and manifest in broad political debate and specific policies. But despite obvious contrasts across the ten countries and our three broad 'culture/regime' groups, it is still possible to find commonalities. We would suggest that the following four linking themes emerge from our analysis (the importance of each varies between countries and regimes and the nature of these variations is also noted). The summaries provided here lead into a more detailed final discussion in the next chapter.

Social exclusion. Occurs to a greater or lesser extent everywhere, but is particularly significant in the unstable policy regimes and is a product of low state provision, a weak rental market, a reliance on sale market provision and restrictive planning control. In the laissez-faire policy regimes, it tends to concentrate (in housing terms) where restriction is tighter or where concentrated tourist incursion coincides with pockets of economic deprivation. Such is the case in Spain. Under the regulatory policy regimes, the most visible example of social exclusion is identified on the Swedish west coast where the pricing out of some local groups from the housing market is attributed to the arrival of German nationals seeking second homes. Though social exclusion may occur under different conditions and exhibit a range of characteristics, it can be identified as a common process affecting some, if not all, of the case study countries.

The presence and role of social housing. The (declining) presence of social housing and its role in housing specific groups is another issue that cuts across the case studies. The term social housing is used here in its broadest sense, denoting both public sector and voluntary sector housing in the UK, co-operative forms of provision in Norway, the social housing sector in Italy or the different forms of state sponsored housing provision found in France or the Republic of Ireland. Of key concern in many of the case study countries is the changing size of the social housing stock, its distribution between town and country and the role it plays in either satisfying need outside the general market or offering a realistic and attractive alternative to market housing. In Norway, it may well perform the latter role, while in England, Scotland and Wales, need-based allocation policies have driven the social sector into a residual role: though this situation may change as more authorities launch choice-based lettings initiatives (which seek to make social housing a more inviting and comparable alternative to private letting).

The relationship between town and country. Throughout much of the discussion presented in this chapter, the relationship between town and country emerged as a recurrent theme. Cultural separation between the two, through history, accident or design, has been a driving force behind the development of current political debate and also the form that policy takes in respect of the countryside. We have already argued that unstable policy regimes are underpinned by a divisive urban–rural culture and regulatory regimes by a more coherent culture and centrist approach to policy design. When we return to this issue in the next chapter, we will consider the practical (policy) implications of this relationship tying some of the examples unearthed into a broader statement of impact.

Creating a competitive rural economy. The objective (and importance) of creating a more competitive rural economy is clear from all ten case studies irrespective of cultural condition or policy regime. In the Republic of Ireland, the informality of planning regulation is partly explained in terms of a fear of unduly hindering development. In Italy, the same informality aims at promoting innovation, and in Spain, considerable weight is being placed on extending the success of coastal tourism to the rural interior (albeit in a different form). In the UK, a more competitive rural economy is seen as at least one part of the antidote to strong external housing demand and a means for allowing local people to compete in the marketplace for rural property. In Norway and Sweden, sensitive tourism and diversification are objectives that have both been pursued with some vigour.

Again, these four themes emerge from the comparative overview provided in this chapter and are discussed more fully in the conclusions presented in the next chapter.

Conclusions

The 'divergent school' within the comparative housing studies literature has produced a series of typologies to explain housing policy differences between countries. Following the tradition established by Gosta Esping-Andersen (1990), these typologies have been derived from an analysis of how political ideologies produce different 'regimes' of housing provision. For example, Jim Kemeny's comparative analyses of housing in Britain, Australia and Sweden (1981, 1992) resulted in the identification of 'collectivist' and 'privatist' regimes.

Allen's chapter (this volume) noted that there has been an absence of comparative rural housing studies. In this chapter, we have attempted to correct this anomaly by undertaking a comparative analysis of rural housing in the various countries that have been discussed in this book. In doing so, we found Esping-Andersen's 'political regime' typological approach to be of limited use. We therefore developed our own typologies. The typologies that we have developed essentially constitute a 'power regime'[2] approach to comparative analysis. While this 'power regime' approach appears more accurate than 'political regime' theory in representing patterns of divergence in rural housing markets, at this stage it is nascent. Nevertheless, such an approach might not only provide a useful guide for further comparative analyses of rural housing markets, but also a reasonable tool for more general comparative studies of housing policy in the remainder of Europe and beyond.

Though there is perhaps limited value in summarising the detail of this chapter, it is perhaps pertinent to emphasise the central message. There *are* outward similarities between the ten case study countries that can be expressed in terms of core challenges. These relate to the extent of social exclusion, the role of social housing, the relationship between town and country and economic competitiveness. But the use of the 'power regime' approach has revealed that these outward similarities are the products of quite different cultural conditions and consequent political discourse and policy. Our hope is that this chapter has gone some way towards explaining how commonalities may be drawn from different national experiences without relying solely on cursory observation.

Notes

1   By repressive, we do not mean that power is exercised in a purely negative way, which might be regarded as oppressive. We are simply suggesting that power can be a reactive force that recognises and responds to changes by regulating or minimising their impact.

2   While Esping-Andersen and Kemeny are concerned with power, their interest is limited to who possesses and uses it rather than the ways in which it is possessed and used. This latter aspect is the focus of power regime theory.

Chapter 14
Conclusions

Mark Tewdwr-Jones, Nick Gallent and Mark Shucksmith

Introduction

We conclude this book by drawing out key themes from the ten case study chapters: these were summarised in the last chapter but are dealt with in more detail here. Following this overview of themes, we go on to assess a range of future policy options for dealing with rural housing pressure and also look at the role a revised spatial policy process may play in assisting the future provision of housing, and the rectifying of other housing pressures, across the European countryside.

All ten case studies reveal that government and government agency actors in each country are concerned about the pressure on housing supply across the different parts of their countryside. We believe that despite underlying differences between the countries, four key themes emerge that should be addressed through future strategy and policy. These are:

1   social exclusion;
2   the presence and changing role of social housing;
3   the relationship between town and country, and its implications for policy; and
4   creating a competitive rural economy.

We now take each of these in turn and consider the broad nature of the issue and how it is expressed in examples of different countries.

Social exclusion

With the exception of Shucksmith and Conway, few of the contributors refer directly to the term social exclusion. The authors of the Scotland case study however, point out that planning systems, which are a key vehicle for restraint policies in rural areas, often link with market distortions and cause either disadvantage to, or the exclusion of, lower income groups from many rural areas.

This process was confirmed in the majority of case studies, but for a variety of different reasons. In England and Wales, the loss of council housing over the last twenty years, combined with the strong desire of many to escape urban living, is creating overwhelming demand for housing in some of the most attractive rural areas. In Sweden and Norway, the acquisition of second homes by foreign buyers is bringing a comparable pressure, particularly on the Swedish west coast, though in Scandinavia the automatic conflict between town and country that seems to exist across Britain is absent, replaced on occasions by more sporadic concerns over this foreign encroachment. Folkesdotter notes that the exclusion of the young from housing in many of the smaller fishing villages is a cause of growing concern. In Italy, a similar process of exclusion seems to be on the horizon as government initiates moves to strengthen planning control. This will mean that the natural venting of housing pressure manifest in illegal housebuilding may be curtailed and hence a process of creeping exclusion will set in as housing acquires a greater scarcity value.

The link between income and exclusion, brought on by increasing housing demand and tightening regulation – in the name of environmental protection and under the auspices of sustainability – is apparent throughout Europe. But it does not always result in, or stem from, an urban–rural conflict over housing consumption. There are many processes at work: changes in the agricultural economy; the opening of markets to foreign consumption interests; the de-skilling of the rural population; the growth of tourism; the aims and nature of housing strategy and policy; and many other factors too. These are all ingredi-ents that display a different balance of importance across western Europe, and add up to clear patterns of exclusion: patterns that may require some remedial response if countries wish to avoid a rural society fractured along income lines.

The present and changing role of social housing

Another common theme running through the studies is the role of social housing. Clearly, the term 'social housing' itself has a wide variety of meanings across Europe. In Britain we tend to associate it with 'state landlordism' and traditional council housing, though in recent years it has assumed a variety of different guises and is predominantly delivered and managed by a voluntary housing sector. In Scandinavia, social housing might be thought of as that provided through co-operative housing schemes and would therefore include different forms of owner-occupied provision. Elsewhere, particularly in France and Italy, it is perhaps closer in type to British social housing and in recent years has followed the same downward trajectory – in terms of its diminishing volume and shrinking social role.

A critical issue across many, if not all of the ten countries, is the changing role of social housing in the countryside and how this role has changed in relation to the importance of market housing. Across Britain, the relative importance and availability of social housing of all types has declined at a time when the rural housing market has become far more competitive in many areas. This has acted to amplify the processes of social exclusion noted above. In Italy, state housing has traditionally been rejected in many rural areas (particularly in the south of the country) as families choose to look inward rather than outward for social support. But as government seeks to reign-in illegal development and perhaps centralise the delivery of welfare services, it is possible that social housing in Italy will take on a new importance. In the Scandinavian examples, and perhaps also in France, an abundance of relatively cheap rural housing has meant a reduced need for this form of state provision. In Norway and Sweden, attempts to control the use of private property have been partially successful in offsetting the need for this type of response. However, tighter occupancy and private property use rules look likely to fall prey to European Union Law, meaning that in the future this type of housing provision for lower income groups may become more important. In Spain too, the coincidence of strong tourist growth and relative poverty could increase the need for state-sponsored housing alternatives.

Therefore, relative to market changes and given the economic problems afflicting some sections of rural society (noted below), the role of social housing across western Europe may need to be revisited. All the countries examined in this book have different views towards (and types of) social housing. All, however, may need to consider how best to manage future population growth and therefore housing demand, which will be a product of both natural population change and immigration. But at the same time, these countries need to ensure that social housing does not become the last choice of the most deprived immigrants, as has happened recently in parts of England, and as has happened in the past in both Italy and France. Across Britain, authorities are attempting to increase the appeal of social housing through choice-based lettings policies, which give prospective tenants greater say over where they are housed and in what type of housing. Elsewhere in Europe, the challenge will be to promote state housing as a real alternative to home ownership, which will be no mean feat given the degree to which the virtues of ownership have been extolled by European governments in recent years.

Town and country

The relationship between town and country is central to the way that policy has evolved in all ten case study chapters. We have already argued that policy is, in part, merely an expression of underlying social values. Policy in Britain, for example, has shaped and been shaped by a particularly problematic relationship between town and country, resulting in constant policy challenges and patterns of housing production that commonly reflect underlying politic suspicions and backbiting rather than levels of need. Elsewhere, there has been a better relationship between town and country. In Spain, for example, policy has sought to strike a balance between the needs of agricultural communities and the importance of allowing controlled growth for the benefit of a developing rural tourist industry. In Norway, the way in which housing policy has been pinned upon an underlying philosophy of social equity has helped stave off urban–rural conflict. And in the Netherlands, a broader approach to spatial planning has been used to set wider policy objectives that are not determined by a town versus country mentality.

We have already suggested, in Chapters 1 and 13, that more divisive cultures, fractured by strong town or country allegiances, frequently create divisive regulatory regimes which have an effectiveness undermined by constant challenge and discord. In England, planning has become a political tool which is hijacked by an elite and used to ward off development that, on many occasions, is designed to meet the needs of the less well off. In the context of a market economy, bestowing particular protections to the countryside and making the *land* itself (rather than communities and the most vulnerable members of society) the subject of that protection, creates a situation where people often come second to environmental factors. In Britain, the whole urban–rural debate often boils down to how much hedgerow will be lost if a development goes ahead, rather than how many people will continue to endure poor housing if it does not. The point is that if the tension between town and country is allowed to persist, then these types of debate will continue to cloud the judgement of policy makers. That is not to say that environmental attributes are unimportant, but rather that policy should seek a wider social equity. For example, where town and country divisions have been traditionally less apparent, policy has tended to focus on fundamental rights or broad spatial strategies. These have driven a welfare agenda that seeks to balance competing interests, but also prioritises the rights of individuals to a decent home. In Sweden, for example, municipalities are ready to provide leisure outlets in the countryside and do not discourage the ownership of second homes. But their priority is with ensuring that people have access to a first home, and they will implement national measures where these two priorities conflict, with the prime objective of ensuring that no one is knocked out of the housing market and becomes homeless. In the Netherlands, the same priorities are reflected in Spatial Planning with the agenda firmly favouring a suitable level of housing provision over other considerations. But balancing social with environmental objectives is clearly the concern of any planning system, and nobody would pretend that achieving this balance is easy. Our point, however, is that the task is made that much more difficult where the countryside is treated as a separate entity and political interest groups are allowed to play a rural agenda off against an urban one. This frequently leads to the denial of rural need and the suggestion that there should be almost zero tolerance to growth in the countryside. In the Netherlands, there is a clear desire to avoid this situation. In Italy, there are concerns that government is heading in this direction. And in England, Wales and Scotland (though England in particular), this problem has already taken hold, revealed by the way in which some groups confuse the government's 'brownfield over greenfield' agenda with a preference for all new housebuilding to be concentrated in cities. It has also resulted in many largely rural authorities rejecting or ducking beneath housing allocations, ostensibly seeing growth as an urban phenomenon.

We would see this urban–rural tension as a barrier to social equity and suggest that governments need to think holistically about the rural housing question, prioritising need and accommodating growth. Though of course, this has to be combined with renewed efforts towards urban renewal and improvement. The conditions need to be created in which people can leave cities if they absolutely want to, but are not forced out by persistent social and physical problems.

Creating a competitive rural economy

The fourth of our key emergent themes is the need to foster and sustain a competitive rural economy. This, we would suggest, is an issue strongly shaping the other three themes. If the rural economy is weak then those engaged in rural employment are likely to find themselves locked into a low-wage economy, unable to compete with consumption interests who derive their wealth from highly-paid and highly-skilled sectors elsewhere. In fact, their weakened position in the housing market will be as much a product of their inability to effectively compete in that market, as any encroachment from outsiders. Unemployment and low wages are the root cause of limited housing access across Europe. No market is completely closed and all 'local' people will find themselves competing for housing against buyers from elsewhere.

These same economic weaknesses also determine the necessary role of social housing in the local market. Ineffective demand will mean a greater need for non-market housing options, if it is not to result in rural homelessness and overcrowding. In Scotland, public sector housing has been traditionally viewed as a suitable alternative to market housing within local low-wage economies. There is an acceptance that such alternatives are needed and play an important social role. In England, Wales and Italy, however, public housing has become increasingly stigmatised over the last twenty years. The issue then is how to turn this situation around, and convince people that until wider economic prosperity can be achieved, social housing is a good alternative to other housing provision. Another problem, however, is that some societies do not merely see housing as a right, but rather home ownership as a right. As a result, they drift into a paradoxical situation where they (wish to) pump in subsidy to enable people to buy a home, but close the doors on migrants who may offer part of the answer to turning around the economic fortunes of an area. In fact, they seem to want growth without growth: new money but no new people. This situation prevails in parts of Wales.

Third, the link between town and country is also critical in terms of fostering a more competitive and stronger rural economy. Cities have undeniably been the engines of economic growth since the industrial revolution, and many rural areas have, in comparison, faded into economic obscurity. If then, the decision is made to separate out rural from urban in policy terms, what hope is there that the countryside will share in future economic growth? There is evidence to show that some industries have chosen to decentralise in recent years, northern Italy and England being obvious examples (see Breheny, 1999) and this has brought some benefits for rural areas. But on the whole, the scope for major manufacturers or finance houses to move to remote rural areas, despite the advent of huge technological advances, is probably limited. The challenge for rural areas, therefore, is two-fold: how to remain open to such investment opportunities where they arise, and also how to foster an enterprise culture. The latter may involve a range of economic diversifications and there are examples of these throughout the ten case studies. It may also mean letting go of the past (often an agricultural past) and embracing a different future. But here again, town–country divisions arise. The rural past is often viewed as one of production (agricultural) while the future is one of consumption (tourism); and this change is frequently painted as former self-sufficiency being replaced by a reliance on urban money. Hence, the town is an exploiter and consumer of the rural. We would suggest that getting beyond this analysis is an important step for rural areas. In England, the Countryside Agency is currently (April 2002) running a rural promotional campaign under the banner 'Your Countryside: You're Welcome'. What they might add is that there is a general perception that visiting the countryside is one thing, staying and moving there is completely different. The tension between town and country persists: were it possible to overcome this tension, then a focus on broader social equity issues would surely be more desirable.

So the question facing all ten countries is how to level the economic playing field between town and country: or rather – in divisive terms – how to improve job prospects and incomes irrespective of location. In Norway, the insistence that agriculture must occupy a revered position in the rural psyche is seen as particularly damaging and a barrier to diversification. But also, the acceptance that the countryside is a legitimate destination for consumption interests helps offset many problems in the agricultural economy. In contrast, the 'look but don't touch' philosophy that permeates rural thinking in Britain has led to a false reliance on agriculture and a diversification strategy drawing on huge public subsidy but with limited yield. In Spain, tourism is seen as an answer, but there is of course concern that the Spanish interior could degenerate into a rural facsimile of the Costa Del Sol. Hence measures to promote 'soft' tourism based less on all-out consumption and more on promoting the cultural and historic attributes of key destinations is being touted. There are no obvious answers to the economic dilemma but it is clear that the authors contributing to this book, and policy makers on the ground, place rural economic issues at the forefront of the wider rural agenda. Without a sustainable and competitive economy, rural areas will continue to be reliant on strong interventionist policy approaches, that can only offer short-term respites from housing and other pressures, but fail to deliver any long-term solutions.

In the final two sections of this chapter, we consider some of the strategy and policy options available to those whose task it is to deal with housing, and wider pressures, across Europe.

Policy responses within spatial planning

The future of rural areas within the European territory has emerged as one of the key important aspects of the spatial planning policy frameworks of the EU (Tewdwr-Jones and Williams, 2001). Important spatial policy documents have emerged from the EU recently, including *Europe 2000+*, the *Sixth Framework Report on Economic and Social Cohesion* and the various drafts of the *European Spatial Development Perspective* process. These have all highlighted the particular challenges and opportunities that face rural areas, and especially peripheral regions (White *et al.* 2000). At the EU level, policy responses have emerged to support rural regions, from the Common Agricultural Policy and Structural Funds to specific initiatives such as the INTERREG IIIC Community Initiative and Article 10 of the European Regional Development Fund.

This book has been produced at a time when there are significant developments emerging in the spatial planning frameworks of the European Union and within member states through policy development. These developments in spatial planning concerned with the future of rural areas are mirrored by developments in theory on rurality. All these attempt to provide a framework for considering forces of convergence and divergence of urban and rural areas in Europe. Associated with these theoretical developments has been the development of the sustainability debate over the last decade and this has considerable implications for the development of rural regions and is an important factor influencing the future shape of spatial planning responses to key development issues, or housing policy priorities, in different countries.

In addition to the theoretical developments witnessed in relation to rurality in recent years, policy debates surrounding the future of rural areas have also developed considerably. These have developed through, for example, the European Spatial Development Perspective and the reform of the Structural Funds and Common Agricultural Policy at the European level. Furthermore, within countries, the moves towards enhanced regionalism, the sustainable development agenda, the transport policy agenda, and the need to respond to demographic change and urban–rural population shifts will all impact on strategic state priorities. All these policy arenas have implications for rural regions and, as such, an important element of the research has been to examine forms for housing policy responses for rural areas.

The key questions we pose here relate to searching for a suitable forum or policy mechanism appropriate for tackling problems associated with rural housing:

1   How important could the EU spatial planning framework be in informing future policy on rural areas, and rural housing in particular?
2   The term rurality is often synonymous with accessibility and peripherality, competitiveness and inequalities (exclusion/inclusion) and sustainable development. The linkages between these various forces, or cross-cutting issues is of key importance in informing our understanding of the opportunities and challenges facing rural areas.
3   To what extent should member states explicitly compensate rural areas for their higher housing costs? What policy mechanisms could be utilised, or adapted to reflect the housing problems of rural areas?

It has been stressed throughout the book that the current problems and future prosperity of rural areas need to be addressed with regard to a broad range of policy areas at all levels of government. Rural problems manifest themselves in local areas in different ways and they are impacted upon by wider sectoral policies not related simply to housing, but also to access, employment and economic development, the environment, agriculture and tourism. Rural problems therefore need to be assessed as a whole and take into account these far-reaching issues.

Planning systems have a key role to play in encouraging sustainable development in rural areas and this is to be best achieved through integrated policies that encompass various cross-cutting development issues, particularly related to transport and accessibility, economic development, community inclusion and housing provision for groups in need. Promoting sustainable development is supporting policies that will assist in ensuring that the economic, social and environmental well-being of communities in the future.

From rurality to territory within policy debates

The problems of rural areas have been assessed by policy makers as criteria for identifying regions within the European Union eligible for support from one or other of the Structural Funds and a range of other EU initiatives. Rural concerns have been addressed through many economic development and infrastructure projects that have received millions of euros over the last ten years. While rural regions have generally acquired the label of 'economic disadvantaged', there may be many exceptions to this rule. Similarly, the interchangeable use of the terms 'disadvantaged rural areas' and 'peripherality' is problematic in the field of economic and spatial policy. The European Spatial Development Perspective (European Commission, 1999) aims to forge the national spatial development policies of each of the EU member states with EC sectoral policies, taking into account subsidiarity. The long-term trends of the European Union, together with reform of both the Structural Funds and the Common Agricultural Policy, are intended to be built upon to create new policy opportunities on a variety of spatial scales. The European context for these changes, as stated in the ESDP, are:

1   the progressive economic integration and related increased co-operation between member states;
2   the growing importance of local and regional communities and their role in spatial development; and
3   the anticipated enlargement of the EU and the development of closer relations with its neighbours.

This context will additionally be influenced by global and technological developments in addition to general demographic, social and ecological trends. Nevertheless, the prime objective is to secure increased territorial and social cohesion within the EU.

Within the EU, the ESDP's impact on government policies will result in an opportunity for re-examination of the problems and characteristics associated with rural areas. This changing political context will occur on two levels: at the political and administrative level within member states; and at the European territorial level.

At the political and administrative level, existing sectoral policies within traditional political and administrative boundaries will continue. Devolution, decentralisation and local policy making provide opportunities for local regions and communities to address their own rural problems. On the European territorial level, European policies and regional co-operation will seek alternative ways of conceptualising urban and rural problems that transcend existing political and administrative boundaries within member states.

The future relationship between the rural and urban, or periphery and core, could be directly affected by these policy developments. Depending on member states' decisions as to which of the arenas of focus to concentrate on, problems associated with rural areas could in future be viewed as part of a wider political solution to resolving urban or regional issues. Labour market changes, retirement migration, agricultural decline, land use conflicts and the conservation of historical and cultural assets within the region could all be viewed from the perspective of the rural community and the potential offered by the urban area. Similarly, problems at the urban level might stem from rural locations.

The urban–rural relationship is complex but this could be the focus of future policy initiatives – the dynamics of the rural and urban together – rather than sectoral policies addressing urban or rural issues, devised by separate policy makers and promoted through separate funding mechanisms.

A territorial and intra-regional perspective of rural areas

This broader perspective, on the dynamics of the rural and the urban, transposes academic and policy makers' attempts to address distinctly rural problems and, in turn, policy solutions, into a much broader laboratory for study. The ESDP suggests that future study should occur on the integration of town/city with countryside/rural areas, the relationships between them, and the intra-regional solutions that could be formulated to address them. This represents a challenge to existing EU and national state policies and the boundaries and delivery mechanisms within which they presently reside. Essentially, the issue for examination becomes how the second level of policy (EU territorial) impacts upon the first level (national political and administrative). But possibilities are also offered to address urban–rural problems by diverting policies and resources to dynamic growth zones that transcend urban areas and their rural hinterlands.

The focus on core–periphery (or urban–rural) relationships necessitates an analysis of *territory*, rather than periphery, urban or rural alone. Achieving growth zones within regions that benefit existing urban areas and the rural areas surrounding them could lead to a strengthening of regional cohesion both economically and socially, and could also take into account cultural, language, environment and historical linkages that are presently key features of rural locations but which often fail to be taken into account sufficiently through policy development. This would also result in attention focusing on infrastructure relationships between the core and periphery, transportation links, accessibility to communication and services, labour market opportunities and housing provision.

Conclusion

The aim of this book was to provide a comprehensive text on rural housing in Europe, stretching from concerns over the nature of housing pressure to debates focused on the way forward in terms of policy responses. It is hopefully clear, particularly from this final chapter and the analysis presented in Chapter 13, that a number of different underlying factors have, to a certain extent, resulted in some similar problems. The challenge for pan-National policy makers is to arrive at a response that addresses the problems while being sensitive to these under-lying factors. It is impossible, we believe, to develop a specific 'European policy' for dealing with housing pressure. It is possible, however, to arrive at a strategy for pooling the skills and resources, for tackling the broad challenges identified within this book.

References

Chapter 1

Alberdí, B. and Levenfeld, G. (1996) 'Spain', in P. Balchin (ed.) *Housing Policy in Europe* (Routledge: London), pp. 170–187

Allen, C., Gallent, N. and Tewdwr-Jones, M. (1999) 'The limits of policy diffusion: comparative experiences of second housebuilding in Britain and Sweden', in *Environment and Planning C: Government and Policy* 17(2): 227–244

Balchin, P. (ed.) (1996) *Housing Policy in Europe* (Routledge: London)

Barlow, J. and Duncan, S. (1994) *Success and Failure in Housing Provision: European Systems Compared* (Pergamon: Oxford)

Clapham, D., Hegedus, J., Kintrea, K. and Tosics, I. (eds) (1996) *Chasing the Market: Housing Privatisation in Eastern Europe* (Greenwood: London)

Doling, J. (1997) *Comparative Housing Policy: Government and Housing in Advanced Industrialised Countries* (Macmillan Press: Basingstoke)

Gallent, N. and Tewdwr-Jones, M. (2000) *Rural Second Homes in Europe: Examining Housing Supply and Planning Control* (Ashgate: Aldershot)

Gallent, N. and Tewdwr-Jones, M. (2001) 'Second homes and the UK planning system', in *Planning Practice and Research* 16(1): 59–70

Golland, A. (1998) *Systems of Housing Supply and Housing Production in Europe* (Ashgate: Aldershot)

Harloe, M., Ball, M. and Martens, M. (1988) *Housing and Social Change in Europe and the USA* (Routledge: London)

Kemeny, J. (1981) *The Myth of Home Ownership: Public Versus Private Choices in Housing Tenure* (Routledge: London)

Kemeny, J. (1992) *Housing and Social Theory* (Routledge: London)

McCrone, G. and Stephens, M. (1995) *Housing Policy in Britain and Europe* (UCL Press: London)

Oxley, M. and Smith, J. (1996) *Housing Policy and Rented Housing in Europe* (E&F Spon: London)

Padovani, L. (1996) 'Italy', in P. Balchin (ed.) *Housing Policy in Europe* (Routledge: London), pp. 188–209

Stephens, M., Burns, N. and MacKay, L. (2002) *Social Market or Safety Net? British Social Rented Housing in a European Context* (Policy Press: Bristol)

Struyk, R. (ed.) (1995) *Economic Restructuring in the Former Soviet Bloc: Evidence from the Housing Sector* (The Urban Institute Press: Washington DC)

Turner, B., Hegedus, J. and Tosics, I. (eds) (1992) *The Reform of Housing in Eastern Europe and the Soviet Union* (Routledge: London)

van Vliet, W. (ed.) (1990) *International Handbook for Housing Policies and Practices* (Greenwood Press: London)

Winn, M. (ed.) (1984) *Housing in Europe* (Croom Helm: London)

Chapter 2

Allen, C. (1999a) 'Disablism in housing and comparative community care discourse – towards an interventionist model of disability and interventionist welfare regime theory', *Housing Theory and Society* 16(1): 3–16

Allen, C. (1999b) 'Towards a comparative sociology of residence and disablement – Britain and Sweden in interventionist welfare regime perspective', in *Housing Theory and Society* 16(2): 49–66

Allen, C., Gallent, N. and Tewdwr-Jones, M. (1999) 'The limits of policy diffusion: comparative experiences in residential tourism in Britain and Sweden', in *Environment and Planning C: Government and Policy* 17(2): 227–244

Ball, M., Harloe, M. and Martens, M. (1988) *Housing and Social Change in Europe and USA* (Routledge: London)

Barlow, J. and Duncan, S. (1994) *Success and Failure in Housing Provision: European Systems Compared* (Pergamon: Oxford)

Bell, D. (1960) *The End of Ideology* (Free Press: Illinois)

Bielckus, C.L., Rogers, A.W. and Wibberley, G.P. (1972) *Second Homes in England and Wales: A study of the distribution and use of rural properties taken over as second residences* (Wye College, School of Rural Economics and Related Studies)

Dartington Amenity Research Trust (1977) *Second Homes in Scotland: a report to Countryside Commission for Scotland, Scottish Tourist Board, Highlands and Island Development Board, Scottish Development Department* (Totnes, DART Publication No. 22)

Doling, J. (1997) *Comparative Housing Policy: Government and Housing in Advanced Industrialised Countries* (Macmillan: London)

Dolowitz, D. and Marsh, D. (n.d.) *Who Learns What from Whom: a Review of the Policy Transfer Literature* (Glasgow, University of Strathclyde Department of Government)

Donnison, D. (1967) *The Government of Housing* (Penguin: Harmondsworth)

Dower, M. (1977) 'Planning aspects of second homes', in J.T. Coppock (ed.) *Second Homes: Curse or Blessing?* (Pergamon Press: Oxford)

Downing, P. and Dower, M. (1973) *Second Homes in England and Wales* (Countryside Commission, HMSO: London)

Eyden, J. (1965) 'The growth and development of the social services and the welfare state', in D. Marsh (ed.) *An Introduction to the Study of Social Administration* (Routledge: London)

Freeman, R. and Tester, S. (1996) 'Social policy diffusion', paper presented to the Social Policy Association Conference, Social Policy in Europe: Convergence or Divergence, 16–18 July, Sheffield Hallam University

Gallent, N. and Tewdwr-Jones, M. (2000) *Rural Second Homes in Europe: Examining Housing Supply and Planning Control* (Ashgate: Aldershot)

Gallent, N. and Tewdwr-Jones, M. (2001) 'Second homes and the UK planning system', *Planning Practice and Research* 16(1): 59–70

Gould, A. (1990) *Capitalist Welfare Systems: A Comparison of Japan, Britain and Sweden* (Longman: London)

Harloe, M. (1985) *Private Rented Housing in the United States and Europe* (Croom Helm: London)

Harloe, M. (1995) *The People's Home: Social Rented Housing in Europe and America* (Blackwell: Oxford)

Kemeny, J. (1981) *The Myth of Home Ownership: Private versus Public Choice in Housing Tenure* (Routledge and Kegan Paul, London)

Kemeny, J. (1992) *Housing and Social Theory* (Routledge: London)

Kemeny, J. (1995) *From Public Housing to the Social Market: Rental Systems in Comparative Perspective* (Routledge: London)

Kemeny, J. and Lowe, S. (1998) 'Schools of comparative housing research: from convergence to divergence', *Housing Studies* 13(2): 161–176

Kerr, C. (1962) *Industrialism and Industrial Man* (Heinemann: London)

Lipset, S.M. (1963) *Political Man* (Anchor Books: New York)

Marshall, T.H. (1967) *Social Policy: 2nd Edition* (Hutchinson: London)

Marshall, T.H. (1970) *Social Policy: 3rd Edition* (Hutchinson: London)

Mishra, R. (1973) 'Welfare and industrial man', *Sociological Review* 21(4): 535–560

O'Connor, J. (1973) *The Fiscal Crisis of the State* (St. Martins Press: New York)

Power, A. (1993) *Hovels to Highrise: Social Housing in Europe since 1850* (Routledge: London)

Pyne, C.B. (1973) Second Homes (Caernarvonshire County Planning Department: Caernarfon)

Rose, R. (1991) 'What is lesson drawing?', *Journal of Public Policy* 11(1): 3–30

Shucksmith, M. (1981) *No Homes for Locals?* (Gower: Farnborough)

Shucksmith, M. (1990) *Housebuilding in Britain's Countryside* (Routledge: USA and Canada)

Shucksmith, M., Tewdwr-Jones, M. and Gallent, N. (2000) *International Experience of Pressured Rural Areas*, Report Commissioned by Scottish Homes (Department of Land Economy, University of Aberdeen) p. 96

Soley, C. (1990) 'Seconds out', *Roof* 15(2): 38–39

Wedderburn, D. (1965) *The Facts and Theories of the Welfare State: 1965 Socialist Register* (Merlin Press: London)

Wilensky, H. (1975) 'Leftism, catholicism, and democratic corporatism: the role of political parties in recent welfare state development', in P. Flora, and A.J. Heidenheimer (eds) *The Development of Welfare States in Europe and America* (Transaction Books: New Jersey)

Wolman, H. (1992) 'Understanding cross-national policy transfers: the case of Britain and the US', *Governance* 5(1): 27–45

Zald, M. (1965) *Social Welfare Institutions* (Wiley: New York)

Chapter 3

Aanesland, Normann and Holm, Olaf (2000) *Offentlig regulering av markedet for land-brukseiendommer – virkninger for verdiskapning og bosetting* (Landbruksforlaget: Oslo)

Annaniassen, Erling (2002) 'Vendepunktet for "den sosialdemokratiske orden": 1970 – tallet og boligpolitikken', *Tidsskrift for Samfunnsforskning* 43: 155–189

Falkanger, Thor (2000) *Tingsrett* (Universitetsforlaget: Oslo)

Gulbrandsen, Lars (1983) *Boligmarked og boligpolitikk. Eksemplet Oslo* (Universitetsforlaget: Oslo)

Gulbrandsen, Lars (1988) 'Norway', in Hans Kroes, Ymkers Frits, and Andre Mulder (eds) *Between Owner-Occupation and Rented Sector. Housing in ten European countries.* (The Netherlands Christian Institute for Social Housing: De Bilt, The Netherlands), pp. 121–143.

Gulbrandsen, Lars (1989) *Boligomsetning under nye rammebetingelser* (Oslo INAS. Notat 89:6)

Gulbrandsen, Lars (1998) *Husholdningenes boligfinansiering* (Oslo: NOVA, Skriftserie 3/98)

Myklebost, Hallstein (1960) *Norges tettbygde steder 1875–1950* (Universitetsforlaget: Oslo)

Myklebost, Hallstein (1989) 'Migration of elderly Norwegians', *Norsk geografisk tidsskrift* 43: 191–213

Nordvik, Viggo and Lars Gulbrandsen (2001) *En bolig ekstra. Ekstraboligers betydning som utleieobjekt og boligkapital* (Byggforsk. Prosjektrapport 312: Oslo)

NOU (1981:5) *Fast eiendom*

Rasmussen, Tor Fr. (1988) 'Urbanisering – et onde?' *Nytt Norsk Tidsskrift*, 5 årgang no. 2: 40–52

Rasmussen, Tor Fr. (1995) 'De lange linjer i norsk distriktspolitikk og urbaniseringsdebatt', in Håvard Teigen, Ragnar Nordgreen and Olav Spilling (eds) *Langtidsliner i distriktspolitikk og tiltaksarbeid* (Stabæk. Vett og Viten a/s)

Sevatdal, Hans m. fl. (2002) *Boligpolitiske konsekvenser av jordpolitisk lovgivning, retningslinjer og prakis m.v. Elektronisk vedlegg til* (NOU 2002:2. Boligmarkedene og politikken) http://odin.dep.no/krdvedlegg/01/09/bolig028.pfd

Statistisk sentralbyrå (1923) *Folketellingen i Norge* 1 desember 1920. Syvende hefte. Boligstatistikk. (Byer. Kristiania) NOS VII 98

Statistisk sentralbyrå (1924) Folketellingen i Norge 1 desember 1920. Ottende hefte. Boligstatistikk. – Bygder. Kristiania, NOS VII 144

Statistisk sentralbyrå (1957): Folketellingen 1 desember 1950. Tiende hefte. NOS XI 253. Oslo

St.meld. nr 35 (1999–2000) Om praktiseringen av jord- og konsesjonslovgivningen i 1996–1999 (Report to the Storting)

Sundt, Eilert (1976) Om bygnings-skikken på landet i Norge (Gyldendal: Oslo) (original 1862)

Chapter 4

Amcoff, Jan (2000) 'Samtida bosättning på svensk landsbygd' (Contemporary settling in the Swedish countryside) *Geografiska regionstudier* 41, 222 pp. (Uppsala University: Uppsala) Swedish text with a summary in English

Andersson, Roger (2001) 'The Swedish area-based urban strategy', in Christoferson (ed.) *Swedish Planning – in Times of Diversity* (The Swedish Society for Town and Country Planning: Gävle)

Ayala, P.F. (1980) *Svenska folkets idealort, En jämförelse mellan önskade, befintliga och planerade boendeförhållanden* (Swedes' Ideal Places, A comparison between wanted, existing and planned dwelling conditions) Forskningsrapport no. 65, Kulturgeografiska institutionen (Uppsala universitet: Uppsala)

Böhme, Kai (2001) 'Swedish spatial development perspectives', in Christofersen (ed.) *Swedish Planning – in Times of Diversity* (The Swedish Society for Town and Country Planning: Gävle)

Borgström, Bengt-Erik and Ann-Kristin Ekman (1992) *Lantbrukares villkor och värderingar* (Farmers' conditions and values) Rapport no. 3: 1992 (Sveriges lantbruksuniversitet: Uppsala)

Christoferson (ed.) (2001) *Swedish Planning – in Times of Diversity* (The Swedish Society for Town and Country Planning, with grants from Formas and the Swedish Board of Housing, Building and Planning: Gävle)

Enochsson, Pia (2001) *Dagens Nyheter*, 5 July 2001, Section A, p. 4

Fehler *et al.* (2001) 'Environmental and resource management – programme for the archipelago', in Christoferson (2001) (ed.) *Swedish Planning – in Times of Diversity* (The Swedish Society for Town and Country Planning: Gävle)

Folkesdotter, Gärd (1986) *Housing Construction and Rural Settlement – a Descriptive Biography* (The National Swedish Institute for Building Research, bulletin M85:23: Gävle)

Folkesdotter, Gärd (1987) 'Research and policy for rural housing in Sweden', in B.D. MacGregor, D.S. Robertson and M. Shucksmith (eds) *Rural Housing in Scotland, Recent Research and Policy* (Aberdeen University Press: Aberdeen)

Folkesdotter, Gärd (1995) *Vilka har styrt bebyggelseutvecklingen på landsbygden?* (Who has controlled the settlement development in rural areas?) (Meyers: Gävle)

Gustafsson, Maria (2001) 'Trends in Swedish sparsely-populated and rural communities', in Christoferson (ed.) *Swedish Planning – in Times of Diversity* (The Swedish Society for Town and Country Planning: Gävle)

Halfacree, K. (1995) 'Talking about rurality: social representations of the rural as expressed by six English parishes', in *Journal of Rural Studies* 11(1): 1–20

Hedman, Eva (2001) 'Swedish housing and housing policy', in Christoferson (ed.) *Swedish Planning – in Times of Diversity* (The Swedish Society for Town and Country Planning: Gävle)

Johansson, Lars (2001) 'Strömstad bygger för norska köpare' (Strömstad builds for Norwegian buyers), *Dagens Nyheter* 24 July 2001

Johansson, Mats (2001) 'The crisis of small and medium-sized towns – dual Sweden revisited', in Christoferson (ed.) *Swedish Planning – in Times of Diversity* (The Swedish Society for Town and Country Planning: Gävle)

Johnson, Ylva (2001) 'Kommuner struntar i strandskyddet' (Municipalities ignore waterfront protection), *Dagens Nyheter*, 26 July 2001

Lundström, Stellan (2001) 'Swedish housing – from regulation to market', in Christoferson (ed.) *Swedish Planning – in Times of Diversity* (The Swedish Society for Town and Country Planning: Gävle)

Müller, Dieter (1999) *German Second Home Owners in the Swedish Countryside. On the Internationalization of the Leisure Space* (Department of Social and Economic Geography, Umeå University and Östersund, European Tourism Research Institute, Mid-Sweden University: Umeå)

Nilsson, Annika (2000) 'Oro för upptrissade fastighetspriser' (Worry for property prices driven up), *Dagens Nyheter*, 23 July 2000

Nordström, Maria and Mårtensson, Fredrika (2001) *Att bo på landet är olika*. (To live in the countryside is to live different lives), Sveriges lantbruksuniversitet, rapport 01:4, Institutionen för landskapsplanering: Alnarp. (English summary)

Planering för hållbar utveckling (Planning for sustainable development) (2000) (Boverket, The National Board for Housing, Building and Planning: Karlskrona)

Rimsén, Fredrik (2001a) 'Sökes: Hälsingegårdar, Finnes: Kapitalstarka köpare' (Wanted: farms in the province of Hälsingland; there are buyers with capital), *Ljusnan*, 26 June 2001

Rimsén, Fredrik (2001b) 'Generösa Söderhamn, Tillåter många nybyggen på stränder med skydd' (Generous Söderhamn, allows many new constructions on protected shores), *Ljusnan*, 27 July 2001

Rundblad, Bengt (1951) *Forestville. A Study of Rural Sociological Change*. (Sociologiska Institutionen, Uppsala Universitet: Uppsala)

Stenbacka, Susanne (2001) 'Landsbygdsboende i inflyttarnas perspektiv. Intention och handling i lokalsamhället' (Countryside living from the perspectives of new-comers. Intentions and actions in the local community.) *Geografiska regionstudier* no. 42, 266 p. (Department of Social and Economic Geography, Uppsala Universitet: Uppsala) (English summary)

Chapter 5

Atzema, O. and Dam, F. van (1996) 'Binnenlandse migratie en regionale inkomenson-twikkeling', *Bevolking en Gezin* 1996/2, pp. 19–51

Council for Rural Areas (1997) *Urban and Rural Areas: The Green Connection. Advice on the Spatial Planning of Urban and Rural Areas* (Council for Rural Areas: Amersfoort)

Dam, F. van (2000) 'Revealed and stated preferences for rural living. Evidence from the Netherlands', T. Haartsen, P. Groote and P.P.P. Huigen (eds), *Claiming Rural Identities. Dynamics, Contexts, Policies*, pp. 80–91

Dam, F. van and Buckers, D. (1998) 'Twee vliegen in een klap? Wonen als nieuwe economische drager van het platteland', *Tijdschrift voor de Volkshuisvesting* 4(1): 27–31

Dam, F. van and Heins, S. (2000) 'Huisje, bomen, beesten. Een analyse van rurale woonpreferenties met behulp van het WBO', *Tijdschrift voor de Volkshuisvesting*, 6(2): pp. 22–26

Dam, F. van, Heins, S. and Elbersen, B. (2002) 'Lay discourses of the rural and stated and revealed preferences for rural living. Some evidence of the existence of a rural idyll in the Netherlands' (forthcoming)

Elbersen, B. (2001) *Nature on the Doorstep. The Relationship between Protected Natural Areas and Residential Activity in the European Countryside* (Alterra: Wageningen)

European Commission (2000) 'The (re)population of rural areas' decline? What decline?', *Leader Magazine* no. 22, Spring 2000

Heins, S., Dam, F. van and Goetgeluk, R. (2002) 'A tragedy of the Dutch commons? The pseudo-countryside as compromise between spatial planning goals and consumers' preferences for rural living', *Built Environment* (forthcoming)

Ministry of Housing, Physical Planning and Environment (1997) *Woonverkenningen MMXXX, Wonen in 2030* (Ministry of Housing, Physical Planning and Environment: The Hague)

Ministry of Housing, Physical Planning and Environment (1999) *Volkshuisvesting in Cijfers 99* (Ministry of Housing, Physical Planning and Environment: The Hague)

Ministry of Housing, Physical Planning and Environment (2001) *What People Want Where People Live. Housing in the 21st Century* (summary) (Ministry of Housing, Physical Planning and Environment: The Hague)

Strijker, D. (2000) 'Agriculture: still a key to rural identity?', in T. Haartsen, P. Groote and P.P.P. Huigen (eds), *Claiming Rural Identities. Dynamics, Contexts, Policies*, pp. 47–54

Chapter 6

Not all the books listed for this chapter are referred to in the text.

Auclair, E., Durand, F., and Vanoni, D. (1998) 'Le logement et l'insertion en milieu rural des exclus de la ville', *Recherche Sociale* no. 145

Besset, J.P. 'Les exclus convergent vers les zones rurales démunies', *Le Monde*, 9 January 1999

Burgel, G. (1993) *La ville aujourd'hui* (Hachette: Paris)

Collier, E. 'Le revenu minimum du soleil', *Le Monde*, 26 March 1996

'Développement local: accueil des urbains au village, un cadeau empoisonné', *Vie Publique*, October 1997

Fougerouse, C. (1996) *Le renouveau rural* (Edition l'Harmattan: Paris)

'Ils ont choisi la campagne', *Le Point*, 18 May 1996

'Ils quittent la ville' (1996) *Village*, no. 21

INSEE/INRA (1998) *Les campagnes et leurs villes*, INSEE, collection 'Contours et caractères'

INSEE (1999) *Recensement général de la population*, http://www.recensement.insee.fr

Joly, C. 'La pauvreté moins dure à la campagne', *Le Pelerin magazine*, 10 July 1998

Kayser, B. (1993) *Naissance de nouvelles campagnes* (Edition de l'Aube: Paris)

Kayser, B. *et al.* (1994) *Pour une ruralité choisie* (Edition de l'Aube: Paris)

'Le monde rural en mouvement' (1999) *Territoires*, Hors série no. 398 bis

'Le rural en mouvement' (1998) *Sciences de la Société*, no. 45

'Les RMIstes aux champs', *L'Express*, 25 June 1998

'Loin des villes, l'exode des exclus', *Le Figaro*, 30 May 1998

Matthieu, Nicole 'La campagne renvoie à la solidarité et à une image de dignité', *Le Monde*, 9 January 1999

Perben, M. (1999) 'Les logements dans l'espace rural', *Indicateurs de l'Economie du Centre* no. 27

'Quitter la ville, la campagne est-elle prête à accueillir' (1997) *Territoires et Villages*, hors série no. 379 bis

Rochefort, R. (1999) *Dynamique de l'espace français et aménagement du territoire* (Edition l'Harmattan, collection Géographie en liberté: Paris)

Séchet, R. 91996) *Espaces et Pauvretés: la géographie interrogée* (L'Harmattan: Paris)

Vanoni, D. and Lainé, F. (1999) 'L'exclusion du logement: état des connaissances sur les situations, les personnes concernées et les facteurs excluants', *Recherche sociale* no. 151

Vanoni, D. *et al.* (1998) 'Le logement des personnes défavorisées 1', *Recherche Sociale* no. 150

Vanoni, D. *et al.* (1999) 'Le logement des personnes défavorisées 2', *Recherche Sociale*, no. 152

Vanoni, D. *et al.* (2000) 'Le logement des personnes défavorisées 3', *Recherche Sociale*, no. 156

Chapter 7

Aniacap (1992) *Le leggi per la casa*, vol. 2 (Editrice Edilizia Popolare: Roma)

Bagnasco, A. (1977) *Tre Italie* (Il Mulino: Bologna)

Bagnasco, A. (1988) *La costruzione sociale del mercato* (Il Mulino: Bologna)

Becattini, G. (1989) (ed.) *Modelli locali di sviluppo* (Il Mulino: Bologna)

Bodo, G. and Viesti, G. (1997) *La grande svolta* (Donzelli: Roma)

Castles, F.G. and Ferrera, M. (1996) 'Home ownership and the welfare state: is southern Europe different?' in *South European Society and Politics* 1 (2): pp. 163–185

Cencini, C., Dematteis, G. and Menegatti, B. (1983) (eds) *L'Italia emergente* (Angeli: Milano)

Dematteis, G. (1983) 'Deconcentrazione metropolitana, crescita periferica e ripopolamento di aree marginali', in C. Cencini, G. Dematteis and B. Menegatti (eds) *L'Italia emergente* (Angeli: Milano)

Eurostat Press Releases, n. 6998 – 14 September 1998, 'A quarter of all income goes to "richest" 10%', Service Press Eurostat

Fuà, G. and Zacchia, C. (1983) (eds) *Industrializzazione senza fratture* (Il Mulino: Bologna)

Garofoli, G. (1991) *Modelli locali di sviluppo* (Angeli: Milano)

Istat (1998) *Rapporto annuale* (Istat: Roma)

Istat (1999) *Famiglie, abitazioni e sicurezza dei cittadini* (Istat: Roma)

Istat (2000) *Note Rapide*, n. 4 July

Laino, G. and Padovani, L. (2000) 'Le partenariat pour rénover l'action publique. L'expérience italienne', in *Pole Sud*, 12, May, pp. 27–46

Leone, U. (1996) *Una politica per l'ambiente* (La Nuova Italia Scientifica: Roma)

Merlo, M. (1986) 'Agricoltura, foreste e territorio. La Formazione dei paesaggi rurali italiani e l'evoluzione nell'uso del territorio', in M. Fabbri (ed.) *Pianificazione del territorio agricolo* (INVET/ Franco Angeli: Milano)

Merlo, V. (1997) *Sociologia del verde* (Angeli: Milano)

Padovani, L. (1984) 'Italy', in M. Winn (ed.) *Housing in Europe* (Croom Helm, London and Canberra, St Martin's Press, New York), pp. 247–280

Padovani, L. (1988) 'Housing provision in Italy: the family as emerging promoter. Difficult relationships with public policies', in *Quaderni del Dipartimento di Ingegneria* (Università degli Studi di Trento: Trento)

Padovani, L. (1996) 'Italy', in P. Balchin (ed.) *Housing Policy in Europe* (Routledge: London), pp. 188–209

Padovani, L. (1998) 'Public and private partnerships in urban regeneration programs', in *Housing in Transition*, Conference Proceedings, B. Cernic, K. Dimitrovska and B. Turner (eds) (Urban Planning Institute: Lubiana)

Tosi, A. (1987) 'La produzione della casa in proprietà: pratiche familiari, informale, politiche', in *Sociologia e ricerca sociale* 22, pp. 7–24

Tosi, A. (1994) *Abitanti: Le nuove strategie dell'azione abitativa* (Il Mulino: Bologna)

Tosi, A. (1995) 'Shifting paradigms: the sociology of housing, the sociology of the family, and the crisis of modernity', in R. Forrest and A. Murie (eds) *Housing and Family Wealth* (Routledge: London)

Vettoretto, L. (1996) 'Morfologie sociali territoriali', in A. Clementi, G. Dematteis and P.C. Palermo (eds) *Le forme del territorio italiano* (Laterza: Roma-Bari)

Chapter 8

Abellán, A. (1993) 'La decisión de emigrar en las personas de edad', *Estudios Geográficos,* LIV (220): 5–17

Barreiro, M.A. and Novoa, X. (n.d.) 'La rehabilitación rural en Galicia', *La práctica de la rehabilitación* (Patronat Municipal de l'Habitatge: Palma de Mallorca), pp. 73–80

Beltrán, C. (1994) 'Acciones institucionales en relación con el Desarrollo Rural en España', *Revista de Estudios Agro-Sociales* 169: 287–309

Blanco, R. and Benayas, J. (1994) 'El turismo como motor del Desarrollo Rural. Análisis de los proyectos de turismo subvencionados por el LEADER I', *Revista de Estudios Agro-Sociales* 169: 119–147

Fundación de Estudios Inmobiliarios (1999) *Libro Blanco del Sector Inmobiliario* (Ministerio de Fomento-Centro de Publicaciones: Madrid) 648 pages

Jessen, O. (1955) 'La vivienda troglodita en los países mediterráneos', *Estudios Geográficos* 58: 137–156

Ministerio de Obras Públicas y Urbanismo (MOPU). Gabinete Técnico de Instituto de Promoción Pública de la Vivienda (1983) 'Calidad ambiental del habitat rural y su protección pública', *Coloquio Hispano-Francés sobre Espacios Rurales*, vol. II, pp. 341–349 (Servicio de Publicaciones del Ministerio de Agricultura, Pesca y Alimentación: Madrid)

Valenzuela, M. (ed.) (1997) *Los turismos de interior. El retorno a la tradición viajera* (Ediciones de la Universidad Autónoma de Madrid: Madrid) 745 pages

Chapter 9

Bacon, P. and Associates (1999) *The Housing Market* (Stationery Office: Dublin)

Barlow, J. and Duncan, S. (1994) *Success and Failure in Housing Provision* (Pergamon: Oxford)

Central Statistics Office (2001) *Population and Migration Estimates, April 2001* (Central Statistics Office: Dublin and Cork)

Centre for Local and Regional Studies, NUI, Maynooth and Brady Shipman Martin (2000) *Irish Rural Structure and Gaeltacht Areas*, www.irishspatialstrategy.ie/docs/report10

Cork Planning Authorities (2001) *Joint Housing Strategy* www.corkcoco.com/cccmm/services/planning/devplan/housing/

Department of Agriculture (1999) *White Paper on Rural Development* (Department of Agriculture: Dublin)

Department of the Environment and Local Government (annually) *Housing Statistics Bulletin* (Department of the Environment and Local Government: Dublin)

Department of the Environment and Local Government (2001) *National Habitat Report for Ireland* (Department of the Environment and Local Government: Dublin)

Department of the Environment and Local Government, website at www.environ.ie

Department of Finance (2000) *Ireland, National Development Plan, 2000–2006* (Stationery Office: Dublin)

Donegal County Council (2000) *Donegal County Development Plan 2000* (www.donegal.ie/doc/)

Downey, D. and Devilly, I. (1998) 'Changing circumstances, latest consequences: new data on rents, conditions and attitudes in the private rented sector, 1998', in B. Harvey (ed.) *Private Rented Housing – Issues and Options* (Threshold: Dublin)

Drudy, P.J. (2001) 'Towards affordable housing: the case for a new approach', in P.J. Drudy and A. MacLaran (eds) *Dublin: Economic and Social Trends* (Trinity College Dublin: Dublin)

Drudy, P.J. (1999) *Housing – A New Approach* (Dublin: The Labour Party)

Economic and Social Research Institute (1999) *National Investment Priorities for the Period 2000–2006* (ESRI: Dublin)

Finnerty, J. (2000) 'Minister Dempsey's 20 per cent solution', *The Property Professional*, Spring 2000

Goodbody Economic Consultants and Department of Regional and Urban Planning UCD (2000) *Development Restraint and Urban Growth Management*, www.irishspatialstrategy.ie/docs/report9

Guerin, D. (1999) *Housing Income Support in the Private Rented Sector* (Combat Poverty Agency: Dublin)

Heanue, K. (1998) 'The affordability gap for housing in peripheral rural areas', *Administration* 46(2), Summer: 47–64

Interdepartmental Review Group (2001) *An Interdepartmental Review of The Pilot Tax Relief Scheme For Certain Resort Areas* (Department of Trade, Tourism and Recreation: Dublin)

Jackson, J. and Hasse, T. (1996) 'Demography and the distribution of deprivation in rural Ireland', in C. Curtain, T. Hasse and H. Tovey (eds), *Poverty in Rural Ireland* (Oak Tree Press and Combat Poverty Agency: Dublin)

Kerry County Council, *County Development Plan 2000* (www.kerrycoco.ie/planning/)

National Economic and Social Council (1997) *Population Distribution and Economic Development: Trends and Policy Implications* (NESC: Dublin)

National Economic and Social Forum (1997) *Rural Renewal – Combating Social Exclusion* (NESF: Dublin)

National Economic and Social Forum (2000) *Social and Affordable Housing and Accommodation: Building the Future* (National Economic and Social Forum: Dublin)

Nolan, B. and Maitre, B. (2000) 'Income inequality', in B. Nolan *et al.* (eds) *Bust to Boom?* (Institute of Public Administration: Dublin)

Nolan, B., Whelan, C. and Williams, J. (1998) *Where are Poor Households? The Spatial Distribution of Poverty and Deprivation in Ireland* (Combat Poverty Agency: Dublin)

O'Brien, T. (2001) 'Plans for Wicklow, Meath and Kildare threatened', *Irish Times*, 6 January 2001

Government of Ireland (1997) *Sustainable Development: A Strategy for Ireland* (Stationery Office: Dublin)

Chapter 10

Barclay, C. (1997) *The Location of New Households*, House of Commons Library Research Paper 97/56, London

Barlow, J. and Savage, M. (1986) 'The politics of growth: cleavage and conflict in a Tory heartland', *Capital and Class* 30: 156–182

Bell, M.M. (1994) *Childerley: Nature and Morality in a Country Village* (University of Chicago Press: Chicago)

Bevan, M. (2000) *Social Housing in the Future: The Rural Perspective* (Institute for Public Policy Research: London)

Bird, S.E. (1982) 'The impact of private estate ownership on social development in a Scottish rural community', *Sociologia Ruralis* 22: 43–55

Bowler, I.R. and Lewis, G.J. (1987) The decline of private rented housing in rural areas: a case study of estate villages in Northamptonshire, in D. Lockhart and B.W. Ilbery (eds) *The Future of the British Rural Landscape* (Geo Books: Norwich), pp. 115–136

Bowley, M. (1945) *Housing and the State 1919–1944* (Allen and Unwin: London)

Boyne, G.A. and Powell, M. (1993) Territorial justice and Thatcherism, *Environment and Planning C: Government and Policy* 11: 35–53

Bramley, G. (1994) *Homelessness in Rural England – Statistical Update to 1992/93* (Rural Development Commission: Salisbury)

Bramley, G. and Smart, G. (1995) *Rural Incomes and Housing Affordability* (Rural Development Commission: Salisbury)

Bridgen, P. and Lowe, R. (1998) *Welfare Policy under the Conservatives 1951–1964* (HMSO: London)

Brownill, S. and Sharp, C. (1992) 'London's housing crisis', in A. Thornley (ed.) *The Crisis of London* (Routledge: London) pp. 10–24

Byrne, D.S. (1976) 'Allocation, the council ghetto and the political economy of housing', *Antipode* 8(1): 24–29

Chaney, P. and Sherwood, K. (2000) 'The resale of right to buy dwellings: a case study of migration and social change in rural England', *Journal of Rural Studies* 16: 79–94

Chapman, P., Phimister, E., Shucksmith, M., Upward, R. and Vera-Toscano, E. (1998) *Poverty and Exclusion in Rural Britain: The Dynamics of Low Income and Employment* (York Publishing Services: York)

Cloke, P.J. and Thrift, N.J. (1987) 'Intra-class conflict in rural areas', *Journal of Rural Studies* 3: 321–334

Cloke, P.J., Milbourne, P. and Widdowfield, R. (2001a) 'The geographies of homelessness in rural England', *Regional Studies* 35: 23–37

Cloke, P.J., Milbourne, P. and Widdowfield, R. (2001b) 'Interconnecting housing, homelessness and rurality: evidence from local authority homelessness officers in England and Wales', *Journal of Rural Studies* 17: 95–111

Cooper, S. (1985) *Public Housing and Private Property: 1970–1984* (Gower: Aldershot)

Countryside Agency (1999) *The State of the Countryside 1999*, Cheltenham

Davies, J.G. (1972) *The Evangelistic Bureaucrat* (Tavistock: London)

Deacon, D. (1991) *Deterioration of the Public Sector Housing Stock* (Avebury: Aldershot)

Dennis, N. (1972) *Public Participation and Planner's Blight* (Faber and Faber: London)

Dorling, D.F.L. (1994) 'The negative equity map of Britain', *Area* 26: 327–342

Dunleavy, P.J. (1981) *The Politics of Mass Housing in Britain 1945–75* (Clarendon: Oxford)

Elson, M.J., Macdonald, R. and Steenberg, C. (1995) *Planning for Rural Diversification* (HMSO: London)

Elson, M.J., Steenberg, C. and Mendham, N. (1996) 'Green belt barrier to affordable housing', *Town and Country Planning*, June, 178–179

Elson, M.J., Waller, S. and Macdonald, R. (1993) *The Effectiveness of Green Belts* (HMSO: London)

Eurostat (2001) *Eurostat Yearbook Edition 2001* (Office for Official Publications of the European Communities: Luxembourg)

Fielding, A.J. (1993) 'Migration and the metropolis: an empirical and theoretical analysis of inter-regional migration to and from South East England', *Progress in Planning* 39: 71–166

Flynn, A. (1986) 'Political ideology: the case of the Housing Act 1980', in P.D. Lowe, T. Bradley and S. Wright (eds) *Deprivation and Welfare in Rural Areas* (Geo Books: Norwich), pp. 55–74

Forrest, R. and Murie, A. (1988) *Selling the Welfare State: The Privatisation of Public Housing* (Routledge: London)

Francis, D.R. (1982) 'Community initiatives and voluntary action in Rural England', Ph.D. thesis, Wye College, University of London

Gallent, N. and Tewdwr-Jones, M. (2000) *Rural Second Homes in Europe* (Ashgate: Aldershot)

Gould, P.R. and White, R.R. (1986) *Mental Maps*, 2nd edn (Allen and Unwin: Boston)

Greve, J., Page, D. and Greve, S. (1971) *Homelessness in London* (Scottish Academic Press: Edinburgh)

Greve, J. (1991) *Homelessness in Britain* (Joseph Rowntree Foundation: York)

Hamnett, C.R. (1992) 'House-price differentials, housing wealth and migration', in A.G. Champion and A.J. Fielding (eds) *Migration Processes and Patterns: Volume One – Research Progress and Prospects* (Belhaven: London), pp. 55–64

Hamnett, C.R. (1993) 'The spatial impact of the British housebuilding market slump', 1989–91, *Area* 25: 217–227

Hamnett, C.R. (1995) 'Housing inheritance and inequalities', *Journal of Social Policy* 24: 413–422

Harloe, M. (1995) *The People's Home?* (Blackwell: Oxford)

Herington, J. and Evans, D.M. (1979) 'The spatial pattern of movement in "key" and "non-key" settlements', Loughborough University Department of Geography Working Paper 3

Herington, J., Day, S. and Lavis, J. (1995) *Section 106 Agreements and Private Finance for Rural Housing Schemes* (Rural Development Commission: Salisbury)

Hoggart, K. (1997) 'Home occupancy and rural housing problems in England', *Town Planning Review* 68: 485–515

Hoggart, K. (1998) 'National regulation and district council housing provision in rural Mid-Bedfordshire 1900–1996', in R. Epps (ed.) *Sustaining Rural Systems in the Context of Global Change* (University of New England, Department of Geography: Armidale), pp. 75–84

Hoggart, K. (1999) 'Where has social housing gone? Politics, housing need and social housing construction in England', *Space and Polity* 3: 35–65

Hooper, C.-A. (1996) *Rural Lone Parents: The Evaluation of a Self-Help Support Project* (York Publishing Services: York)

Housing Corporation (2001) *Homes in the Countryside: A Rural Position Paper*, London

Kirby, D.A. (1979) *Slum Housing and Residential Renewal: The Case of Urban Britain* (Longman: London)

Langton, E. (2000) 'Rural England finds a guardian angel', *The Guardian*, 14 October (see Guardian Unlimited at: http://www.societyguardian.co.uk/regeneration/story/0,7940,395021,00.html/ read on 31.5.01)

Maclean, U. (1974) 'Environmental perceptions in a deprived area', in J.T. Coppock (ed.) *Environmental Quality* (Scottish Academic Press: Edinburgh), pp. 178–188

Mandler, P. (1997) *The Fall and Rise of the Stately Home* (Yale University Press: New Haven)

Milbourne, P. (1998) 'Local responses to central state restructuring of social housing provision in rural areas', *Journal of Rural Areas* 14: 167–184

Monk, S. and Whitehead, C.M. (1996) 'Land supply and housing', *Housing Studies* 11, 407–423

Mullins, D. (1993) *An Evaluation of the Housing Corporation Rural Programme* (Rural Development Commission: Salisbury)

Murdoch, J. and Marsden, T.K. (1994) *Reconstituting Rurality* (UCL Press: London)

Newby, H.E. (1986) 'Locality and rurality: the restructuring of rural social relations', *Regional Studies* 20: 209–215

Orbach, L.F. (1977) *Homes for Heroes: A Study of the Evolution of British Public Housing 1915–1921* (Seeley Service & Co.: London)

Page, D. (1993) *Building for Communities: A Study of New Housing Association Estates* (Joseph Rowntree Foundation: York)

Phillips, D. (1987) 'The rhetoric of anti-racism in public housing allocation', in P. Jackson (ed.) *Race and Racism* (Allen and Unwin: London), pp. 212–237

Phillips, D.R. and Williams, A.M. (1982) *Rural Housing and the Public Sector* (Gower: Farnborough)

Power, A. and Mumford, K. (1999) *The Slow Death of Great Cities?* (Joseph Rowntree Foundation: York)

Rao, N. (1990) *The Changing Role of Local Housing Authorities* (Policy Studies Institute: London)

Richmond, P. (1985) 'The state and the role of the housing association sector in rural areas: a case study in Devon', Ph.D. thesis, University of Exeter

Rose, D., Saunders, P., Newby, H.E. and Bell, C. (1976) 'Ideologies of property', *Sociological Review* 24: 699–730

Rugg, J. and Jones, A. (1999) *Getting a Job, Finding a Home: Rural Youth in Transition* (Policy Press: Bristol)

Rural Housing Trust (2000) 'Second home help for rich outstrips rural housing subsidies', press release, 5 October 2000. (See http://ruralhousing.org.uk/press_releases/002.htm/ read on 31.5.01)

Shucksmith, M. and Henderson, M. (1995) *A Classification of Rural Housing Markets in England* (HMSO: London)

Swenarton, M. (1981) *Homes Fit for Heroes: The Politics and Architecture of Early State Housing in Britain* (Heinemann: London)

Tetlow, R., Auchincloss, M. and Haddrell, K. (1996) *Rural Needs in Local Authority Housing Strategies* (Rural Development Commission: Salisbury)

Thornley, A. (1993) *Urban Planning Under Thatcherism* (Routledge: London)

Tinker, A., Wright, F. and Zeilig, H. (1995) *Difficult to Let Sheltered Housing* (HMSO: London)

UK Department of the Environment, Transport and the Regions (2000) *Planning Policy Guidance Note 3: Housing* (The Stationery Office: London)

UK Department of the Environment, Transport and the Regions (2001) *Planning Policy Guidance Note 7: The Countryside – Environmental Quality and Economic and Social Development* (The Stationery Office: London)

UK Office of National Statistics (1997) *Key Statistics for Urban and Rural Areas: Great Britain* (The Stationery Office: London)

Warrington, M. (1994) 'A new role for housing associations: at what cost?' (University of Cambridge, Homerton College: Cambridge)

Chapter 11

Alexander, D., Shucksmith, M. and Lindsay, N. (1988) *Scotland's Rural Housing: Opportunities for Action*, Shelter (Scotland) and Rural Forum.

Church of Scotland (1988) *Housing Scotland's People*, Report of the Church of Scotland's Independent Inquiry into Scottish Housing (St Andrew Press: Edinburgh)

Cloke, P., Milbourne, P. and Widdowfield, R. (2001) 'The local spaces of welfare provision: responding to homelessness in rural England', *Political Geography*, 20(4): 493–512

Communities Scotland (2002) Draft Corporate Plan

Corbett, G. (1996) 'Local authority house waiting lists in Scotland 1995', *Scottish Housing Monitor* 20: 6

Gallent, N. (1997) 'Planning for affordable rural housing in England and Wales', *Housing Studies*, 12(1): 127–137

Hall, P., Thomas, R., Gracey, H. and Drewett, R. (1974) *The Containment of Urban England*, London, Allen and Unwin

Jessop, B. (1991) 'The welfare state in the transition from Fordism to post-Fordism', in B. Jessop *et al.* (eds) *The Politics of Flexibility: Restructuring State and Industry in Britain, Germany and Scandinavia* (Edward Elgar: Aldershot)

Jessop, B. (1994) 'From the Keynesian welfare state to the Schumpetarian workfare state', in R. Burrows and B. Loader (eds) *Towards a Post-Fordist Welfare State?* (Routledge: London)

Kirk, B. and Shucksmith, M. (1990) *Rural Housing Market Studies: A Summary* (Scottish Homes, Research Report, No. 13)

Lipietz, A. (1987) *Mirages and Miracles* (Verso: London)

Midwinter, A., Keating, M. and Mitchell, J. (1991) *Politics and Public Policy in Scotland* (Mainstream: Edinburgh)

Newby, H. (1985) *Green and Pleasant Land?* (Penguin: Harmondsworth)

Scottish Homes (1990a) *The Rural Housing Challenge* (Scottish Homes: Edinburgh)

Scottish Homes (1990b) *Rural Policy* (Scottish Homes: Edinburgh)

Scottish Homes (1998) *Tackling Rural Housing: Policy Satement 1998* (Scottish Homes: Edinburgh)

Scottish Development Department (1987) *Housing: The Government's Proposals for Scotland*, CM242 (HMSO: Edinburgh)

Scottish Executive (2000) *Rural Scotland: A New Approach* (HMSO: Edinburgh)

Scottish Office (1998) *Towards a Development Strategy for Rural Scotland* (HMSO: Edinburgh)

Shucksmith, M. (1987) 'Rural housing policy in Scotland', in B. MacGregor, D. Robertson and M. Shucksmith (eds) *Rural Housing in Scotland: Recent Research and Policy* (Aberdeen University Press: Aberdeen), pp. 17–27

Shucksmith, M. (1990a) *Housebuilding in Britain's Countryside* (Routledge: London)

Shucksmith, M. (1990b) *The Definition of Rural Areas and Rural Deprivation*, Research Report 2 (Scottish Homes: Edinburgh)

Shucksmith, M. and Watkins, L. (1990) *The Development of Housing Associations in Rural Scotland*, Research Report 1 (Scottish Homes: Edinburgh)

Shucksmith, M. and Watkins, L. (1991) 'Housebuilding on farmland: the distributional effects in rural areas', *Journal of Rural Studies* 7(3): 153–168

Shucksmith, M., Chapman, P. and Clark, G. (1994a) *Disadvantage in Rural Scotland: How it is Experienced and How it Can be Tackled* (Rural Forum: Perth)

Shucksmith, M., Henderson, M. and Conway, E. (with CR Planning) (1994b) *Monitoring and Evaluation of Scottish Homes' Rural Demonstration Areas*, Research Report 34 (Scottish Homes: Edinburgh)

Shucksmith, M., Chapman, P. and Conway, E. (1996a) *Review of Scottish Homes' Rural Policy*, Research Report 53 (Scottish Homes: Edinburgh)

Shucksmith, M., Chapman, P. and Clark, G. (1996b) *Rural Scotland Today: The Best of Both Worlds?* (Avebury: Aldershot)

Shucksmith, M., Conway, E. and Henderson, M. (unpublished) *The Potential of Local Housing Agencies in Rural Scotland*

Swain, N. (1999) 'Conceptualising late modernity as a "shock"', paper given at 18th Congress of the European Society for Rural Sociology, Lund, Sweden

Chapter 12

Aitchison, J.W. and Carter, H. (2000) *Language, Economy and Society* (University of Wales Press: Cardiff)

Beresford, M. (1989) *Affordable Housing in Welsh Villages*, Brecon Beacons National Park Committee

Bollom, C. (1978) *Attitudes and Second Homes in Rural Wales* (University of Wales Press: Cardiff)

Champion, A.G. and Watkins, C. (1991) *People in the Countryside: Studies of Social Change in Rural Britain* (Paul Chapman: London)

Cloke, P.J. (1977) 'An index of rurality for England and Wales', *Regional Studies* 11: 21–46

Cloke, P.J. (1978) 'Changing patterns of urbanisation in rural areas of England and Wales', *Regional Studies* 12: 603–617

Cloke, P. (1995) 'Housing in open countryside: windows on "irresponsible planning" in rural Wales', *Town Planning Review* 67(3): 291–308

Cloke, P. and Davies, L. (1992) 'Deprivation and lifestyles in rural Wales. I: Towards a cultural dimension', *Journal of Rural Studies* 8(4): 349–358

Cloke, P. and Edwards, G. (1985) *Cymdeithas Tai Dyffryn and local authority housing provision in mid Wales.* Working Paper No. 8, Department of Geography, Saint David's University College, Lampeter

Cloke, P.J. and Edwards, G. (1986) 'Rurality in England and Wales 1981; a replication of the 1971 index', *Regional Studies* 20: 289–306

Cloke, P. and Milbourne, P. (1992) 'Deprivation and lifestyles in rural Wales. II: Rurality and the cultural dimension', *Journal of Rural Studies* 8(4): 359–371

Cloke, P., Goodwin, M. and Milbourne, P. (1994) 'Life-styles in rural Wales', unpublished (Welsh Office: Cardiff)

Cloke, P., Goodwin, M. and Milbourne, P. (1995a) ' "There's so many strangers in the village now": marginalization and change in 1990s Welsh rural lifestyles', *Contemporary Wales* 8: 47–74

Cloke, P., Goodwin, M. and Milbourne, P. (1997a) 'Living lives in different ways? Deprivation, marginalization and changing lifestyles in rural England', *Transactions of the Institute of British Geographers* 22: 210–230

Cloke, P., Goodwin, M. and Milbourne, P. (1997b) *Rural Wales. Community and Marginalisation* (University of Wales Press: Cardiff)

Cloke, P., Goodwin, M., Milbourne, P. and Thomas, C. (1995b) 'Deprivation, poverty, marginalization in rural lifestyles in England and Wales', *Journal of Rural Studies* 11(4): 351–365

Cymuned (2001) *Housing, Work and Language* (Y Lolfa: Aberystwyth)

Davies, R.B. and O'Farrell, P.N. (1981) 'A spatial and temporal analysis of second homes in Wales', *Geoforum* 12: 161–178

Department of the Environment (1996) *Circular 13/96 Planning and Affordable Housing* (HMSO: London)

Devolution Unit (1999) *Making the Difference in Wales: A Guide to the Powers of the National Assembly* (Welsh Office: Cardiff)

Dyfed County Planning Department (1980) *Second Homes in Dyfed* (Dyfed County Council: Carmarthen)

Dyfed County Planning Department (1983) *Second Homes in Dyfed* (Dyfed County Council: Carmarthen)

Dyfed County Planning Department (1989) *Affordable Housing: Some Possible Solutions* (Dyfed County Council: Carmarthen)

Edwards, W.J. (1995) *Demand for Housing and Housing Needs in Radnorshire*, report to Montgomery District Council and Mid Wales Housing Association (Rural Surveys Research Unit, University of Wales: Aberystwyth)

Edwards, W.J. (1996) *Housing Circumstances in Ceredigion*, report to Cyngor Dosbarth Ceredigion (Rural Surveys Research Unit, University of Wales: Aberystwyth)

Edwards, W.J. (1998a) *Regional Survey of Antur Cwm Taf: Report to ACTT LEADER Group* (Rural Surveys Research Unit, University of Wales: Aberystwyth)

Edwards, W.J. (1998b) 'Charting the discourse of community action: perspectives from practice in rural Wales', *Journal of Rural Studies* 14(1): 63–77

Fevre, R., Borland, J. and Denney, D. (1999) 'Nation, community and conflict: housing policy and immigration in North Wales', in R. Fevre and A. Thompson *National Identity and Social Theory* (University of Wales Press: Cardiff) pp. 129–148

Fisk, M.J. (1996) *Home Truths: Issues for Housing in Wales* (Gomer Press: Llandysul. Ceredigion)

Fisk, M.J. and Hall, D. (1997) *Building our Future: the Housing Challenge in Wales* (Institute of Welsh Affairs: Cardiff)

Gallent, N. (1997) 'The alternative route to affordable housing provision: experiences in rural Wales', *Journal of Rural Studies* 13(1): 43–57

Gallent, N. (1998) 'Local housing agencies in rural Wales', *Housing Studies* 13(1): 59–81

Gallent, N. and Tewdwr-Jones, M. (2000a) *Rural Second Homes in Europe: Examining Housing Supply and Control* (Ashgate: Aldershot)

Gallent, N. and Tewdwr-Jones, M. (2000b) 'Housing in rural Wales', in R. Smith, T. Stirling and P. Williams (eds) *Housing in Wales* (Chartered Institute of Housing: Cardiff)

Gallent, N., Tewdwr-Jones, M. and Higgs, G. (1997) 'Planning for residential tourism in Wales', *Contemporary Wales* 10: 103–126

House of Commons (1992/3) 'Welsh Affairs Committee Third Report', *Rural Housing 2* (HMSO: London)

Harrington, V. and O'Donoghue, D. (1998) 'Rurality in England and Wales 1991: a replication and extension of the 1981 Rurality Index', *Sociologia Ruralis* 38(2): 178–201

Higgs, G. and White, S.D. (1997a) 'A comparison of community level indices in measuring disadvantage in Wales', *Contemporary Wales* 10, 127–169

Higgs, G. and White, S.D. (1997b) 'Changes in service provision in rural areas, Part 1: the use of GIS in analysing accessibility to services in rural deprivation research', *Journal of Rural Studies* 13(4): 441–451

Housing Management Advisory Committee (1993) *Taking Stock: A Guide to Local Housing Needs Assessment* (Cardiff)

Institute of Welsh Affairs (1988) *Rural Wales* (Cardiff)

Littler, S., Tewdwr-Jones, M., Fisk, M. and Essex, S. (1994) *Compatibility of Planning and Housing Functions in Welsh Local Authorities* (Centre for Housing Management and Development, University of Wales: Cardiff)

Milbourne, P. (1997) 'Housing conflict and domestic property classes', *Environment and Planning A* 29, 43–62

Milbourne, P. (1998) 'Local responses to central state restructuring of social housing provision in rural areas', *Journal of Rural Studies* 14(2): 167–185

Milbourne, P. (1999) 'Changing operations? Building society and estate agency activities in rural housing markets', *Housing Studies* 14(2): 49–63

National Assembly for Wales (1998) *Welsh Housing Statistics* (Cardiff)

National Assembly for Wales (1999a) *Welsh Housing Statistics* (Cardiff)

National Assembly for Wales (1999b) *Welsh House Condition Survey* (Cardiff)

National Assembly for Wales (1999c) *A Better Wales: A Consultation Paper on Values, Service Priorities and Spending Plans* (Cardiff)

Ribchester, C. and Edwards, B. (1999) 'The centre and the local: policy and practice in rural education provision', *Journal of Rural Studies* 15(2): 49–63

Shucksmith, M. (1990) 'A theoretical perspective on rural housing: housing classes in rural Britain', *Sociologia Ruralis* 30(2): 210–229

Shucksmith, M. and Chapman, P. (1998) 'Rural development and social exclusion', *Sociologia Ruralis* 38(2): 226–242

Tai Cymru [Housing for Wales] (1990a) *The Demand for Social Housing in Rural Wales* (Housing for Wales: Cardiff)

Tai Cymru [Housing for Wales] (1990b) *The Housing Aspirations of Young People in Rural Wales* (Housing for Wales: Cardiff)

Tai Cymru [Housing for Wales] (1992) *An Atlas of Housing Conditions in Welsh Districts* (Housing for Wales: Cardiff)

Tewdwr-Jones, M. (1998) 'Rural government and community participation: the planning role of community councils', *Journal of Rural Studies* 14(1): 51–62

Tewdwr-Jones, M., Gallent, N., Fisk, M. and Essex, S. (1998) 'Developing corporate working approaches for the provision of affordable housing in Wales', *Regional Studies* 32(1): 85–91

Wales Rural Forum (1994) *A Strategy for Rural Wales: Consultation Document* (Gomer Press: Llandysul, Dyfed)

Welsh Affairs Committee (1993) *Rural Housing: Third Report* (Welsh Office: Cardiff)

Welsh Language Society (1971) *Tai Haf* (Cymdeithas Yr Iaith Gymraeg: Aberystwyth)

Welsh Language Society (1989) *Houses, Migration, Prices: Community Control of the Property Market* (Cymdeithas Yr Iaith Gymraeg: Aberystwyth)

Welsh Language Society (1992) *Llawlyfr Deddf Eiddo* (Cymdeithas Yr Iaith Gymraeg: Aberystwyth)

Welsh Language Society (1998) *Agenda for the National Assembly of Wales* (Cymdeithas Yr Iaith Gymraeg: Aberystwyth)

Welsh Office (1986) *Welsh House Condition Survey* (Welsh Office: Cardiff)

Welsh Office (1988) *Circular 53/88 The Welsh Language Development Plans and Planning Controls* (Welsh Office: Cardiff)

Welsh Office (1990–1996) *Welsh Housing Statistics* (HMSO: Cardiff)

Welsh Office (1990) *Planning Policy Guidance (Wales): Land for Low Cost Housing* (Welsh Office: Cardiff)

Welsh Office (1992a) *Planning Policy Guidance Note 3 (Wales): Housing* (Welsh Office: Cardiff)

Welsh Office (1992b) *Planning Policy Guidance Note 7* (Welsh Office: Cardiff)

Welsh Office (1992c) *Planning Policy Guidance Note 12 (Wales)* (Welsh Office: Cardiff)

Welsh Office (1996a) *A Working Countryside for Wales* (Welsh Office: Cardiff)

Welsh Office (1996b) *Planning Guidance (Wales): Planning Policy* (Welsh Office: Cardiff)

Welsh Office (1996c) *Technical Advice Note 2: Planning and Affordable Housing* (Welsh Office: Cardiff)

Welsh Office (1997a) *A Voice for Wales*, Cardiff

Welsh Office (1997b) *A Working Countryside for Wales*, 1997 review, Cardiff

Welsh Office (1998) *Local Housing Needs Assessment Guide*, Cardiff

Welsh Office (1999) *The Welsh Language – Unitary Development Plans and Development Control* (Welsh Office: Cardiff.)

White, S.D., Guy, C.M. and Higgs, G. (1997) 'Changes in service provision in rural areas. Part 2: Changes in post office provision in mid Wales: a GIS based evaluation', *Journal of Rural Studies* 13(4): 451–467

Chapter 13

Bell, C. and Newby, H. (1971) 'Theories of community', in Colin Bell and Howard Newby (eds) *Community Studies* (Praeger: New York) pp. 21–53

Clegg, S. (1989) *Frameworks of Power* (Sage: London)

Esping-Andersen, G. (1990) *Three Worlds of Welfare Capitalism* (Polity Press: Cambridge)

Kemeny, J. (1981) *The Myth of Home Ownership* (Routledge: London)

Kemeny, J. (1992) *Housing and Social Theory* (Routledge: London)

Rhodes, R.A.W. (1997) *Understanding Governance: Policy Networks, Governance, Reflexivity and Accountability* (Open University Press: Buckingham)

Chapter 14

Breheny, M. (ed.) (1999) *The People: Where Will They Work?* (Town and Country Planning Association: London)

European Commission (1999) *European Spatial Development Perspective* (CEC: Luxembourg)

Tewdwr-Jones, M. and Williams, R.H. (2001) T*he European Dimension of British Planning* (Spon Press: London)

White, S., Tewdwr-Jones, M., Alden, J. and Phillip, L. (2000) *Peripherality and Spatial Planning*, Report commissioned by DETR (DETR: London)

Index

Major discussions of topics are given in **bold** type; references to figures or tables in *italic* type.

Aberconwy *195*, *196*, *198*, 205(n4), 206(n12)
access to housing 92, 147, 233; England
    158–9, 162; Ireland 129, 131, 132, 133,
    137, 139, 142, 143; Scotland 174, 179–80;
    Wales 191, 192, 201
affordable housing 27, 52, 53, 216; England
    148, 153, 158, 159, 160, 161, 162, 163,
    164; France 71, 77, 79; Ireland 89–90,
    129, 131, 132, 133, 135, 137, 139, 140,
    142, 143; Italy 110; Netherlands 60, 63,
    67; Scotland 149, 171, 172, 173, 174, 176,
    177, 178, 182; Spain 119, 120, 126; Wales
    150, 189, 190, 192–6, 197, 198, *198*, 199,
    200, 204, 206(n13–14)
ageing population 61, 63, 76, 103–4, 118,
    119, 128, 188, 193, 201, 204, *212*
*Agence Nationale pour l'Amélioration de
    l'Habitat* (ANAH), France 82
Agenda 2000 (Wales) 200
Agrarian Amelioration Agencies (Spain) 121
Agrarian Development Plans (Spain) 121
agriculture and farming 24, 25, 214, 216,
    227, 231, 233; decline 230, 235; European
    Union 59; France 73, 75; Ireland 134, 138,
    139–40, 143; Italy 95–6, *97*, 101, 103,
    105, 108, 113(n14); Netherlands 61, 62,
    68; Norway 29, 31, **37–41**, 42, 232; Spain
    88, 117–18, 119, 120, 122, 128, 229;
    Sweden 46, 49, 51, 55; Wales *213*; Western
    Europe 168
agro-business sector (Spain) 128
agro-industrial systems (Italy) 103
Almería 126
Amcoff, J. 46, 47–8, 241
Amsterdam 63
Andalucía 118, 120, *125*, 126, 127, 128
Andalusian Housing Plan 125
anti-development interests (Scotland) 149
Antur Cwm Taf (Carmarthenshire) 205(n7)
Apennines 103

Aragón 117, 118, 124
Ardèche (France) 80
Area Renewal Schemes 190
Arfon *195*, *198*, 205(n4), 205–6(n10),
    206(n13)
åsetestakst (deceased's estate appraisement) 38
Association of District Councils 157
atomistic cultures, laissez-faire regimes
    87–145, 210, 211, 218–19, 220–1, 223,
    224; Ireland 129–45; Italy 91–115; preface
    87–90; Spain 116–28
Atzema, O. and Dam, F. van 65, 243
Autonomous Communities (Spain) *122*, 123
Auvergne 77
Aveyron (France) 80

Bagnasco, A. 113(n10), 245
Bala (Gwynedd) *203*
Balearic Islands 118, 123, 124
Basque Country (País Vasco) 118, 124
Bastia 77
Becattini, G. 113(n10), 245
Bell, C. and Newby, H. 216, 258
Bell, M.M. 159, 249
Bergen 35
Bodo, G. and Viesti, G. 113(n10), 245
Bohuslän province (Sweden) 51
borough corporations (Ireland) 144(n7)
Brecknock *195*, *196*, *198*, 205(n4)
Brecon Beacons National Park 190
Brown, G. (Chancellor of Exchequer) 153
brownfield sites 158, 161, 162, 167(n4), 230
BTS (Below Tolerable Standard) Housing
    172
Bubal (Huesca province) 126
building permits (Italy) *105*
building re-use 163, 167(n6)
building sector: informality (Spain) 11–12
El Burgo (Málaga) 126
Bustadsbanken (Norway) 32

Cáceres province 126
Cádiz 126
Care in the Community 179, 193
Care and Repair (Scotland) 174, 179, 182
Carmarthen *195*, 205(n4–5), 206(n12, n14), 207(n21)
Castilla and León 117, *125*, 126, 127
Castilla La Mancha 120
casualisation 168
Catalonia/Cataluña 118, 120, *122*, 128
cave-housing *125*, 126
censuses of population 33, *34*, 38, *75*, 76, 112(n1), 166(n2)
Ceredigion *195*, *196*, *198*, 205(n4, n5), 205–6(n10)
Champagne-Ardennes (France) 75
change of dwelling use 13–14, 18; holiday home to permanent occupation (France) 81; Norway *218*; 'property conversion' 199; Spain 126; Sweden 46, 48, 53, 57
Chapman, P. 186
Cloke, P.J. 190, 254
Circular 53/88 The Welsh Language: Development Plans and Planning Control 194, 257
co-operative housing 32–3, *35*, 35, 126, 223, 227
coastal development 55–6, 103, 224
Code de l'urbanisme (urbanism legislation, France) 81–2
collectivist regimes (Kemeny) 225
Colwyn 205(n4)
Common Agricultural Policy (European Union) 232, 233, 234
communes (Italy) *95*, 98, *100*, *101*, 102, *105*, 107, 113(n12)
Communities Scotland (2001–) **184–5**, 186, 187(n3)
Community Councillors (Wales) 200
Community Initiative Leader 108
community involvement (Scotland) 180
commuting 26, 45, 48; extension 57; France 79, *212*; Ireland 135; Scotland 170, 171; Spain 119
comparative analysis 10, **13–21**, **208–25**, **238–40**, **258**; divergence method 15–19; levels *17*; policy transfer and the rural housing problem 13–15; sequence of research questions 20; theoretical debates 15
competitive rural economy 224, 225, **230–2**
compulsory purchase powers (Scotland) 182

Comunidad Valenciana 120, 123, 128
conservation 39, 235
Conservative Party 147, 154, 155, 156, 158, 161, 166(n1), 178, 180, 185, 186
convenzione 105, 114n
convergence thesis 15–16, 208–9
Conwy 205(n5)
Cork viii, ix, 130
Cork City and County: Joint Housing Strategy (2001), 143, 247
cortijos (multi-functional buildings) *125*, 126
Cortina (Italy) 114(n17)
Costa del Sol 232
council estates (England) 155
council housing (United Kingdom) 148, 227
counter-urbanisation 48, 216
counties/*comarca* (Spain) *122*
Countryside Agency 157, 158, 163, 167(n2–3), 231, 249
Countryside Alliance 160
county borough corporations (Ireland) 144(n7)
County Clare 141
county councils (Ireland) 138, 140, 144(n7); (Sweden) 56
county development plans (Ireland) 142
County Donegal 136, 140–1, 247
CR Planning 176, 253
craft industries 118
credit unions (Ireland) 131
Cymdeithas Tai Clwyd *203*

Dagens Nyheter 56
Dam, F. van 65, 243
Dam, F. van and Heins, S. 65, 243
Dam, F. van, Heins, S. and Elbersen, B. 65, 243
Delyn 205(n4)
Dematteis, G. 113(n10), 245
demography 11, 26–7, 113(n12), 116, 128, 130, 143, 191, 192–3, 201, 234
Den Haag 63
Denbighshire 205(n5)
depopulation: France 72, 75, 84; Ireland 129, 134, 136, 137, 140, 143, 144(n5); Italy 87, 103; Netherlands 61, 63; rural 7; Spain 117–19, 124, *125*; Sweden 44, 45, 56, 57; Wales 188
deprivation 87, 92, 93, 112(n5), 156; rural 80, 88, 96, *97*, 103–4, 138; urban 68; urban versus rural 80, 109; *see also* poverty

devolution 12, 169, **184–5**, *219*, 235
'diffused cities' (Italy) 87, 100, 102–3, 109, 113(n11, n13)
Dinefwr *195*, *196*, *198*, 205(n4, n10), 206(n12), 207(n21)
divergence theory **15–19**, 209, 224, 225
DoELG *see* Ireland: Department of the Environment and Local Government
Dublin 89, 130, 134, 135, 137, 138, 141, 143
Dwyfor *195*, *196*, *198*, 205(n4)
Dyfed *195*, *198*, 206(n12)

economic diversification 200, *212*, 231; barriers (Norway) 232; Norway 224; Spain 88–9, 118, 119, 124–5, 126, 128; Sweden 224
economic growth 8; Ireland **129–37**, 142, 143, *219*, 221; Spain 221; Wales *213*
edge-development 26
edilizia agevolata (subsidised housing) *105*, 106, 108–9, 114n
edilizia convenzionata 105
Elbersen, B. 65, 243
elderly people 92, 164; England 159, 166(n1); Ireland 143; parents 106; Scotland 149, 169, 171, 172, 174; sheltered housing (England) 166(n1); Wales 192, *196*
emigrant workers (Italian) *97*, 98
employment 31, 68, 109, 198; England 163; France 77; Ireland 130, 134; rural Ireland *213*; rural Spain 120; rural Sweden 46, 47; Spain 127; urban Spain 120; Wales 195, *196*
empty triangle (*la diagonale du vide*), France 76
energy efficiency *125*, 125–6, 183, 189
England: Town and Country Planning Act (1947), 217
Enochsson, P. 53, 242
environmental protection 7, 8, 9, 25, 26, 215, 216, 227, 229–30, 233; England 161–2, *219*, 222; France 73, 81–2; Ireland 136–7, 141; Italy 88, 103, 104, 108, 110, 112; Netherlands 69, *218*; Scotland 181; Sweden 52, 54–6; Wales 150, 201
Environmental and Resource Management (Sweden) 54–6
Eryri National Park *195*, 197, *198*
Esping-Andersen, G. 225, 225(n2), 258
ethnic minorities 44, 155
Europe 2000+ (European Union) 232

European Commission (EC) 234
European Regional Development Fund (ERDF) 121; Article 10, 232
European Spatial Development Perspective, ESDP (European Commission, 1999) 232, 233, 234–5
European Union 1–2, 4, 13, 25, 55–6, 108, *122*, *125*, 126, 130, 144(n2), 209, 232–3, 234; cultural and political differences 3; enlargement 59, 234; household disposable income 153, *154*; Objective One programme 108, 189, 190, 201
European Union Structural Fund 121, 124, 232, 233, 234
Extremadura 117, 120

Falköping (Sweden) 48–9
farming *see* agriculture
Fehler *et al.* (2001) 55, 242
Fifth National Policy Document on Spatial Planning (Netherlands) 67–8
fishing villages 227
Fisk, M.J. 205(n8), 255
Fisk, M.J. and Hall, D. 205(n8), 255
Fjällbacka (Sweden) 51
Fonds Européen d'Orientation et de Garantie Agricole (FEOGA) 121
Fonds Solidarité Logement (FSL), Housing Solidarity Fund 83
France: Housing and Urban Planning Act (2000) 82
France: *Loi Besson* (1990) 83
France: *Loi d'Orientation pour l'Aménagement et le Développement Durable du Territoire* (LOADDT 1998) 85
France: *Loi d'Orientation pour la Ville* (1991) 83
France: *Loi Solidarité et Renouvellement Urbain* (SRU, 2000) 84–5
France: *Plan Départemental d'Action en Faveur du Logement des Personnes Défavorisées*: housing plan for the disadvantaged (1990–) 83
France: *Plan Local d'Urbanisme* (PLU) 82
France: *Plan d'Occupation du Sol* (POS) 82
France: *Politique de la ville* 72
Francis, D.R. 157, 250
Fuà, G. and Zacchia, C. 113(n10), 245

Galicia 118, 120, 124, *125*, 127
Galway 130, 134

Garofoli, G. 113(n10), 245
general elections: Sweden (2002 forthcoming) 53
Germans 24; holiday homes in Denmark 54; holiday homes in Sweden 45, 47, 49–50; second homes in Sweden 223
Gers (France) 80
Glyndwr 205(n4)
Gothenburg 44, 51
Government White Paper on Rural Development in Ireland (Department of Agriculture, 1999) 138, 139–40, 247
Granada 126
Granadilla (Cáceres province) 126
grants: purchase and improvement of housing (Spain) 121, 123
Grants for Rent or Ownership (GRO) 174, 178
Greece 114(n29)
green belts 230; England 148, 158, 161, 163; Italy 113(n9); Netherlands 67, 70
Guerin, D. viii, 12, 89–90
Gulbrandsen, L. viii, 9–10, 11, 23, 24
Gustafsson, M. 46, 242
Gwynedd *195*, *198*, 205(n5)

Halfacree, K. 46–7, 242
Hålsingland (Sweden): photographed 58
hamlets (*nuclei abitati*), Italy 94
Hautes Alpes (France) 80
Henderson, M. 186
Herington, J., Day, S. and Lavis, J. 162, 250
Hermansö (Sweden): photographed 58
Highland Council 184
holiday homes 13, 14, 25, 27, 29, 42, 57; France 74, 80–1; Ireland 89–90, 136–7, 142, 144(n4–5); Italy 98, 100; Scotland 170, 171; Sweden 45, 51, 54
homelessness 230; England 159, 161; France 80, 83; Italy 106; Scotland 177, 179; United Kingdom 154; Wales 150, 190, 193, 201
home ownership 23, 228, 231; England 148, 156, 160, 161; Europe 60; France 72, 73, 79, 82; Ireland 130, 131, 132, 135, 136, 138–9; Italy 104, *105*, 106; Netherlands 60, 68; Norway 35; Scotland 175, 177, 178, 185; Sweden 53; United Kingdom 153; *see also* owner-occupation
House Builders' Federation 167(n4)

house prices 19, 25, 33, 39; England 148, 156, 158, 163; France 77; inflation (Ireland) 130, 132, 133, 135, 136, 137, 139, 142, 144(n5); Ireland 89, 144(n3); Italy 102, 103, 114n; Netherlands 26, 63; Norway 35, 38, 41; ratio to average earnings (Ireland) 130; rural/urban England 158; Scotland 170; South-East England 156; Spain 88, 119; Sweden 44, 47, 50, *50*, 51, 52, 53, 57; United Kingdom 153, 155; Wales 206(n13)
housebuilding 13–14, 26, 29; co-operative (Norway) 32; England 216; France 72, 81–3, 84; illegal (Italy) 9, 11; Ireland 90, 130–1, 136–7, 144(n3); Italy 92, 100, *100*, *105*, 106, 107, 112(n3), 114n; Norway **32–3**, 34, 35–6; private 215; restrictions (Netherlands) 62, 63–4, 67, 68, 69; rural Scotland 178; rural Spain 116, 123, 126; Scotland 186; second 15, 18, 19, 20; sporadic (Ireland) 11; United Kingdom 230
household formation: England 158
Houses in Multiple Occupation (HMOs) 190
housing: 'scattered' (south Italy) 111; characteristics (France) *78*; low quality (rural France) 26–7; ownership (Norway) 38; private 18; public 18; re-let or resale (Wales) 199, 200, 206(n12), 207(n18, n20–1); recreational 23, 24, 29, *212*; residence and operation obligations (Norway) 40, 41–2; rural supply (Netherlands) 62, 68; scarcity value 227; types (Norway) *34*; uninhabited (Norway) 37
Housing Act (1980) 161, 190
Housing Act (1988) 155, 156
Housing (Scotland) Act (2000) 172, 186–7(n2–3)
Housing (Scotland) Act (2001) 184
Housing Association Grant (HAG) 174–5, 178, 179, 181
housing associations *178*, 200, *203*; England 155, 156; non-profit (England) 162; Scotland 171–5, 184, 186–7(n2); Wales 188–9, 192, 195, 199–200, 206(n13)
housing co-operatives 32–3, *35*, 35, 126, 223, 227
housing conditions (England) 156
Housing Corporation 157, 164, 251; Rural Programme 164, 251

Housing Corporation (England) 162–3
Housing Corporation (Scotland) 187(n3)
housing market 9, 10, 101, 217; centralised
    approach (Sweden) 25; distortions 216;
    exclusion of locals 19; farm properties
    (Norway) 38, *39*; formal (Italy) 102; France
    77; German second-homes (elsewhere in
    Europe) 49–50, 54; higher-income
    newcomers 7; Italy 109, 110; Norway 23–4,
    29, 35–6, 39, 41; rural Scotland 169–70,
    177; rural Spain 116; rural Sweden *218*;
    Scotland 149, 170, 171, 183; supply
    constraints (Netherlands) 62; Sweden *212*;
    types 18; Wales 190, 191, 204, 205(n10)
housing quality 51, 53; France 71, 78–9, 82;
    Ireland 131, 138, 143; Italy 88, 91, 92–3,
    97, 98, 100, 104, 108, 110; public sector
    (United Kingdom) 155; Scotland 172, 176,
    177, 179, 182; Spain 89, 116, 118, 123,
    126, 127, 128; United Kingdom 229;
    Wales 204(n2)
Housing Revenue Account (HRA): non-HRA
    (Scotland) 179
housing rights (*le droit au logement*) 11, 83,
    218, 231
Housing Statistics Bulletin (Ireland) 144(n3)
housing supply 51, 209; constraints (Scotland)
    149, 170, 171, 172, 175; England 217;
    France 81–3; Scotland 173, 174, 176,
    177–8; United Kingdom 223; Wales 192–3
Howard's Garden Cities concept 64
Huesca province 126
hunting 120, 147

illegal housebuilding: Ireland 221; Italy 9, 11,
    87, 88, 93, *97*, 103, 104, 108, 110, 112,
    112(n3), 215, *218*, 221, 227; Spain 89, 221
immigration: England 228; France *212*, 228;
    Italy 228; into Italy 87, 92, *97*, 103, 109,
    112(n2), 115(n32); into Spain 120, 128;
    trans-national 44–5
Improvement Grants 174
in-migration xi, 7, 16, 48–9, 52, 57, 231; low-
    income rural (France) 27, 80; rural England
    148, 159, 164; rural England and Wales
    227; rural Scotland 170; rural Spain 118;
    rural Wales 150, 190, 192, 193, 201;
    South-East England 156; Stockholm 57;
    Wales 150, 188, *213*
income inequality: Ireland 130; Italy 93,
    112(n4); Portugal, Greece, Spain 112(n4)
'industrial districts' (Italy) *97*, 113(n11)

industrialisation 30, 32, 214, 215–16; Italy 96,
    113(n12)
industry/industries: Italy 96, 108; light
    113(n14); new (Italy) 87; small local (Italy)
    109; Spain 117, 124; traditional 7,
    113(n14)
infrastructure 51, 81, 93, 107, 174, 234, 236;
    France 73; Ireland 136, 137, 140, 141,
    143; Italy *97*; Spain 89, 118, 121, 123,
    124, 127
'inhabited centres' (*centri abitati*, Italy) 94,
    113(n8)
inheritance 23, 24, 36, *37*, 38, 41, 166
*Institut National des Statistiques et des Études
    Économiques* (France) 74, 244
International Monetary Fund 13
Interreg III initiative 56
INTERREG IIIC Community Initiative
    (European Union) 232
Ireland: Community Development Projects
    139
Ireland: Department of Agriculture 138, 247
Ireland: Department of the Environment and
    Local Government (DoELG) 140, 144(n7),
    247; Strategic Planning Guidelines (SPGs)
    141
Ireland: Economic and Social Research
    Institute 135, 247
Ireland: Minister of Agriculture 139
Ireland: National Economic and Social
    Council (NESC) 134, 248
Ireland: National Spatial Strategy 129, 135,
    140, 143, 144(n1, n7)
Ireland: Planning and Development Act
    (2000), 140, 142, 143
Ireland: Seaside Resort Renewal Scheme
    (SRRS) 136
Ireland: Town Renewal Scheme (2000–02)
    140
Istat *see* Italy: Central Institute of Statistics
Italy: Act No 167 (1962) *105*, 114n
Italy: Central Institute of Statistics (Istat)
    101–2, 112–14(n5, n7–8, n12, n16), 245–6
Italy: *Condono edilizio* 112(n3)
Italy: Housing Act (1978), 104, 106,
    114(n21)
Italy: Housing Financing Act *105*

Jackson, J. and Hasse, T. (1996), 138, 248
Jessop (1991, 1994), 169
Jigso Community Development Initiative
    190–1

Powys *195*, *198*, 205(n5)
Preseli *195*, *198*, 205(n7, n10)
Preseli Pembrokeshire 205(n4)
prêt à l'accession à la propriété (PAP loans)
72
prêt à taux zero (housing loans, France) 72
private rented sector *213*, 224; England 160,
161; Ireland 130–1, 135, 139, 142; Italy
105, 112(n1); Scotland 149, 172, 182;
United Kingdom 153–4, 155; Wales
193
'privatist regimes' (Kemeny) 225
pseudo-countryside 64, 68, 70
public access rights (*allemansrätt*) 52
public bodies: local (Italy) 114n
public funds (Italy) *105*, 106–7, 114n,
115(n30)
public sector housing 155, 160, 161, 223,
230–1; stigmatised (England, Wales, Italy)
231
public–private partnership (Italy) 114n

quality of life 66, 68, 77, 103, 109, 113(n15),
121, 191

racial bias 109, 115(n32)
Radnor *196*, 205(n10), 206(n11)
Radnorshire *195*, *198*, 205(n4), 207(n17,
n19)
Rågårdsvik (Sweden): photographed 57
Randstad (Netherlands) 25, 63
recreation 25, 39, 214, 220; Netherlands 61,
62, 63, 65, 67; Sweden 47–50, 52, 53
refurbishment 122; *see also* rehabilitation
regional planning: France 73, 81, 85, 220;
Ireland 140, 141–2; Sweden **54–6**
regionalism (European Union) 233
regions (European Union) 235
regulatory regimes 11, **23–85**, 208, 210, 211,
218, 220, 223, 224, 225(n1)
rehabilitation *105*, 107, 114n, 119, 123, *125*,
126, 177, 189, 190, 199, 204(n2), 205(n9)
rent control 23, *105*
rented housing/accommodation: France 79;
Ireland 89, 132, 133, 139; Italy 102;
Netherlands 60–1, 68; Norway 32; Scotland
169, 170, 174, 177, 182, 184, 185;
Sweden 45; Wales 150, 194, 197, 199, 200,
206(n13)
restrictions on second homes: Denmark 50,
54; Sweden 53–4, 56
retirement 7, 14, 36

retirement migration 65, 216, 235; England
156, 160; France 81; Italy *97*; Scotland
170, 171; Spain 119, 120; Wales 188, 201,
213
right-to-buy: England 161, *219*; Italy 106;
Scotland 171, 172, 184, 186, *219*; United
Kingdom 154, 155; Wales 188
Riviera (France) 73
ROI (Republic of Ireland) *see* Ireland
Rome 93
Romeo error 16, 20, 21(n1), 209, 215
Rosslare Strand (County Wexford) 137
Rotterdam 63
Ruimte voor Ruimte, Space for Space (Ministry
of Agriculture, Netherlands) 68
rural areas 7; Britain 148; consequences of
rural dynamism 76–7; definition (France)
74; definition (Ireland) 129; definition
(Netherlands) **61–2**; definition (Scotland)
186(n1); definition (Spain) **117**; definition
(Wales) **190–1**; definition problems (Italy)
87; definitions (England) 148, 157, 162,
163–4, 167(n3); definitions (Italy) 94–6;
definitions (Sweden versus elsewhere) 46–7;
demographics (France 1962–99), 75–6, 85;
different places, different pressures (Italy)
101–4, 113(n12); England 158, 160–1,
167(n5); external demand (Sweden) 45, 53,
54, 57; France **73–7**; housing pressure
(Sweden) **45–52**; in urban agglomerations
(Netherlands) 62; Ireland 90, 133, 134,
135, 138–9; Italy 87, 88, **93–104**, 107,
109, 110, *111*, 112; *landsbygd* (Sweden) 47;
low priority (Ireland) 143; Norway 23;
patterns of change (Spain) **117–19**;
population revival (France 1975–) 26; post-
productivist 26; postmodern (Netherlands)
62; remote France 71, 80; renaissance
(France) 71, *75*, 76–7, 84; romanticised
view 64; Scotland 149, 168, 169, 170,
172–86, 186–7(n2); second homes
(Norway) 36–7; socially-exclusive (England)
160; Spain 88; sustainability (Wales) 197–8,
201, 204; Sweden 44, 59; territorial and
intra-regional perspective **235–6**; two kinds
(Ireland) 129, 133, 144(n5); United
Kingdom 147; urban demand for homes
24, 25; Wales 150
Rural Demonstration Areas (RDAs) 176, 177,
178, 179, 180, 185, 186
rural economy 8, 51–2, 75, 96, 110, 140,
143, 200–1

Rural Empty Properties Grant (REPG) 179, 182
Rural Home Ownership Grants (RHOGs) 174, 178
Rural Housing Challenge (Scottish Homes, 1990a) 149, 173, 174, 175, 177, 253
Rural Housing Trust 160, 161, 252
Rural and Islands Forum of Housing Associations 183
Rural Partnership for Change Initiative (Scotland) 184
Rural Policy (Scottish Homes, 1990) **173–6**, 186, 253; review **176–81**, 182–3, 186
Rural Scotland: A New Approach (Scottish Executive, 2000) 184, 253
Rural Scotland: People, Prosperity and Partnership (Scottish Office, 1995) 176, 180, 253
rural shops 46–7, 51, 66, 159
rural sustainability 233
Scottish Enterprise 175, 186
Scottish Executive 170, 184, 253
Scottish Homes vii, xi, 4, 16, 149, 169, 171, 172–3, **173–6**, 177–81, 184, 185–6, 187(n3), 253; replaced by 'Communities Scotland' (2001) 184; resource allocation 177, 183; rural policy statement (1998) **182–3**, 253
Scottish Office 149, 169, 175, 176, 253
Scottish Parliament 184, 187(n2)
Scottish Secure Tenancy 184
Scottish Special Housing Association 187(n3)
second homes 5, 8, 9–10, 13, 14, 216; demand 19, 21(n3); England 160, *213*; 'extra houses' (Norway) 9, 24, 36–41; foreign buyers 227; France *212*; German (in Denmark) 54; German (in Sweden) 47, 49–50, 223; Ireland 89–90, 131, 136–7, 142, 144(n4–5); Italy 92, 93, *97*, 100, *101*, 103, 106, 114(n17); Netherlands 67; Norway *212*, 227; photographed (Sweden) 57–8; purpose-built 18, 19, 21(n2); recreational 29, 36, 38, *39*, 39, 41, 42; repercussions on rural communities (Sweden) 49; Scotland 149, 170; Spain 88, 116, 118, 119, 120, 123, 124, 126, 128, *212*, *218*; Sweden 45–50, 227; Wales 192, *203*, *213*; *see also* holiday homes
Section 106 agreements (England and Wales) 175, 193, 199, 200, 204, 207(n18, n20–1); same as Section 50 agreements (Scotland) 178, 187(n4)

self-build housing 102, 103, 116, 132, 149, 174, 200, *212*, *219*
sensitive tourism (Norway and Sweden) 224
Sevilla 126
Shucksmith, M. ix, xi, 7, 8, 12, 14, 147, 148–9, 171, 226, 239–40, 253
Shucksmith *et al.* 169, 253
Shucksmith, M., Chapman, P. and Conway, E. (1996) **176–81**, 182–3, 253
SIFO (*Svenska institutet för opinionsundersökningar*) 45
Single Social Tenancy (Scotland) 186–7(n2)
single-person households 119, 149, 169, 171
Sixth Framework Report on Economic and Social Cohesion (European Union) 232
social class 46; professional and managerial (England) 159, 160, 161, 164; professional and managerial (Scotland) 168; white-collar 163
social exclusion 45, 223, 225, **226–7**, 228, 233; England 216; France 77, 80, 82, 83, 84; Ireland 130, 139; Italy 92, 227; Netherlands 63; Scotland 149, 170, 171, 183; Wales 150
social housing 4, 27, *213*, 223–4, 225, 230, 231; central Wales 163; choice-based lettings policy (United Kingdom) 228; England 156, 160, 161, 162–3, 166(n1), 167(n5), *219*, 222, 227; France 82, 84–5; Ireland 89, 130, 131, 132, 133, 140, 142, 143; Italy *91*, 104–7, 114n, 223, 227, 228; Netherlands 61, 63; present and changing role **227–8**; Scotland 170–3, 175, 184, 186, 186–7(n2), *213*, *219*, 223; sell-off (Italy) 106; status problems (England) 164; United Kingdom 154, 155, 209; Wales 150, 188, 189, 192, 193, 201, 204, 205(n9), 222, 227
social rental sector (*edilizia sovvenzionata*) *105*, 106, 114n
societies: 'leader' and 'laggard' 13, 15–16; lesson-learning **19–20**
Soley, C. 14, 240
Soria province 125–6
South Italy 9, 103
South Pembrokeshire *195*, *196*, *198*, 205(n4, n7, n10), 206(n13), 207(n19)
South Pembrokeshire Action with Rural Communities (SPARC) 205(n10)
South Wales 190
South-East England 5, 158, 163, 168, 222

Södermanland (Sweden) 54
Spain: *Fundación de Estudios Inmobiliarios* 126, 246
Spain: General Directorate of Housing, Architecture and Planning *122*
Spain: Ministry of Agriculture, Fishing and Food 121, *122*
Spain: National Housing Plans 116, 121
Spain: Population and Housing Census (1991), 116
Spain: *White Book of Housing* (1999), 126, 248
Spanish National Statistics Institute (INE) 117
spatial planning 11, 26; Ireland 129, 133, 135, 140, 142, 143, 144(n1, n7); Italy 108; Netherlands 62, **67–8**, *218*, 220, 229–30; policy responses **232–4**; Sweden 229
special needs housing 83, 164, 171, 184, 189–90, 193, 201, 234
State Housing Bank (Norway) 32–3, 42
Stefano, P. de 111n
Stockholm 44, 51, 54
Stratford-on-Avon *165–6*
Strömstad (Sweden) 51–2
subsidiarity 234
subsidies 44, 72, 82, 122, 231; Ireland 139; Italy 104, *105*, 106, 108–9, 114n; Scotland 173; Spain 120; Wales 150, 188
suburban areas 73, 75, *75*, *76*, 82, 93, 102, 190, 191
suburbanisation 62, 137
Sudtirol (Italy) 114(n17)
Sundt, E. 33, 241
sustainable development 45, 55, 110, 112, 221, 233, 234
sustainable regeneration (Scotland) 177, 181, 182–3, 186
Swain (1999), 168
Sweden: Environmental Protection Agency 56
Sweden: National Board of Housing, Building and Planning 45
Sweden: National Rural Agency (*glesbygdsverket*) 46, 53
Sweden: Planning and Building Act (*planoch bygglagen*) 53–4
Sweden: Real Estate Purchasing Act (*jordförvärvslagen*) 53–4
Sweden: Shore Act (*Strandlagen*) of 1952, 52

Tackling Rural Housing: Policy Statement 1998 (Scottish Homes, 1998), **182–3**, 253

Tai Cymru (Housing for Wales) 190–1, 256
Taking Stock (Housing Management Advisory Committee, 1993) 205(n3), 256
Tanum municipality (Sweden) 51
tax relief *105*, 131, 132, 136, 140, 160
taxation 9, 25; England 155; France 83; Italy *105*, 109; Sweden 44, 51, 53, *218*; VAT (Scotland) 177
tenure *35*, 114n, 150, 189, 193
tertiary sector *see* service sector
Tetlow, R., Auchincloss, M. and Haddrell, K. 159, 162, 167(n5), 252
tettsted (small settlement) 31
Tewdwr-Jones, M. ix–x, xi
Thatcher, M./Thatcherism 147, 154, 169
Tidaholm (Sweden) 48–9
Tinker, A. Wright, F. and Zeilig, H. 159, 166(n1), 252
Tosi, A. 115(n31), 246
Toulouse 77
tourism 49, 62, 74, 87, 214, *218*, 227, 231, 233; coastal and interior (Spain) 224; Ireland 138; Italy 96, *97*, 100, 103, 108; residential 19, *212*; rural 18, 229; Spain 89, 118, 119, 124–8, 221, 224, 228; Wales 201, *203*
transport 24, 57, 63, 201, 233, 234, 236; France 73, 76–7, 81; Ireland 137, 144(n5); lack of effective policy (Ireland) 135; Scotland 170; Spain 127
Trentino (Italy) 114(n17)
Trondheim 35
Turin 93
Tuscany 114(n18)
Tywi (Carmarthenshire) 205(n7)

Umbria 114(n18)
UMCOBASE data 50
UN Habitat Programme 125
unemployment 7, 45, 76, 106, 130, 131, 138, 194, 197, 230
unitary authorities (Wales) 190, 205(n9)
United Kingdom: Department of the Environment, Transport and the Regions (DETR): (2000) 161, 252; (2001) 161, 252
United Kingdom: Office of National Statistics 157, 163, 252
United Kingdom: Office of Population Censuses and Surveys 157
United Kingdom: Town and Country Planning Acts 6

University of Aberdeen: Arkleton Centre for Rural Development Research i, ix, 176, 182
Uppsala 54
urban compaction (principle) 67, *218*
urban district councils (Ireland) 144(n7)
urban spill-over (Ireland) 135–6, 140, 141, 144(n5)
urban and village renewal (Ireland) 140
urban–rural divide 5, 6–7, 8, 11, 157, 211, 233, 235; absent (Scandinavia) 227; barrier to social equity 229–30, 231; blurred 100, 102, 214; England 147; lacking 214; Norway **30–2**; Scotland 149; sharp 11, 12; United Kingdom 222–3; Wales 151, 190; weak 10–11, 12, 23–7
urbanisation 7, 8, 23, *212*, 214, 215–16; Italy 93–4, 96, 113(n12); Ireland 134, 135–6, 140; 'interstitial' (France) 74, 76–7, 78; France 82; Netherlands 62; Norway **30–2**, 33, *34, 35, 37*, 42; Spain 123
'urbanised countryside' (Italy) 102–3, 109, 113(n14)
Utrecht 63

Valdicio (Cantabria) 125–6
Vanoni, D. x, 11, 26–7, 214
Vanoni, D. *et al.* 80, 85(n2), 245
Vendée département 73
Veneto (Italy) 113(n15)
village exception policies (Wales) 198, *198*, 199–200, 207(n19–20)

village services 51, 118, 137, 162
villages 23, 51, 73, 148, 159–64, 167(n5), 188, 191, 198, *198*, 206(n16)
Villalbilla (Soria province) 126
VINEX (*Fourth National Policy Document on Spatial Planning*, Netherlands) 67, 69–70
voluntary sector 130, 139, 143, 168–9, 170, 171, 223, 227; *see also* housing association

Wales: Housing Act (1980) 190
Wales: Housing Management Advisory Committee 205(n3), 256
Wales: Planning Policy Guidance (PPG) 189; PPG 7 (Welsh Office, 1992b) 199, 257; PPG 12 (Welsh Office, 1992c) 192, 257
Wales: Technical Advice Notes (TANs) 189
Wales/Welsh Rural Forum 193, 205(n8), 257
Waterford 130
Welsh Assembly Government: national housing strategy 189, 190
Welsh Office 194, 205(n9), 257; 'Rural White Paper' (1996) 193, 257
West Germany *94*
West Wales 190
Western Europe 11, 12, 23, 30, 63, 168–9; differences and commonalities 10; *see also* European Union
Wexford (county) 137
White Paper on Housing in Scotland (1987), 172